Resplendent Dress from Southeastern Europe

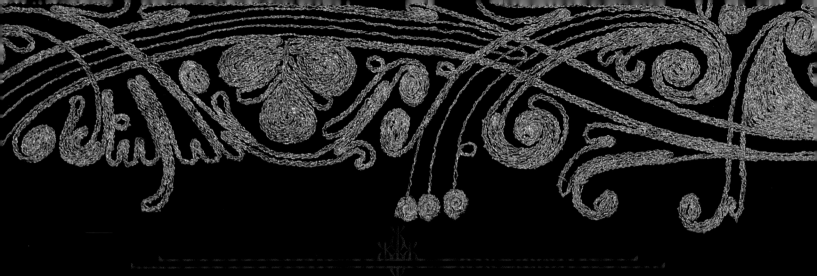

Resplendent Dress from Southeastern Europe

A HISTORY IN LAYERS

with essays by

ELIZABETH WAYLAND BARBER

JOYCE CORBETT

ELSIE DUNIN

CHARLOTTE JIROUSEK

BARBARA BELLE SLOAN

Fowler Museum Textile Series, No. 11

Elizabeth Wayland Barber
and Barbara Belle Sloan

Fowler Museum at UCLA
LOS ANGELES

FOWLER
MUSEUM
Textile Series

Major funding for this publication
and the accompanying exhibition is provided by
Patricia Anawalt, R. L. Shep, and the R. L. Shep
Endowment Fund at the Fowler Museum.
Additional support comes from
Lee Bronson in memory of Rada (Radmilla) Bronson,
Norma Greene, Carolyn and Charles Knobler,
Michael Rohde, and members of
the Fowler Textile Council.

The Fowler Museum is part of
UCLA's School of the Arts and Architecture

Lynne Kostman, *Managing Editor*
Danny Brauer, *Designer and Production Manager*
Don Cole, *Photographer*
David L. Fuller, *Cartographer*

Fowler Museum at UCLA
Box 951549
Los Angeles, California 90095-1549

Requests to reproduce material from this volume should be sent to
the Fowler Museum Publications Department at the above address.

Printed and bound in Hong Kong by Great Wall Printing Company, Ltd.

Title font is Bulgaria Moderna designed by Yanko Tsvetkov.
http://alphadesigner.com

ISBN 978-0-9847550-4-2 (casebound)
ISBN 978-0-9847550-3-5 (paperback)

FRONT COVER, see fig. 6.10; BACK COVER, see figs. 4.5, 1.71. 1.89, 1.93, 1.9;
PAGE 1, see fig. 6.9; TITLE PAGE, see fig. 2.12; THIS PAGE, see fig. 6.20;
OPPOSITE PAGE, see fig. ; PAGE 6, see fig. 1.28; PAGE 8, see fig. 3.21; PAGE 10, see
fig. 1.41; PAGE 13, see fig. 6.10; PAGE 254, see fig. 3.20; PAGE 280, see fig. 2.12.

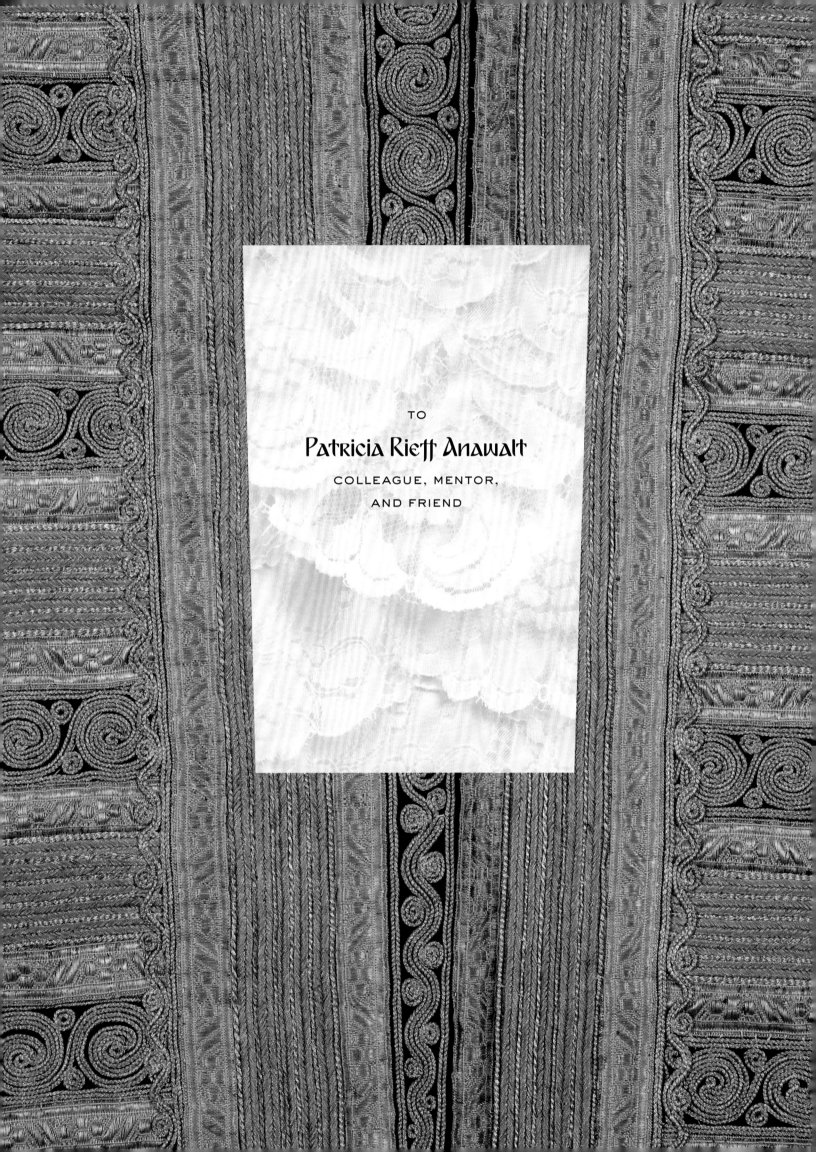

TO

Patricia Rieff Anawalt

COLLEAGUE, MENTOR,
AND FRIEND

Contents

Foreword

When the Center for the Study of Regional Dress opened, as part of the Fowler Museum, over twenty years ago, I envisioned a range of activities taking place: scholarly research would be carried out; books with long shelf lives would be written; classes on the world's range of non-Western textiles and clothing would be taught; unique garments relating to those classes would be displayed. And, happily, all of that has come to fruition. What never occurred to me, however, was that the Center might someday serve as a magnet to draw further attire from distant lands into the Fowler Museum's collections. That, too, has come to pass, as this exhibition of the resplendent attire of southeastern Europe illustrates. But this did not, could not, would not have happened without the dedicated efforts of three outstanding women.

In 1984 Professor Elsie Dunin of UCLA's Dance Department mounted an exhibition of traditional costumes at the Museum of Cultural History (as the Fowler was then known): *Dance Occasions and Festive Dress in Yugoslavia.* This exhibition made a highly favorable impression on those who visited it. Subsequently, Professor Dunin generously donated many of those garments to our Museum, creating the core of the Fowler's collection of eastern European traditional dress.

The second powerful influence on the collection was Barbara Belle Sloan, Associate Director of the Center for the Study of Regional Dress. As soon as Barbara became aware that there was a cache of authentic "Yugoslavian" costumes stored in a crowded closet of UCLA's Women's Gym (now Glorya Kaufman Hall), she went into action. And it is a good thing she did! As it turned out, those garments—subsequently donated to the Fowler by Robert Leibman—had to be removed immediately or they would have been destroyed during the impending renovation of the building. No sooner had Barbara rescued that treasure trove than word began to spread that there existed at UCLA a highly regarded repository where a family's traditional dress could be donated with the secure knowledge that those beloved garments would be carefully studied, stored, and perhaps even eventually displayed. As a result, the Fowler collection now includes over eighty complete ensembles as well as an additional several hundred individual garments. From the start Barbara saw the potential for organizing this remarkable body of material for presentation. She has been instrumental in virtually every aspect of the development of this book and the accompanying exhibition.

The third force behind this long-awaited project is Dr. Elizabeth (Betchen) Barber, an internationally known authority on the early history of eastern European cloth and clothing, as well as on that region's dance and oral traditions. Betchen grew up involved with her parents' folk-dance group, an enthusiasm she nurtured throughout her college years, her professional life, and on into the present day. Her passion has extended to creating and sustaining her own folk-dance group, which performs in various Southern California venues. Indeed, Elizabeth Barber truly knows the range of eastern Europe's dances and their attendant costumes, as well as the region's complex history and its effect on the area's rural populations, the people whose unique and colorful festive dress is so beautifully displayed in this memorable exhibition.

Dr. Patricia Rieff Anawalt
DIRECTOR
CENTER FOR THE STUDY OF REGIONAL DRESS
FOWLER MUSEUM AT UCLA

Preface

Resplendent Dress from Southeastern Europe: A History in Layers represents that rarest of Fowler Museum projects, an exploration of a European art form. Only a very small number of our major projects in recent years, notably *¡Carnaval!* (2005), have included a substantial portion of European material considered together with closely related arts from elsewhere in the world (even though some of the earliest objects to enter the Fowler collections were indeed from Europe). Equally rarely have we dealt with hybrid forms that involved a European component, most recently in *Order and Disorder: Alighiero Boetti by Afghan Women* (2010). Occasionally a small project has come along like the photographic exhibition *The Northern Fiddler: Irish Traditional Fiddle Playing in Donegal and Tyrone 1977-1979* (2001). But one has to go back to the earliest years of the Museum in the 1960s, a time when our institution's primary focus—now defined as the arts of Africa, Asia and the Pacific, and ancient, indigenous, and diasporic communities in the Americas—was just beginning to be established, to find any substantially recurring emphasis on European projects. These included *Lithuanian Folk Art* (1966) and *Swiss Folk Art* (1969, circulated by the Smithsonian Institution), each accompanied by a publication bearing the same title.

This limited history of European projects of course reflects the nature of the Museum's holdings. Among all of our diverse collections, only two sets of European material stand out as top-tier internationally. One is the Fowler family collection of European (and American) silver, published in *The Francis E. Fowler, Jr. Collection of Silver* (1991). The other is our extensive collection of items of dress from southeastern Europe. This collection has been featured in two past exhibitions: *The Balkans: Costumes and Folk Art from Albania, Bulgaria, Greece, Yugoslavia, and Romania* (1969) and *Dance Occasions and Festive Dress in Yugoslavia* (1984). The latter project was accompanied by a publication with the same title, authored by Elsie Ivancich Dunin, who has returned to contribute again to *Resplendent Dress*. The impressive time depth of Professor Dunin's work is put fully to advantage in her contributions in the present volume (chapters 4 and 5). The collection has continued to grow since the project of 1984, and the Museum has long anticipated and planned this opportunity to feature it anew.

The intellectual *force majeure* of the project this time—its "superior and irresistible" power—derives from the energy and lifelong work of Elizabeth Barber, one of the world's leading scholars of the textile history of a vast region stretching from the Danube to the deserts of Central Asia. Professor Barber is renowned for her previous publications including *Prehistoric Textiles: The Development of Cloth in the Neolithic and Bronze Ages with Special Reference to the Aegean* (1992), *Women's Work, the First 20,000 Years: Women, Cloth, and Society in Early Times* (1995), and *The Mummies of Urumchi* (2000). This time out, our subtitle "a history in layers" reflects Professor Barber's command of a deep slice of Eurasian history, enabling her to trace (in chapter 1) how past influences have shaped the dress of southeastern Europeans, leaving telltale clues in the accumulated layers of cloth that remain visible today. Professor Barber's long-standing love of the traditional dance of the region also informs her work, as the clothing she discusses expresses its deepest social meanings in the context of village dancing.

While Professor Barber uncovers "layers" whose origins can be traced to periods ranging from the Neolithic to the Renaissance, Charlotte Jirousek's contribution (chapter 2) provides further insights regarding the last great premodern cultural impulse that profoundly re-made southeastern Europe. This was the conquest of much of the region by the Ottoman Empire, whose Muslim, Turkish culture brought with it new ways of dressing.

Jirousek and all of the contributing authors have appropriately focused primarily on items of dress (drawn almost entirely from the Fowler Museum collection), their historical development, and their use in the communities where they were made. Thoughtful readers, however, cannot help but be aware of certain complex, powerful, and challenging narratives that underlie this subject matter. Our authors have not shied from these issues, and indeed they are evident throughout the book, but it has not been their primary purpose to explore them overtly or analytically. I would like to devote a few words to placing a couple of these issues in context.

The first has to do with how the items of dress featured in this book evolved over the course of the twentieth century from best dress that would have been worn at least weekly if not daily (the more elaborate items were always "special" dress) by a large segment of the population. In so doing, these articles of clothing became something very different: deliberately self-conscious statements of identity in some cases "put on" by limited numbers of people for special situations such as festivals or performances for tourists. Joyce Corbett's discussion (in chapter 3) of the circumstances underlying the promotion of embroidery in several communities in Slovakia provides excellent examples of such developments. A full exploration of this subject—well beyond the scope of this brief preface—would require long detours through the history of nineteenth-century romanticism and nationalism; Eric Hobsbawm's "Invention of Tradition"; the copious literature about how identity is negotiated; a review of the reasons why the term "folk" has become contested in academic discourse; and perhaps, with regard to the reception of Ottoman forms of dress in Europe, even Edward Said's concept of "Orientalism." Given the recent history of the region, this narrative continues to be extraordinarily powerful especially in the former Yugoslavia, as evidenced by Elsie Dunin's coverage of the determination with which the citizens of the Croatian village of Čilipi reconstituted their performances for tourists in the twenty-first century after their village was destroyed by war (chapter 4).

A related issue—the elephant in the room—is of course the divisive conflict or "balkanization" of southeastern Europe, to use a term that has by now grown so toxic that even the quotation marks cannot rehabilitate it. The linguistic map of this region looks much like linguistic maps of other regions frequently featured in Fowler Museum publications (Southeast Asia, for example, or Papua New Guinea): a stippled overlay of one group of people living cheek-by-jowl with multiple others. This is the root of the region's greatest wealth—its magnificent human and cultural riches—but also, when combined with its history of strategic conflict, undeniably the source of it greatest recurring agony. In the aftermath of the genocidal brutality and wars of the 1990s, the tinge of communal conflict is implicit and inescapable. Our authors are to be commended for avoiding descending into lachrymose litanies while at the same time not sweeping conflict under the rug with happy portrayals of multiculturalism. The Fowler Museum thanks all of them for their careful work, based in each case on a deep personal attachment to the region and its diverse peoples. With this book we celebrate the creativity southeastern Europeans exercised with spindle and loom, needle and thread. A fitting conclusion to the book is offered by Barbara Sloan in her contribution (chapter 6) highlighting the resilience of some of the individuals and families whose resplendent textiles eventually entered the Fowler Museum's collections.

In addition to the authors, many people have contributed in a variety of ways to the realization of this publication and the accompanying exhibition. We are extremely grateful to Dr. Patricia Anawalt, the director of the Center for the Study of Regional Dress at the Fowler Museum, for her generous support, without which this volume could not have seen the light of day. Dr. Anawalt has been a staunch supporter of this project from its inception, putting other work at the Center aside so that Barbara Sloan would be free to dedicate extended periods of time to *Resplendent Dress*. R. L. Shep not only contributed to the book through the R. L. Shep Endowment Fund at the Fowler Museum—which makes possible the Fowler Museum Textile Series, of which the present volume forms the eleventh entry—but made an additional donation specifically for this book project. We also thank Lee Bronson, who contributed in memory of his late wife Rada (Radmilla) Bronson, Norma Greene, Carolyn and Charles Knobler, Michael Rohde, and members of the Fowler Textile Council.

No project of this size and complexity could be accomplished without the commitment and professionalism of the Fowler staff (listed at the back of this publication). Special thanks are due to Barbara Sloan for her wholehearted dedication to the collection and for gracefully managing the plethora of details that arise in the preparation of a book and an exhibition. The production of this handsome volume is the work of the Fowler Museum's Publications Department: Lynne Kostman, our editor, who brought her usual care and attention to detail to the task; Danny Brauer, our director of publications, who created a truly resplendent design to showcase the garments; and Don Cole whose beautiful photographs grace these pages.

Roy W. Hamilton
SENIOR CURATOR
FOWLER MUSEUM AT UCLA

Acknowledgments

This project represents a fruitful convergence of the priorities of the Center for the Study of Regional Dress and the Fowler Museum. It unites research emanating from the Center with the exhibition and publication programs of the Fowler. It has been the work of many hands, and we wish to acknowledge all those whose dedication has made possible this volume and exhibition. First and foremost we would like to express our gratitude to Patricia Anawalt, the director of the Center, for her steadfast support and to Fowler Museum Director Marla C. Berns for her continued assistance and for graciously providing us with the opportunity to exhibit the Fowler's extensive collection of textiles from southeastern Europe. Our gratitude extends as well to Senior Curator Roy Hamilton for his enthusiasm and guidance throughout this process. We join Roy in thanking the entire Fowler Museum staff for their efforts in producing the book and the exhibition. Our dedicated authors are also to be acknowledged for their hard work, patience, and quick response to many difficult deadlines.

Special thanks are due to Robb Shep for his continued—and additional support—for this volume, and to Lee Bronson, Norma Greene, Carolyn and Charles Knobler, Michael Rohde, and members of the Fowler Textile Council for their enthusiasm and donations. Judy Sourakli, Curator of Collections, Henry Art Gallery, University of Washington, Seattle, kindly assisted us in borrowing her institution's Montenegrin man's shirt and pants. These, together with a very few items lent from private collections, are the only objects in the exhibition that are not drawn from the Fowler collection.

Thank you to our esteemed colleagues in Turkey and Croatia who graciously hosted us in their museums: Dr. Cengiz Aydın, Director, Ethnographic Museum, Ismir; Mirjana Menković, Museum Adviser, Ethnographic Museum, Belgrade; Director Damodar Frian, and Senior Curators Vesna Zorić and Aida Brenko, Ethnographic Museum, Zagreb; Marina Desin, Director, Ethnographic Museum, Čilipi, Croatia; and the staff of the Ethnographic Museum, Dubrovnik.

The literally hundreds of magnificent textiles donated to the Fowler by Robert Leibman and Elsie Ivancich Dunin were the inspiration for *Resplendent Dress*. Their love of the textiles, dance, and traditions of the region motivated us to explore the history, mysteries, and details of these clothes. A heartfelt thank you to our new friends—the people who shared memories with us and donated to the Museum textiles that had been in their families for generations—Danilo Bach, Michelle Cheyovich, Helenka Chlebeckova Frost and John Frost, Nicholas Colasanti, and Joel Halpern.

We thank James Snowden, Carol Bowdoin Gil, Helene Baine Cincebeaux, and Joel Halpern for their photographs, and Kelvin Wilson and Elizabeth Barber for their drawings. Martin Koenig is to be thanked for sharing his photographs and expertise on Bulgarian costume and dance. Margaret Hempstead and Naeda Robinson, longtime textile aficionados, were particularly helpful in answering questions about Macedonian aprons and vests. And, a wholehearted thank you to Mary Jane Leland, textile enthusiast extraordinaire, whose expert knowledge of fiber and weave structure was indispensible. It is our hope that *Resplendent Dress from Southeastern Europe: A History in Layers* will provide an insightful and enjoyable experience for all.

Elizabeth Wayland Barber
VISITING CURATOR
PROFESSOR EMERITA, LINGUISTICS AND ARCHAEOLOGY
OCCIDENTAL COLLEGE, PASADENA

Barbara Belle Sloan
ASSOCIATE DIRECTOR
CENTER FOR THE STUDY OF REGIONAL DRESS
FOWLER MUSEUM AT UCLA

Timeline

Elizabeth Wayland Barber

25,000 BCE	20,000 BCE	8000 BCE	7000 BCE	6000 BCE	4000 BCE	3200 BCE	2000 BCE

PALEOLITHIC · · · **NEOLITHIC** · · · **BRO**

- **25,000 BCE** — First clear evidence for spinning fiber into thread and for netting and weaving
- **20,000 BCE** — First evidence for string skirt, belt-bands, string caps
- **8000 BCE** — First evidence for agriculture and domestic animals (Near East)
- Flax domesticated
- **7000 BCE** — First evidence for large mechanized loom (Asia Minor)
- **6000 BCE** — Agriculture reaches Balkan Peninsula from Asia Minor
- First evidence for agrarian fertility motifs, on female figurines
- Through selective breeding, domestic sheep begin to produce usable wool
- First evidence for square-patterned wraparound skirt
- **4000 BCE** — Cities and writing develop in Near East
- More elaborate clothing invented to reflect new social stratification
- **3200 BCE** — Linen tunic/chemise reaches Europe from Near East
- **2000 BCE** — Layered clothing based on chemise begins to develop and with it a new silhouette

1370 BCE

1200 BCE

1000 BCE

800 BCE

700 BCE

500 BCE

229 BCE

0

313 CE

Earliest preserved string skirt

Massive migrations from Eurasian steppes disrupt Europe and Near East

Intruders into Europe bring pants, worn with shirt, belt, boots

Earliest preserved pants, shirt

First evidence for motif of "Protectress" with birds on hands

Earliest preserved jacket with useless sleeves

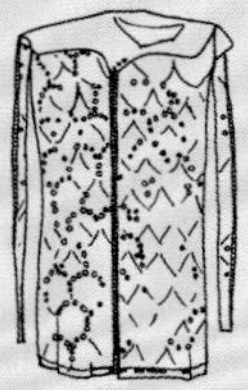

Romans begin conquering Balkan Peninsula

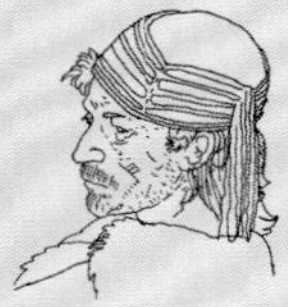

Roman Emperor Constantine accepts Christianity

Old European forms
of dress continue
outside the urban
Classical world

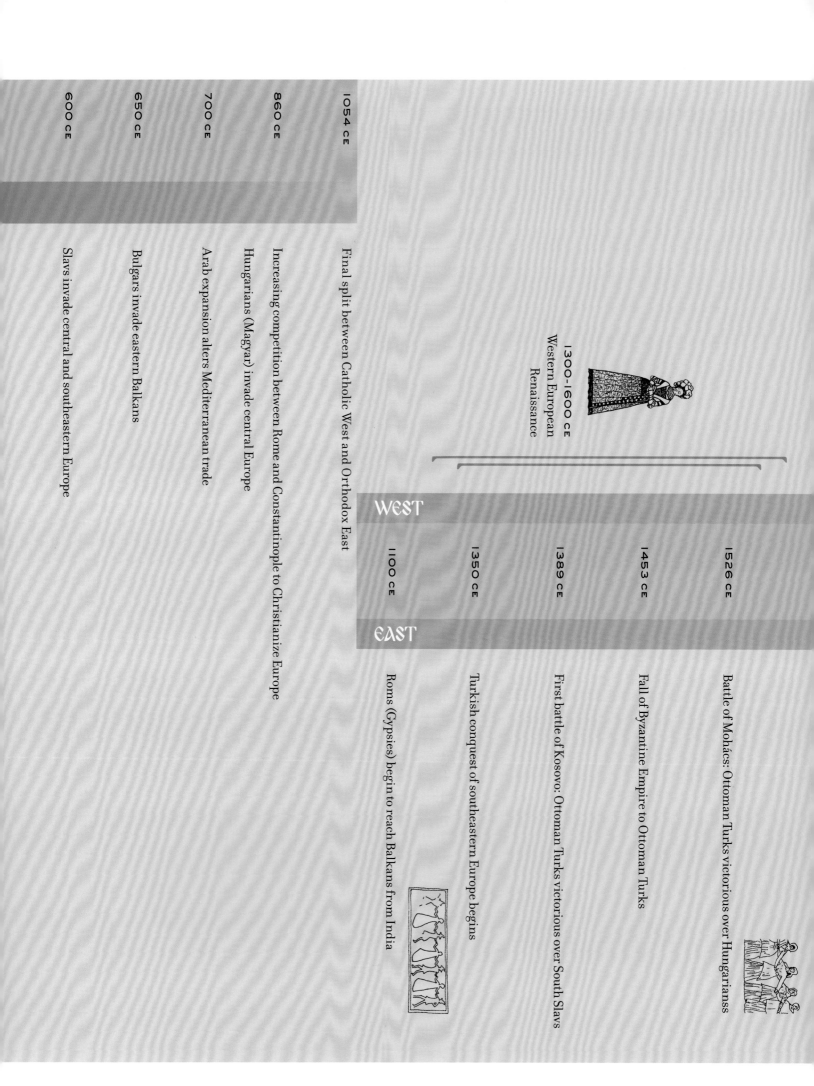

600 CE — Slavs invade central and southeastern Europe

650 CE — Bulgars invade eastern Balkans

700 CE — Arab expansion alters Mediterranean trade

860 CE — Hungarians (Magyar) invade central Europe

Increasing competition between Rome and Constantinople to Christianize Europe

1054 CE — Final split between Catholic West and Orthodox East

1300-1600 CE
Western European
Renaissance

WEST

EAST

1100 CE — Roms (Gypsies) begin to reach Balkans from India

1350 CE — Turkish conquest of southeastern Europe begins

1389 CE — First battle of Kosovo: Ottoman Turks victorious over South Slavs

1453 CE — Fall of Byzantine Empire to Ottoman Turks

1526 CE — Battle of Mohács: Ottoman Turks victorious over Hungarianss

2000 CE Traditional dress worn only in remotest districts or for show

1945 CE World War II ends; rural traditional dress cedes to factory-made fashion

1918 CE World War I ends; local forms of dress begin to disappear

1878 CE Bulgarians gain de facto independence from Ottoman Turks

1867 CE Serbians gain de facto independence from Ottoman Turks

1841 CE

1828 CE Most Greeks gain de facto independence from Ottoman Turks

DMC begins manufacturing mercerized embroidery cottons

1801 CE

Jacquard process invented for mechanically weaving brocades, etc.

DMC Mulhouse (Alsace) founded, begins printing chintz-like cottons

1756 CE

Cheap, colorful, printed cotton chintzes from East India banned

1700 CE

1683 CE Battle of Vienna: Austrians defeat Ottoman Turks and win Hungary

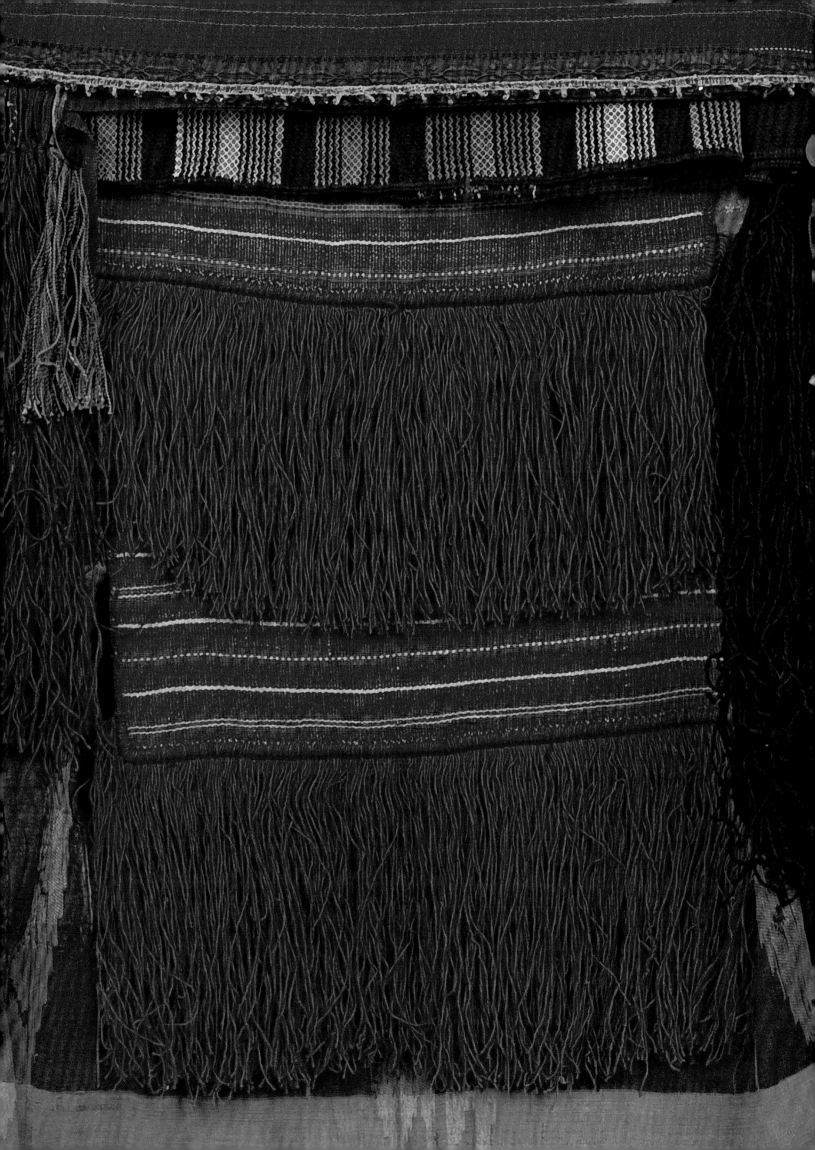

CHAPTER
ONE

From String Skirt to Thirty Pounds of Walking History

A TWENTY-THOUSAND-YEAR-OLD TRADITION OF DRESS

Elizabeth Wayland Barber

Roughly twenty-two thousand years ago, at each end of Europe, someone carved a piece of mammoth tooth into the shape of a plump woman wearing a skirt made of string. Many such hand-size "Venus-figures" were made in the Gravettian era of the Paleolithic, or "Old Stone Age." Most are nude, some have a band around the torso, and an occasional figure sports a cap or hairnet. One from France and another from Russia, however, wear string skirts, our first evidence of a meaning-laden European clothing tradition that persists to this day in remote parts of eastern Europe (fig. 1.1). The significance of this string skirt, as will be discussed in detail below, is that it indicates its wearer is old enough to perform the mystical feat of producing a new human being.

At their very inception, therefore, fiber craft and the making of clothing were linked to women, and women's clothing was linked to the role of women in bearing children. Clothes may make the man, but women made everyone's clothes. By hand. From scratch. This persisted in rural southeastern Europe into the twentieth century and occasionally into the twenty-first. Newer forms of dress entered the tradition bit by bit and were added to the outfit. Moreover, once accepted and endowed with cultural significance, they were not easily shed. By 1900 a village woman's apparel consisted of millennia of layered history. With a glance at her, the onlooker could read not only her marital status but also her religion, wealth, skills, industriousness, village of origin, ethnic/linguistic group, and more. For it was by these traits, and not physical beauty, that a girl was chosen to become a bride.

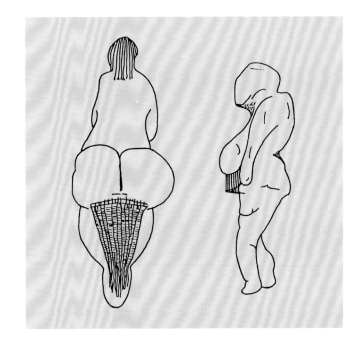

1.1 Paleolithic "Venus-figures," carved circa 20,000 BCE, sometimes wear string skirts, which were apparently already a sign relating to childbearing. The figure from Lespugue, France, wears hers in back (drawing after Musée de l'Homme, Paris), whereas that from Gagarino, Russia, wears hers in front (after Tarasov 1965, fig. 14).

OPPOSITE
Detail of figure 1.41a.

1.2A–G Figurines of mature females from early farming communities continue to wear string skirts, from the Neolithic on through the Bronze and Iron Ages: (a) Šipintsí, Ukraine, 4000 BCE; (b) Vinča, Serbia, 5000 BCE; (c) Crnokalačka Bara, Serbia, 4000 BCE; (d) Sitagroi, Greek Macedonia, 5000 BCE (drawings after Gimbutas 1982, pl. 13, fig. 8, pl. 21; Renfrew, Gimbutas, and Elster 1986, fig. 9.21); (e) bronze figurine from Grevensvænge, Denmark, circa 1200 BCE (after Munksgaard 1974, fig. 50b); (f) clay statuette, Thisbe, Boiotia, Greece, circa 550 BCE (after Louvre, figurine s1643). One string skirt (g) was found actually preserved in the log coffin of an eighteen-year-old girl buried in 1371 BCE (Bronze Age) at Egtved, Denmark (after Munksgaard 1974, fig. 44). Compare the use of the bottom cord to Neolithic figurine c.

As a result, young girls lavished their work, attention, and creativity on the outfits they would don upon reaching physical maturity and childbearing age. The better her ensemble, the better the match a girl could hope for. If far more of this volume concerns women's clothing, it is because it received the most time and effort. Men were merely clothed—young women were costumed. Men wore their clothes out; few of them survive. Women laid away their "bridal" outfits—worn from puberty, with additions upon marrying, until the birth of a first child—and they expected to be buried in them. Above all, the girl's costume was designed to be displayed to best advantage during the dancing that took place on holidays (chiefly Sunday afternoons, during Christian times)—dancing that a girl was not allowed to join until she reached maturity.

By the mid-twentieth century, with the coming of paved roads and then television, times and beliefs had changed. The world no longer centered on the village or on participating in traditional dances, which in some instances dated back to the Stone Age. Excitement and entertainment now came from elsewhere, potential spouses as well.

Some of these treasured dresses were nonetheless preserved, sold to tourists and collectors or given to museums. In this essay and the chapters that follow, we examine the development of this remarkably long-lived tradition of dress throughout southeastern Europe, using precious examples of women's and men's clothing drawn almost exclusively from the collections of the Fowler Museum.

THE STRING REVOLUTION

In our age of machine-made cloth and clothing, most Americans lack awareness of how a few easily breakable fibers, twisted together as a group, can produce string, which is by contrast very strong and can be made as long as needed. We have clear evidence, however, that by 25,000 BCE people had discovered this principle and were busy making thread, string, and rope of plant fiber, using these products to tie things up and also to form nets. String allows for catching and carrying so much more than otherwise that fiber craft began to revolutionize human life. By 20,000 BCE, as the Venus-figures attest (see fig. 1.1), string was being used for another new invention, namely clothing—not only for sewing up the pelt from last night's dinner to use to keep warmer but also for weaving and knotting bands and caps and string skirts.[1]

Unlike a pelt, the string skirt does not contribute to either warmth or modesty, and yet it persisted for thousands of years in Europe, through the Stone Ages and beyond (fig.1.2 and see timeline, pp. 16–19). Being of little practical use, it must have become a cultural signal that sent an important message. Since, as previously noted, the ancient evidence shows that it was worn by women of childbearing age only, it presumably signaled just that. After all, the population density in Europe in the late Paleolithic was rather less than one human per square mile, so being able to determine such information at a considerable distance was helpful. That this was indeed their significance is

1.3 Apron
Mirdite, northern Albania, late twentieth century
Woven wool top; fringe of tightly spun combed wool wrapped around core; belt-band woven of cotton and wool
38 x 46 cm
PRIVATE COLLECTION

This apron, evidence of a still-living tradition, was purchased directly from its maker/wearer in 1997. The old lozenge motif symbolizes female fertility.

corroborated by the fact that string skirts and their stringy derivatives continued to signal exactly the same message into the twentieth century and beyond on rural women's dress in parts of eastern Europe. The Albanian string skirt illustrated in figure 1.3, for example, was purchased directly from its wearer in 1997. The woman said that she intended to continue wearing her traditional costume until she died; and yes, she possessed another string skirt at home to wear in place of the one she agreed to part with. It was her badge of womanhood.

By 8000 BCE, human technology was undergoing a new revolution with the advent of agriculture and domestication, which mark the start of the Neolithic, or "New Stone Age." Having wheat and flax among their earliest domesticates, people no longer had to go searching for food and fibers but could grow as much as they needed at home. Furthermore, around 7000 BCE, evidence from Iraq and Turkey shows that a loom capable of making large pieces of fabric, not just narrow bands, had been invented.[2] With lots of fiber and a big loom, people could start making more substantial clothing.

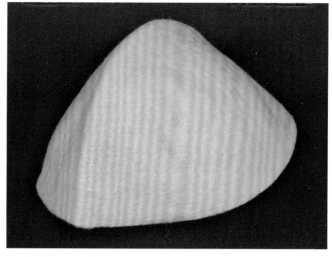

1.4 Figures on a stone vase from Warka (Uruk), southern Mesopotamia, circa 3200 BCE, show clearly the use of clothing to mark social position that first proliferated in the earliest cities: a farmer (naked, offering basket of produce), a king's servant (in a simple kilt), a ruler (mostly destroyed, but his elaborate sash and garment hem visible), and a priestess (in a sari-like wrap she holds on from underneath with her left hand; the goddess Inanna's standard is behind her). DRAWING AFTER PARROT 1961, FIG. 89; FARMER PARTLY RESTORED FROM ANOTHER SUCH FIGURE.

1.5 Man's cap
Serbia, twentieth century
Fiber-felted wool
Diam. 18 cm
FOWLER MUSEUM X96.6.16; GIFT OF PROFESSOR ELSIE IVANCICH DUNIN

This white cap, traditional across much of Eurasia, was made by mashing dampened wool fibers together directly into the desired shape, a process known as felting. It is impervious to wind and will shed light rain.

Interestingly, however, they didn't, if their representations of themselves are to be believed. For several more millennia, figurines of humans show people basically going naked (though often "clothed" in body paint). Beginning around 5000 BCE, female figurines from southeastern Europe occasionally sport a wraparound skirt in a checkerboard pattern, while others continue to wear string skirts. We don't, however, see clothes developing in earnest until the advent of more complex societies at the end of the Neolithic, beginning in the Near East (fig. 1.4).

This also happens to be about the time and place that sheep, domesticated in the Near East by 8000 BCE, started to bear usable wool, a change wrought by four thousand years of selective breeding (wild sheep have a coat more like that of a deer).[3] Wool is a remarkable fiber. Unlike plant fibers it is very stretchy (nice for clothing) and often curly (nice for insulation), and its surface bears little scales that allow it (and only it) to be mashed together, without weaving, into a dense cloth-like covering called felt, still widely used in the colder parts of Europe (fig. 1.5). Wool also comes in various natural hues and absorbs dyes well, making stripes, checkerboards and other color-based patterns possible. The plant fibers available in early Europe, on the other hand, such as linen (from the flax plant), begin life as stem fibers designed *not* to absorb the nutrient liquids they carried up the plant; so linen was generally left white, the whiter the better. In general, in the forms of dress that developed in Europe, linen remained white, whereas wool might be white, black, brown, or any color for which a dye was available. The favorite color, as a cursory glance at the illustrations in this book will show, was red.

THE GREAT COVER-UP: ADDING THE CHEMISE

When the notion of the white linen tunic as the basic body-wrapper reached southeastern Europe from the Near East around 2000 BCE, European clothing took another major step down the path leading to the way we dress today. Although the earliest Near Eastern linen tunic seems to have been an over-one-shoulder wraparound, rather like an Indian sari, it acquired, in migrating to Europe, the form of a sort of chemise: a "T"-shirt with two cylindrical sleeves at right angles to a tubular body (fig. 1.6). This simple garment has the advantage that even in high winds it doesn't have to be held in place the way an unsewn wrapper does.

The "T" shape, however, tends to chafe under the armpits and, if the shirt-body is narrow, to constrict both stride and arm movement. As a result, people in different regions came up with various modifications, which persist to the present. One early solution, attested from 700 BCE on down, was to leave the seams in the armpit unsewn, creating an opening that improved both mobility and ventilation. Other solutions, used for example in much of Macedonia, were to add side-panels for more fullness and/or insert a gusset (see below) in the armpit (fig. 1.7). In what is now Romania and part of Hungary and Croatia, women created roominess by adopting a sort of raglan sleeve, gathered at the neck (fig. 1.8). South Slavic historians of dress call this gathered sleeve the "Pannonian sleeve" as opposed to the older "T" shape, which they call the "Dinaric sleeve," using local geographical names to distinguish them.[4] One can often tell where a chemise came from, in fact, by how it was constructed.

1.6a Woman's chemise
Zadar, Croatia, twentieth
century
*Woven cotton, embroidered linen;
applied wool tassels, braid, metal
button*
100 x 134 cm
FOWLER MUSEUM X68.3068;
MUSEUM PURCHASE

The pure "T" shape of the
original European chemise
without underarm gussets
is preserved in this Croatian
blouse ("Dinaric" type). For
the wearer to be able to walk,
however, extra panels had to
be inserted near the bottom.
Note that the elaborate cross-
stitching on the chest was done
on a separate panel that could
be removed and reused when
the chemise wore out.

1.6b Detail of figure 1.6a.

1.7A Man's shirt
Serbia, twentieth century
Woven and embroidered cotton (cross-stitched, smocked); tatted edging
83 x 152 cm
FOWLER MUSEUM X2011.4.41; GIFT OF DR. JOEL MARTIN HALPERN

This "T"-shaped shirt has gussets in the armpits to facilitate raising the arms, as well as a very wide body-tube controlled by gathering the extra cloth and adding pleats in front.

1.7B Detail of figure 1.7a.

The adoption of the chemise totally changed the European notion of dress. From then on, the soft, white, easily washable plant-fiber chemise lay next to the skin as the foundation garment among rural farmers (as opposed to the urban-oriented Classical Greeks and Romans). Any other garments, especially ones like the string skirt that needed to be visible, were worn over it.

By 2000 BCE the basic secret of making dyes colorfast had been discovered,[5] so people could now also create increasingly brightly colored woolen clothing, which they did with gusto. String skirts, for which red and black were favored, evolved here and there from belt-bands with long fringes, to little aprons with long or medium fringes (fig. 1.10), to big aprons with long, short, or even no fringes (figs. 1.9, 1.11, 1.12). Eventually many apron styles abandoned the fringes altogether, opting for inwoven, appliquéd, or embroidered decoration instead (figs. 1.13–1.15). Red in particular dominated. Being the color of life-giving blood, it was believed to turn away evil spirits and protect against the evil eye.[6]

1.8 Woman's blouse
Romania, twentieth century
Plain-weave cotton, smocked, hemstitched, faggoted, silk and cotton embroidery, cotton tassels
60 x 153 cm
FOWLER MUSEUM X2005.30.3; PROMISED GIFT OF SUSAN FAUX

In the raglan or "Pannonian" sleeve, the cloth tube forming the sleeve goes all the way to the neck, being gathered with the top of the chemise body to make the neck opening. The gathering was often done with elaborate smocking. On this typical Romanian blouse the pre-finished edges are sewn together with a stitch called faggoting (here in dark red), designed to add extra elasticity to the garment.

1.9 Woman's apron
Smiljevo, Macedonia, circa 1930
Woven and fringed with worsted (combed) wool; silk tassels
and embroidery
95 x 47 cm
FOWLER MUSEUM X2008.39.8; GIFT OF GLORIA GRANZ GONICK

The woven cloth forming the apron is folded over the belt to provide
a second layer of the all-important fringes. The yellow silk cord used
here and there was intended to resemble yet more expensive metallic
gold thread.

1.10A Detail of figure 1.10b.

1.10B Woman's apron
Romania, twentieth century
*Wool, cotton, and metallic twill-woven brocade and overshot;
fringes spun of combed wool, cotton*
71 x 66 cm
FOWLER MUSEUM X2012.5.1; GIFT OF JOYCE CORBETT

Tremendously long fringes on a narrow apron woven with lozenge
motifs are typical of Romanian women's dress in the conservative
Banat region that straddles Romania and Serbia. Such aprons are
normally worn in the back, with a fully woven apron in the front.

1.11 Woman's apron
Macedonia, twentieth century
Woven and fringed wool; metallic thread, wool ribbons
75 × 43 cm
FOWLER MUSEUM X99.34.33; GIFT OF ROBERT LEIBMAN

Here, as in many areas in the region, the woven part of the apron
has become larger and the fringes smaller—but still present.

1.12 Woman's apron
Lika, Dalmatia, southern Croatia, twentieth century
*Tapestry-woven wool; inner fringe carded wool, outer fringe combed
wool; commercial metallic braid and brocade silk ribbon; belt of felt with
chain-stitched embroidery, surrounded by heavy cord wrapped with
colored wool*
79 x 71 cm
FOWLER MUSEUM X68.3071; MUSEUM PURCHASE

Apron fringes from this conservative area of Dalmatia tend to be
thick like a lion's mane.

1.13 Woman's apron
Macedonia, twentieth century
Woven wool, glass beads, commercial metallic ribbon, cotton rickrack, lace; cross-panel apparently on linen, with fine metallic thread, sequins
63 x 68 cm
FOWLER MUSEUM X99.9.1;
GIFT OF IRMA SWITZER

In much of Macedonia, fringeless aprons are woven as two heavy rectangles sewn together horizontally, usually—as here— with lace or other trim hiding the seam.

1.14 Woman's apron
Macedonia, twentieth century
Two panels of wool woven in weft-face, with inwoven colored spots; black commercial trim, white silk cord, glass beads, coins, sequins, buttons
50 x 41 cm
FOWLER MUSEUM X96.6.18D; GIFT OF
PROFESSOR ELSIE IVANCICH DUNIN

The top of this apron was subtly shaped by turning the corners under, so as not to cut the cloth. Modern molded plastic buttons mingle with antique Ottoman-period coins stamped in Arabic script.

1.15 Woman's apron
Serbia, twentieth century
Cotton velvet, commercial cotton lace, wool embroidery
53 x 81 cm
FOWLER MUSEUM X68.41; GIFT OF VILMA MACHETTE

Colorful flowers cross-stitched onto black aprons and socks are
especially typical of the Šumadija area of central Serbia.

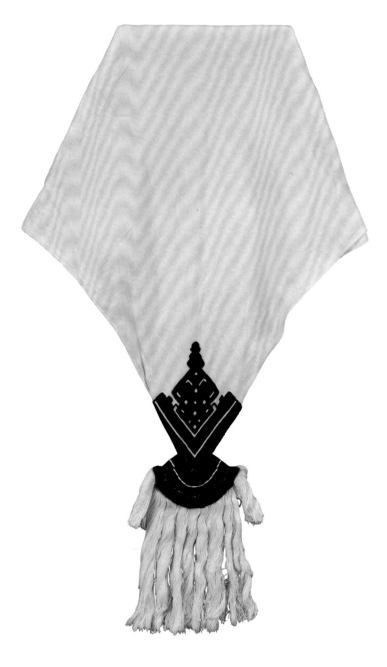

The message of the fringes was sacrosanct, however, and couldn't be left off. So as newer garments usurped the space of the string skirt, the fringes often migrated. The strings might adorn the sash (fig. 1.16), or move upward to the sleeves (fig. 1.17), shoulders (figs. 1.19a,b), and/or head (fig. 1.18).[7] In Ukraine, Belarus, and South Great Russia (the vast area largely east of Ukraine but south of Moscow), however, the main message was taken over by a large apron called a *panyova* that wrapped around the back and bore a checkered or square pattern similar to that on certain Neolithic and Bronze Age figurines (figs. 1.20–1.22), although usually with vestigial fringes or tassels still clinging somewhere. The *panyova* was first offered to a girl when she reached puberty, although, at least in some regions, she had the right to refuse it for up to a year if she felt unready (or wanted to avoid an unwelcome suitor). Once she put it on, she was eligible for marriage and wore it through her adult life.[8] In short, it had the same significance as the ancient string skirt, announcing to all viewers that she could now bear children. The woman's traditional costume across large sections of eastern and southeastern Europe is characterized by two aprons, one worn in front and the other in back, belted on over a chemise.

1.16 Woman's sash
Galičnik, western Macedonia, twentieth century
Woven sash and tassels of hard-spun combed wool; sequins, commercial white tape, metal strip wound around yellow cord
145 x 53 cm
FOWLER MUSEUM X96.6.12D; GIFT OF PROFESSOR ELSIE IVANCICH DUNIN

In parts of both Macedonia and Albania, the sacred fringes took the form of heavy tassels hanging from a sash separate from the apron.

1.17 Woman's over-sleeves
Galičnik, western Macedonia, twentieth century
Tapestry-woven bands of wool and silk connected by twill wool bands; edging and darker panel embroidered on plain-weave linen; combed hard-spun wool fringe
56 x 23 cm
FOWLER MUSEUM X99.9.2A,B; GIFT OF IRMA SWITZER

False sleeves were pulled on over the arm like armbands, covering the plainer sleeves of the ordinary chemise for festive occasions. In the case of a "bride," however, who wore her finery for several years (both as a sign of her status and to chase away evil from her incipient reproductive capacity), she might remove them only when performing tasks like laundry where the heavy but important fringes would be in the way.

1.18 Head cover
Bitola area, southwestern Macedonia, twentieth century
Woven and embroidered cotton; white cotton tassels, tightly wrapped at top, black felt edging.
81 x 41 cm
FOWLER MUSEUM X2012.8.4; GIFT OF GRACE COHEN GROSSMAN

Lightweight white scarves like this one could also carry the significant tassels on the back corner, in either black or white (e.g., head cover in figure 1.48).

1.19A Woman's sleeveless vest
Mariovo, southwestern Macedonia, twentieth century
Woven cotton base, wool embroidery and fringe; sequins, glass beads
100 x 41 cm
FOWLER MUSEUM X99.50.3A; GIFT OF GAIL KLIGMAN

In the conservative uplands of southern Macedonia, the deeply
significant fringes have migrated to many parts of the costume,
such as the shoulders and tails of the vest.

1.19B The long panel hanging in back of figure 1.19a, with its
magnificent red wool fringe, was originally the head cover, which
here has been cut and sewn on so its fringes always fall in the proper
place (cf. figs. 1.61a–f).

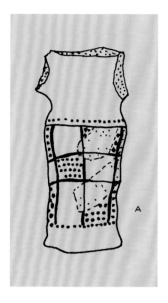   

1.20A-D With woven cloth more common in the late Stone Age, the important message of a woman's childbearing ability sometimes shifted to a checkerboard-patterned wraparound, seen here (a) on a Neolithic figurine (circa 5000 BCE) from Vinča, Serbia (drawing after Gimbutas 1982, fig. 7). The large clay statue from Kličevac (b–d), on the Serbian Danube, shows a female dressed in a full-sleeved embroidered chemise, checkered overskirt, wide sash, and short apron with very long fringes (from Hoernes 1898, pl. 4). Despite its age (roughly 1500 BCE; Bronze Age), this outfit is closely similar to ones worn in much of eastern Europe until recently (see 1.21a–d).

1.21A-D In eastern Europe, when a girl reached maturity, she received a square-patterned back apron to wear over her chemise. (a) The typical Ukrainian costume has a full-sleeved chemise, checkered back apron (*plakhta* or *panyova*), and apron, all with embroidered or inwoven fertility motifs (shown here on a Moiseyev dancer with skirts shortened for the stage). The zigzag on the bottom of her chemise matches that on the Bronze Age statue in figure 1.20b–d. (b) A Ukrainian girl drawn in 1785 shows by her checked back apron that she is beyond puberty; its double layer, displayed by tucking the top layer up, shows she is well off; wearing a wreath and braid rather than covering her hair shows she is unmarried (after Zelenin 1927, fig. 193). (c) The woman from southeastern Belarus wears a chemise, checkered back apron (partly tucked up at an angle), long tassels (far left), and a *namitka*, a married woman's head-wrap (after Ramanjuk 2003, 48). (d) The typical married woman from Oryol region, South Great Russia, wore a chemise, square-patterned back apron (corners tucked up), and cap heavy with fringes (after Vinogradova 1969).

1.22 Square-patterned back apron
Ukraine, twentieth century
Cotton overshot; cotton tassels
69 x 69 cm
FOWLER MUSEUM X70.1220A; GIFT OF ERIC BARKER

The squares in this ritual back apron contain a traditional
eight-pointed "star of the Ukraine" motif.

Still farther north, in yet colder climes, the square-patterned back apron was sewn into a tube that would keep the cold out more effectively by forming a skirt over the chemise, which now functioned as a one-piece blouse and petticoat. The traditional pattern for the crucial back apron in some areas consisted of stripes rather than squares—for example, in Moravian Slovakia,⁹ and in Šumadija (literally, "woodland"), the oak-growing heartland of old Serbia (fig. 1.24). Often, as in northwest Bulgaria and parts of Kosovo and Albania, the important back apron was tightly pleated (fig. 1.23), and in many regions, including Serbia, girls habitually tucked up the corners of the back apron into their belt at the back (see figs. 1.21b–d). This not only produced an interesting beetle-wing shape but sometimes made it necessary to place any embroidery on the inside face of the garment so it would show when hitched up (see fig. 6.36a).

In the lower Danube basin, a quite different type of overgarment appeared, apparently a separate result of the wraparound meeting the chemise. This was a one-piece, sleeveless overdress, known in American English as a jumper. It appears on many a Bronze Age figurine from the area (figs. 1.25a–c) and persisted into the twentieth century in the rural costumes of much of Bulgaria, where it is called a *sukmàn* (figs. 1.26–1.29).

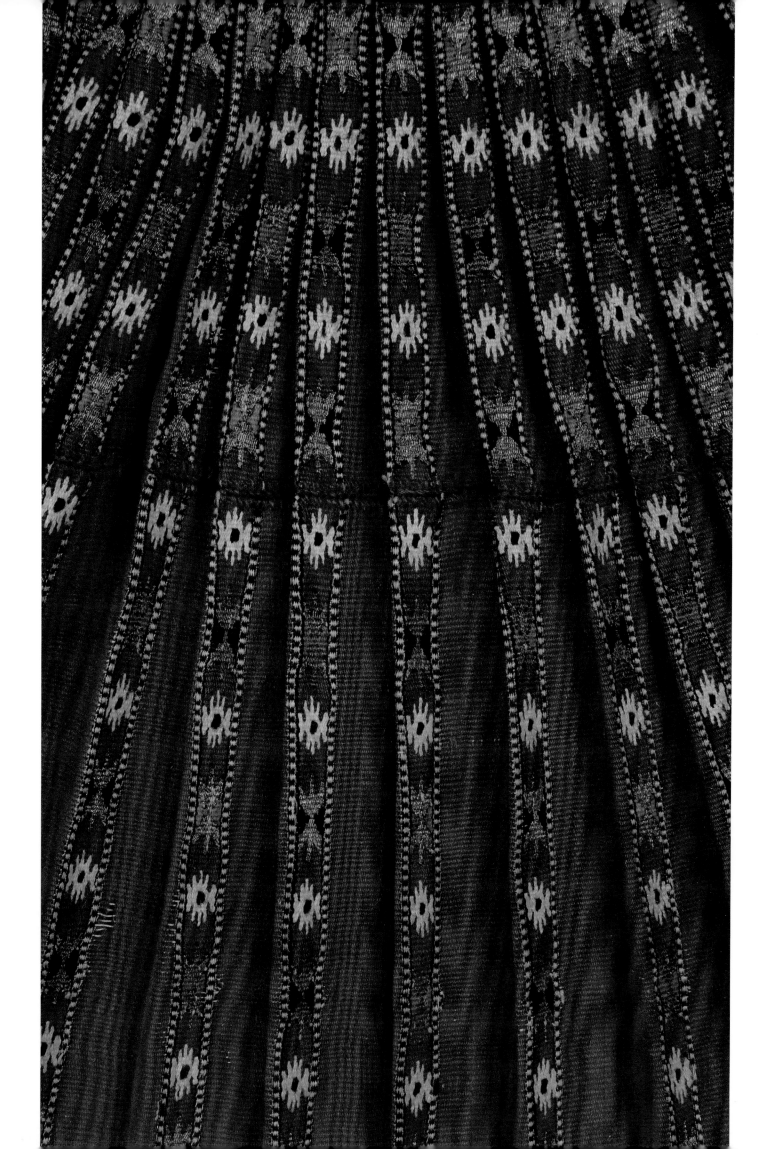

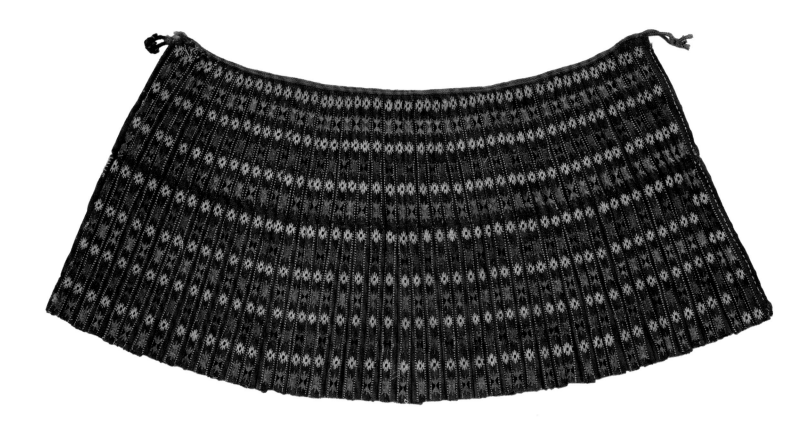

1.23A Detail of figure 1.23b.

1.23B Striped back apron
Serbia, twentieth century
Weft-faced woven wool with tapestry-woven pattern bands, pleated so that plain red between bands is largely hidden; metallic thread in bands
44 x 95 cm
FOWLER MUSEUM X96.6.48; GIFT OF PROFESSOR ELSIE IVANCICH DUNIN

1.24 Striped back apron
Šumadija, central Serbia,
twentieth century
*Woven wool, embroidered,
with crocheted edging*
76 x 102 cm
FOWLER MUSEUM X97.27.5A;
BEQUEST OF MARSHA
LIPMAN

A   B   C

1.25A–C Jumper-dresses first appear on clay figurines of the mid-second millennium BCE (Bronze Age). (a,b) Figurines from Cirna, Romania, typically wear a jumper over a long-sleeved chemise (note the cuffs and fingers ending the curved arms, and the little tie at the neck opening), plus a large, horizontally divided and decorated front apron. The lines down the back of figure b probably represent a string skirt. The boomerang-shaped motifs at the neckline still occur in parts of Bulgaria. (c) The pattern on back of the skirt of this figurine from Novo Selo, Bulgaria, may also represent a string skirt, but it bears a remarkable resemblance to the Bulgarian skirt decoration in figure 1.28a,b. Drawings after Müller-Karpe 1980 (IV), 326 #3, #9; 282 #B.

1.26A Woman's ensemble
Slatina, Sofia district, Bulgaria, twentieth century
FOWLER MUSEUM X99.50.1A,B; GIFT OF GAIL KLIGMAN
(*See Appendix for full details.*)

The jumper-type overdress, or *sukmàn*, in this costume is famous for its handsome pattern of white curlicues of cotton cord on a ground of fine black or royal blue twill. This particular chemise bears an even more famous pattern around its lower hem: a bird on either side of a flowering plant that seems originally to have represented a maiden-goddess.

1.27 Bulgarian girls eligible for marriage donned their best attire, along with borrowed wedding jewelry (note the coin ornaments) and flower-covered headdresses topped with feathergrass, for the Saint Lazarus Day abundance-rituals that marked the "coming out" of young girls each spring. These "Lazarki" from the area around Sofia (the Bulgarian capital) wear exactly the same costume as that illustrated in figures 1.26a,b. REPRODUCED FROM SNOWDEN (1979, 36).

1.26B Back detail view of figure 1.26a.

1.28A Woman's ensemble
Stara Zagora, southeastern Bulgaria (Thrace), twentieth century
FOWLER MUSEUM X93.14.4A–C; GIFT OF DOROTHY DAW
(See Appendix for full details.)

The skirt of the jumper is decorated with stacked circles of colored felt marching in a row down each vertical stripe of the skirt (cf. figure 1.25c). The flowers on the broad apron were created using an unusual embroidery technique that creates large loops rather like chenille, while the vase-like element at the bottom of the two bouquets betrays the influence of patterns from imported Indian chintzes popular in the late seventeenth century (see p. 132).

1.28B Back view of figure 1.28a.

1.29 A young woman carries water in Stara Zagora, Bulgarian Thrace. She wears the same type of costume as illustrated in figures 1.28a–c. REPRODUCED FROM SNOWDEN (1979, 40).

1.28c Detail of figure 1.28b.

I.30 Man's ensemble
Thrace, Bulgaria, twentieth century
FOWLER MUSEUM X93.23.15A–D;
GIFT OF PROFESSOR ELSIE IVANCICH
DUNIN
(See Appendix for full details)

1.31 Man's trousers
Bosnia-Herzegovina, twentieth century
Wool woven in twill, silk cord
107 x 127 cm
FOWLER MUSEUM X68.3199; MUSEUM PURCHASE

These trousers, called *gaće*, are extremely
heavy and durable, being made from tightly
spun combed wool in a dense twill weave.
A two-piece gusset is set in the crotch,
while rows of maroon cord ornament
the edges of the wide fly (not to be
mistaken for pockets).

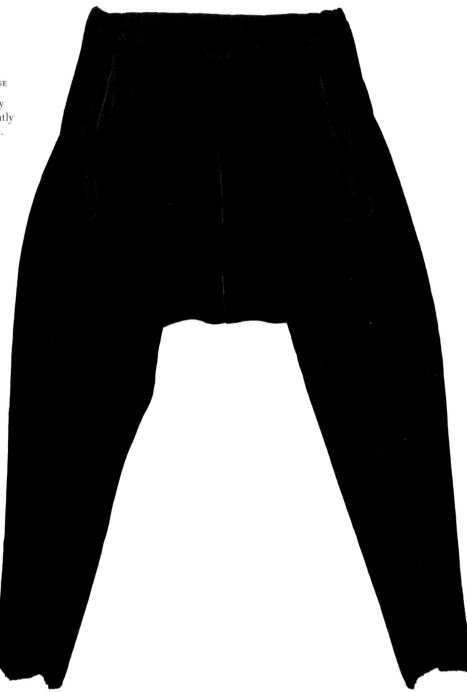

THE MEN'S DEPARTMENT

Men's clothing followed its own line of development (fig. 1.30).
Late Neolithic figurines already show men wearing belts or
sashes, and these persist, not just as a practical garment but
also as a cultural one. In Slavic areas especially, boys were
given a red sash to mark puberty. Like women, men adopted
the sleeved chemise, wearing it sometimes as a long loose
caftan. But their most important innovation was trousers.

Pants seem to have been invented by Eurasian nomadic
herders when they took up riding on the backs of their
domestic horses rather than riding in chariots.[10] Having
sleeve-like tubes for each leg, pants didn't need to be held
on with the hands, and they kept the legs warmer than
either a cloak or chaps when galloping into the stiff winds
of the grasslands. In order to straddle the horse easily,
however, one had to shorten the chemise to hip length
(the English word "shirt" originally meant "shortened")
and provide extra room in the crotch of the pants. Our
earliest preserved examples of pants, worn by Caucasian
horsemen buried in central Eurasia around 700 BCE, have a
biased gusset in the crotch. The "straight" of a woven fabric
(the two directions in which the threads run) doesn't have
much give, but when tugged diagonally (on the bias), cloth
is very stretchy. A gusset is simply a small square of cloth
set in where seams come together (e.g., under the armpit,
see fig. 1.7, or in the crotch, figs. 1.30, 1.31), placed so the
diagonal (bias) crosses the gap, thereby making full use
of that stretchiness. All these sartorial tricks were known
by the end of the Bronze Age.

1.32 Man's trousers
Serbia, twentieth century
Wool woven in a tight twill, heavily felted; black wool braid
102 x 73 cm
FOWLER MUSEUM X96.6.14; GIFT OF PROFESSOR ELSIE IVANCICH DUNIN

Trousers throughout much of Serbia, Bulgaria, and parts of Hungary give much the same impression as these narrow-legged, heavy white trousers with dark trim over the seams and around the fly openings.

1.33 Man's trousers
Skopje, northern Macedonia, twentieth century
Woven linen or cotton, tatted edging, glass beads
79 x 58 cm
FOWLER MUSEUM X69.114; MUSEUM PURCHASE

These summer-weight trousers have a much looser fit than
the heavy woolen trousers normally seen.

1.34 Woman's trousers
Turkey, twentieth century
Woven rayon
86 x 107 cm
FOWLER MUSEUM X2001.10.4; GIFT OF ELAINE ANDERSON

The cut of these trousers, the ultimate in baggy pants, is typical of
Turkish tradition for both women and men but was also taken up
here and there in the former Ottoman domains. One can think of
the design as a very full skirt, sewn up across the bottom with only
a little hole left at each end (or corner) through which the foot and
ankle can protrude. The bright color is also typical of Turkish pref-
erences, contrasting with the predominantly white, black (or dark
brown), and red of the Slavic peoples.

1.35 This Montenegrin man from Risan, Boka Kotorska, wears
pants constructed with large amounts of cloth between the legs,
while the overall shape of his garments resembles that of ceremonial
dress from Montenegro. The artist Nikola Arsenović (1823–1885)
produced this watercolor. REPRODUCED FROM BJELADINOVIĆ (2011, 134,
FIG. 208).

Pants, shirt, and belt or sash thus became the standard model for men's wear from then on, even if the exact cut of each garment might differ. Compare, for example, Serbian pants (see fig. 1.32) with those of Macedonia and Croatia (fig. 1.33 and see fig. 1.83). Balkan farmers were not particularly riders of horses, so they tended not to bother with a gusset, although the very roomy woolen trousers from Bosnia (see fig. 1.31) have one. As villagers became more affluent, they often displayed their wealth by using an extravagant amount of cloth in the breach of their pants (figs. 1.34, 1.35).

Shirttails grew as well, becoming so large in parts of Macedonia (fig. 1.36), Albania, and Greece that it was easier to sew them as a separate garment, girded on like a kilt, with the often enormous fullness added by means of gores (wedge-shaped segments of cloth; fig. 1.37) and/or tight pleats (fig. 1.38 and see fig. 1.62). Men's line dances often include elegant leg movements that emphasize these skirts.

1.36 Man's shirt
Dracevo village, Skopje, Macedonia
Woven cotton, silk and cotton embroidery; black silk cord attached with white silk crochet; hemstitching, smocking
93 x 145 cm
FOWLER MUSEUM X69.113; MUSEUM PURCHASE

1.37A,B Boy's shirt and *fustinela*
Ovče Pole, Macedonia, twentieth century
Woven linen, embroidery, crochet, sequins, plastic buttons
Fustinela: 44 x 114 cm; shirt: 60 x 129 cm
FOWLER MUSEUM X99.34.2A,B; GIFT OF ROBERT LEIBMAN

Shirttails became so large and ostentatious in parts of Macedonia and Greece that they had to be girded on as a separate garment. The father of a bride viewed it as imperative to have a month's warning in which to clean and mend his *fustan* before appearing at the wedding. This boy's *fustinela*, or *fustan*, unlike a man's, has festive ornaments.

1.38 This man from Valona, Albania, wears the national costume, which includes a tightly pleated white skirt (*fustan*) over narrow trousers, topped by a white shirt, fancy vest, belt, and fez. The photograph, taken circa 1928, is from the Emily Blackstone Camp Archive, Fowler Museum (see Sloan, this volume).

MORE LAYERS:
COATS, JACKETS, AND VESTS

The sleeveless vest, which, long or short, forms such a prominent part of southeastern European dress, appears to be a simple garment from which more complex coats and jackets must have arisen; but history seems to have it the other way around. To obtain a fitted outer garment, people appear first to have designed a sleeved overcoat similar to a shirt, though more voluminous (figs. 1.39a,b), and it is this overcoat that apparently led to the vest by successive reduction and elimination of the sleeves. Thus, contrary to modern western wear, we often see the inner garments, not the outer, having the longest sleeves (although medieval western European ladies also affected tops with elbow-length sleeves layered over their long-sleeved chemises, possibly cued by Near Eastern fashions brought back by the Crusaders). Note, for instance, the short-tailed, short-sleeved felt jacket worn over a double-breasted jacket with longer sleeves and longer body in the man's outfit from Macedonia (figs. 1.40a,b).

1.39A Coat
Zagreb, Croatia, twentieth century
Very fine woven and felted wool; fox fur trim, appliquéd silk cord; sheepskin lining, interior belt of woven cotton
103 x 95 cm
FOWLER MUSEUM X99.34.11; GIFT OF ROBERT LEIBMAN

Coats like this with corded decoration were made by skilled furriers.

1.39B Back view of figure 1.39a.

1.40A,B Man's jackets
Lazaropole, western Macedonia, twentieth century
FOWLER MUSEUM X99.34.21A,D; GIFT OF ROBERT LEIBMAN
(*See Appendix for full details.*)

Jackets were made to be shown off, not just for warmth. Therefore
it is the outer jacket, not the inner, that has the shorter sleeves so
that both jackets are visible. Here, the outer jacket is heavy felted
twill, whereas the inner is of a fine worsted wool in plain weave,
a top-quality cloth.

For women in particular, the shorter sleeves or complete sleevelessness of the outer layers allowed the wearer to display rich decoration on the inner garments as well. Many Macedonian women's costumes, in fact, are constructed with several layers of sleeved and sleeveless vests, coats, and jackets. Note, for example, the outfit from Lazaropole, western Macedonia (figs. 1.41a–c), which has a sleeveless woolen coat over a sleeved woolen jacket over a sleeveless cotton and velvet vest over a lightweight sleeved chemise (not to mention extra over-sleeves). This layering explains why most of the shortest vests (e.g., figs. 1.42–1.47) are far more ornate in back than the longer ones. The short ones typically lay outermost and covered up the inner ones at the back. But since the fronts usually flapped open, there the viewer could see all the layers, so those areas are decorated.

1.41A Woman's ensemble
Lazaropole, western Macedonia, twentieth century
FOWLER MUSEUM X99.34.15A–K; GIFT OF ROBERT LEIBMAN
(See Appendix for full details.)

This elaborate outfit, from one of the conservative Mijak villages in the uplands of western Macedonia, consists of many layers of clothing, the topmost of which (sash, apron, head scarf, and over-sleeves—here set to each side) display the masses of fringe associated with the string skirt tradition. Beneath them, but over a white chemise with colored sleeves, lies a long white coat of felted wool that has armholes directly in front of sleeves too slender to use (see fig. 1.58).

1.41B Back view of figure 1.41a.   1.41C Detail of figure 1.41a.

OPPOSITE

1.42A Detail of figure 1.42b.

1.42B Woman's vest
Serbia, twentieth century
Woven wool, couched with metallic and wool braid,
commercial metallic ribbon, egg-shaped buttons with
metallic thread and glass beads; printed cotton lining
33 x 39 cm
FOWLER MUSEUM X93.14.2; GIFT OF DOROTHY DAW

The couching of metal thread to form elegant
designs like those on this series of six vests
(see also figs. 1.43–1.47) was the work of special
craftsmen in the towns and was heavily
influenced by Ottoman styles.

1.43 Woman's vest
Serbia, early twentieth century
Velvet, metallic rope; printed cotton lining
30 x 41 cm
FOWLER MUSEUM X96.6.6; GIFT OF PROFESSOR
ELSIE IVANCICH DUNIN

1.44 Woman's vest
From Skopje, Macedonia,
probably Albanian,
twentieth century
*Woven wool, metallic rope and
braid, perle silk; braided metallic
thread and glass beads on oval
buttons; printed cotton lining*
33 x 40 cm
FOWLER MUSEUM X96.6.44; GIFT OF
PROFESSOR ELSIE IVANCICH DUNIN

1.45 Woman's vest
Probably Serbian, twentieth
century
*Woven cotton or linen couched
with metallic rope, cotton thread;
oval buttons with braided cotton;
printed cotton lining*
33 x 40 cm
FOWLER MUSEUM X2008.30.9;
GIFT OF ANTHONY SHAY

I.46 Vest
Probably Serbian, twentieth century
Silk brocade, metallic rope and braid, commercial metallic ribbon;
printed cotton lining with cotton rope
31 x 41 cm
FOWLER MUSEUM X2009.14.2; GIFT OF YUTTA DARCY-TONKIN

I.47A Detail of figure 1.47b.

I.47B Woman's vest
Probably Serbian, early twentieth century
*Velvet, metallic rope, oval buttons with braided metallic thread
and coral beads; silk braid closures; cotton and silk striped lining*
33 x 38 cm
FOWLER MUSEUM X2008.30.12; GIFT OF ANTHONY SHAY

Because showy sleeves could get in the way of rough farmwork and be damaged, the most heavily embroidered and fringed sleeves were often removable, designed to be pulled on and attached to the costume for festive wear (figs. 1.48a,d, and see fig. 1.17). Possibly for the same reason, short sleeveless vests became particularly popular in men's costumes. Both men's and women's vests ranged from small, purely decorative outerwear (e.g., fig. 1.51; and see figs. 1.42–1.47) to longer vests worn primarily for warmth (figs. 1.49, 1.50, 1.53), and even longer ones that are still heavily decorated to impress the viewer (figs. 1.52, 1.54). This sort of long sleeveless coat, widely known as a *sayà*, gave the characteristic silhouette to women's costumes throughout much of Bulgaria, Macedonia, Albania, and Greece. Among its more interesting variants are the wing-like gores on the woman's padded vest from Titov Veles, Macedonia (see fig. 1.50).

Those women's costumes that developed from placing a closed skirt over the chemise (rather than one or a pair of flat aprons, or open vests) led to a different sort of sleeveless vest, more like a bodice. This type, which reaches only to the waist, fits closely to the body and may be sculpted under the breasts (figs. 1.55a,b, 1.56a,b), facilitating breast-feeding while remaining clothed. The bodice style, as we shall see, became particularly popular in the north, where skirts became the norm.

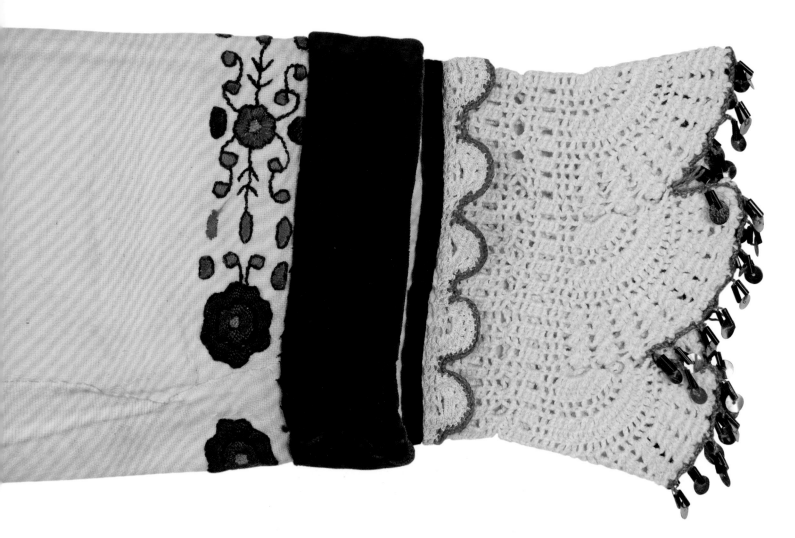

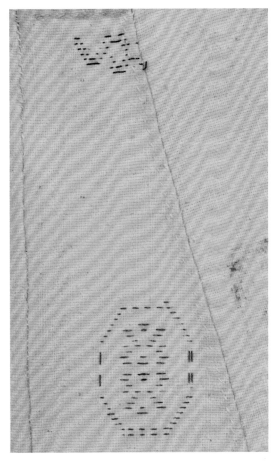

OPPOSITE, TOP
1.48A Detail of sleeve-end in figure 1.48a. Here a false sleeve decorated with crocheted and beaded ruffles has been slipped *under* the end of the embroidered sleeve of the chemise. It was used on festive occasions.

OPPOSITE, BOTTOM
1.48B,C Details of figure 1.48a. The seamstress chose a spot near the waist of the chemise (where it would never be seen) to work out the guide-stitches for the embroidery patterns she then put on the bottom and back of the chemise.

ABOVE
1.48D Woman's ensemble
Bitola, southwestern Macedonia, twentieth century
FOWLER MUSEUM X96.6.17A–I; GIFT OF PROFESSOR ELSIE IVANCICH DUNIN
(See Appendix for full details.)

A starkly geometrical black-on-white scheme of decoration is not unusual in Macedonia and Thrace, nor is the use of old coins as ornaments (here decorating the lower skirts of the long sleeveless vest or *sayà* (*saja*). Note the typically Macedonian vertical oblongs climbing up the back of the skirt (see fig. 1.48e) and the long white tassels on the head scarf.

1.48E Back view of figure 1.48d.

1.49 Woman's vest
Montenegro, before 1920
Velvet, metallic braid; twill
cotton lining
31 x 41 cm
FOWLER MUSEUM X78.469;
GIFT OF DOROTHEA GUDELJ

The shape, color, and sim-
plicity of this vest, with its
understated edging of gold
trim, make it representative
of women's basic vests over
much of central Europe.

1.50 Woman's vest
Titov Veles, central Macedonia,
twentieth century
Woven wool, quilted to rough
plain-weave wool backing;
cotton and wool cord as trim
84 x 109 cm
FOWLER MUSEUM X99.34.4B;
GIFT OF ROBERT LEIBMAN

For winter, vests might be
longer and padded for warmth,
as this one is. As on vests from
the town of Skopje, this one has
distinctive side-panels that
stick out like half-folded wings.

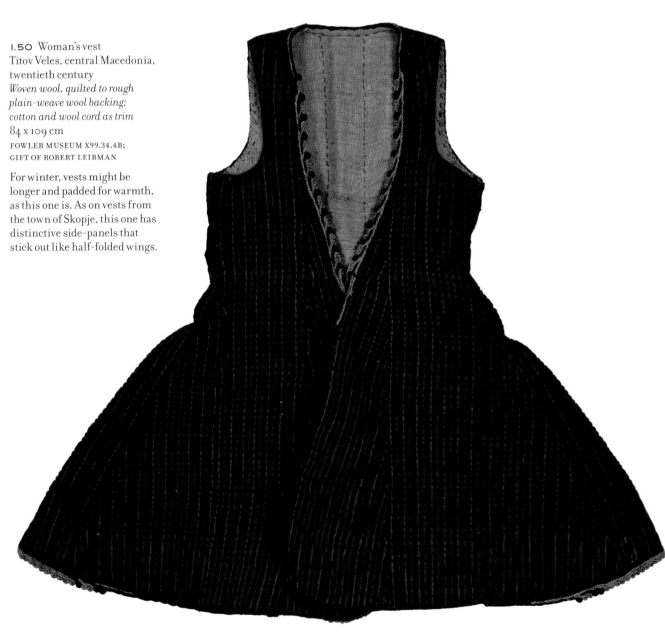

1.51A Detail of figure 1.51b.

1.51B Woman's vest
Bosnia-Herzegovina, twentieth century
Wool woven in twill and felted, couched and embroidered
with perle silk
28 x 41 cm
FOWLER MUSEUM X93.23.3; GIFT OF PROFESSOR ELSIE IVANCICH DUNIN

Vests could be quite small, like this one, yet still add considerable
decoration to an outfit. Along the edges of the inner face, one can
see the orange thread used to fasten (couch) the thick colored cords
to the outer surface.

1.52 Man's vest
Dubrovnik, Dalmatia, southern Croatia,
twentieth century
Fine worsted wool couched with perle silk;
lined with plaid cotton, pattern-woven cotton band
47 x 51 cm
FOWLER MUSEUM X84.1221; GIFT OF LOUISE LASSER

Although of the most traditional cut, this vest was
intended for festive occasions, as shown by the
elaborate designs in Ottoman style. Traces of
sewing show that it had been made smaller with
darts in the back, then let out again—evidence
of how long it had been treasured.

OPPOSITE
1.52B Detail of figure 1.52a.

1.53 Man's vest
Bosnia-Herzegovina, twentieth century
Wool woven in twill, silk cord
50 x 47 cm
FOWLER MUSEUM X68.2492; MUSEUM PURCHASE

This simple vest, long enough to keep one warm
but not so long as to get in the way of work, is
representative of men's basic vests over much of
southeastern and central Europe. It is of the same
materials as the trousers in figure 1.31.

OPPOSITE
1.53B Detail of figure 1.53a.

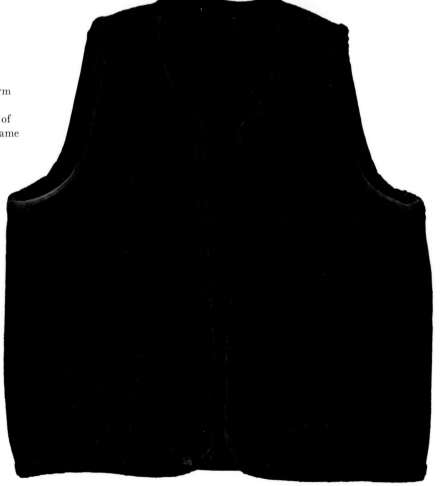

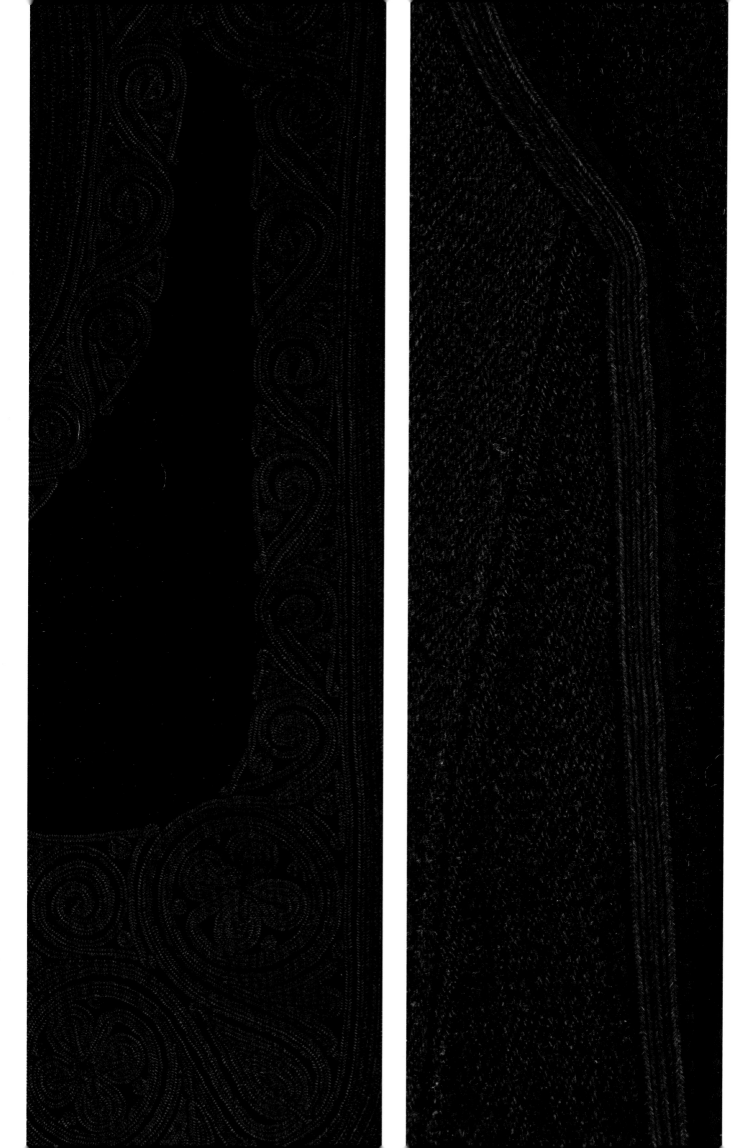

1.54A Detail of back of figure 1.54b.

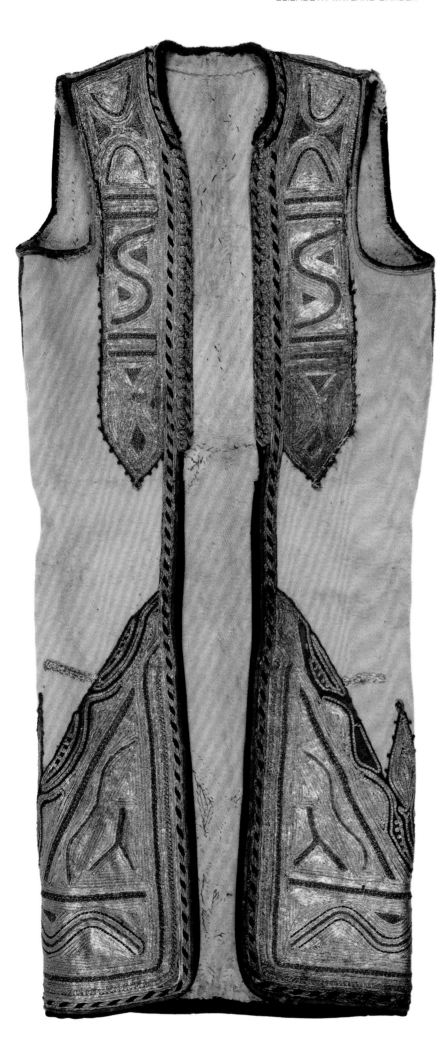

I.54B Woman's vest
Dragas, Kosovo, twentieth century
*Wool woven in twill and felted; metallic and
wool braid, perle silk, fine woven wool (in trim)*
98 x 46 cm
FOWLER MUSEUM X96.6.4; GIFT OF PROFESSOR
ELSIE IVANCICH DUNIN

This handsome vest, made of heavy felted
wool and masses of metal braid, weighs well
over four pounds.

1.55A Woman's vest
Serbian or perhaps Bosnian
Croat, twentieth century
*Velvet, metallic rope and braid,
bits of colored silk, sequins,
open-work metal buttons;
lined with cotton or linen*
39 x 40 cm
FOWLER MUSEUM X97.27.8;
BEQUEST OF MARSHA LIPMAN

Women's vests were sometimes
cut very low in the front, under
the breasts (which of course
facilitated breast-feeding).
The two filigree buttons that
close the vest materialize, in
the jeweler's art, the same sorts
of designs as the tailor produced
in couched gold thread, here
felicitously picked out with
occasional sequins and bits of
colored silk peeking out from
under the gold.

OPPOSITE
1.55B Detail of figure 1.55a.

1.56A Woman's vest
Serbian, twentieth century
*Velvet couched with metallic
thread and braid; sequins; ball-
shaped buttons covered with
metallic braid; cotton lining*
39 x 40 cm
FOWLER MUSEUM X2011.4.71;
GIFT OF DR. JOEL MARTIN HALPERN

The neckline in this vest has
been sculpted to support the
breasts. Both the metallic decoration and the ball-shaped buttons show Ottoman influence.

OPPOSITE
1.56B Detail of figure 1.56a.

The most intriguing development of the sleeved coat, however, has got to be that of the "useless" sleeve, apparently a by-product of slipping one's arms out of the sleeves through the vent-holes left open under the armpits. Underarm vents are already attested around 700 BCE on a woman's dress preserved in the Taklamakan Desert of Central Asia, and images from late Classical times show people with their arms stuck through just such holes when performing messy tasks like laundry, while the empty sleeves dangle behind. Furthermore, in the Katanda River area of the Altai Mountains, archaeologists unearthed a handsome leather man's jacket dating to about 400 BCE and sporting long tubular sleeves that were deliberately sewn so narrow that the wearer could not possibly get his arms into them. This coat could only be worn by slinging it around the shoulders like a cape with the useless sleeves hanging free in back. This jaunty-looking habit of dangling the sleeves developed in three interesting directions.

In one derivative, the vent-hole was deliberately enlarged for easier donning as a cape or long vest, while the vestigial sleeve was narrowed yet more (fig. 1.57). Delightful examples of this form still exist in women's attire from mountainous western Macedonia. Galičnik (fig. 1.58) and Lazaropole (see fig. 1.41), populated by the Mijak group, who are mostly herders, seem to lie near the center of this tradition, but the narrow white vestigial sleeves can be found here and there in Mijak villages from Tetovo in the north all the way to Smiljevo in the south.[11]

1.57 Nineteenth-century "Sart" women in central Asia wore coats with long, narrow, vestigial sleeves hanging down in back, not unlike the vestigial sleeves Mijak women wore in western Macedonia (see figure 1.58). Both costumes have simple armholes in front of these sleeves for actual use as well as decoration on the ends of the sleeves. The name "Sart" was given to settled Muslims of Turkic or Iranian speech living in Russian Turkestan. REPRODUCED FROM MOSER (1885, 72).

1.58 Woman's coat with vestigial sleeves
Galičnik, western Macedonia, twentieth century
Wool woven in twill and felted; velvet, perle silk embroidery, wool and metallic braid sequins; silver filigree balls
56 x 155 cm
FOWLER MUSEUM X96.6.12C; GIFT OF PROFESSOR ELSIE IVANCICH DUNIN

This coat of felted white wool has slits for the arms directly in front of vestigial sleeves that one couldn't possibly use. The "sleeves" consist of narrow tubes tapering to an end the size of a garden hose, with a bit of red cord sewn around the opening like a tiny cuff. The strange affectation of useless sleeves on one's jacket is traceable back at least twenty-five hundred years among Eurasian herders—a fact suggesting some connection between the Mijak tribe and one of the invasions from the Eurasian grasslands.

1.59a Woman's coat
Pristina, Kosovo, twentieth century
Woven silk, metallic thread embroidery, metallic ribbon and braid,
sequins; buttons covered with metallic thread, coral beads; cotton lining
115 x 117 cm
FOWLER MUSEUM X67.2424; GIFT OF MR. AND MRS. THEODORE LOWENSTEIN

Where one expects sleeves, this showy coat has flat, sculpted,
heavily decorated lengths of cloth—quite useless as sleeves. Many
coats and jackets in southeastern and central Europe, especially
those for warriors, had ostentatious "sleeves" of this sort. Eventually
they became a sign of nobility.

OPPOSITE
1.59b Detail of figure 1.59a.

In a second derivative, the tube of the sleeve was left
completely unsewn so as to hang from the shoulder as a
flat, arm-length strip, a convenient canvas for ostentatious
decoration. Figure 1.59 is a woman's garment, but in some
areas, especially Greece, men wore flat pendant sleeves too.

The third offspring of the Katanda jacket tradition was
reflected in the penchant among central Eurasian warriors
for wearing jackets half on and half off. That is, the sleeves
were large enough to be functional when needed, but it was
considered more elegant to leave one or both sleeves hanging down unused. The fashion seems to have persisted in
Albania, Greece, and Bulgaria, where successive waves of
Central Asian warriors—Avars, Huns, Bulgars, Mongols,
and so forth—roared in and then settled down over many
centuries. The half-off jacket trimmed with an abundance
of braid later became an affectation of the military groups
called Hussars. It looked so dashing in fact that presently the
male nobility of Europe adopted the fashion: a jewel-colored,
sleeved jacket encrusted with gold braid worn over one
shoulder only, the other sleeve hanging down behind (fig.
1.60).[12] Ballet princes wear it still, icons of romantic nobility.

So far, we have been looking at the broad lines of development of European clothing. Before moving on to consider historical evolution farther north, however, let's pause to inspect a single outfit closely, one used by a young woman, since those are the most complex. Take, for example, the young woman's outfit from the Mariovo uplands east of Bitola, in western Macedonia (figs. 1.61a–f). Like so much Slavic attire, the overall impression is of flaming red and white, picked out with black and bits of other colors, the inspiration of a widely known folksong: *Makedonsko devojče— kitka šarena!* (Macedonian girl—a many-colored bouquet!).

The innermost garment is a long white T-shaped chemise (*košula*) of heavy handspun, handwoven plant fiber (linen, hemp, or cotton). Its sleeve-ends, neck opening, and hem have been heavily embroidered with locally traditional motifs in mainly red and black wool with a bit of yellow. Highly characteristic of this and other Macedonian costumes are the vertical panels of embroidery rising in the back from the hemline like twin skyscrapers. Behind the front slit for the head to pass through sits a dickie (*grlo, grlce*), which might be embellished with colored buttons,

glass beads, or embroidery. The garment is belted with a 15-foot (5 meter) black cord plaited of wool (*pojas*).

The next layer is the *saja* (or *sagija*), in this case a hip-length sleeveless vest, also of heavy white cloth but open in the front. It has panels of red embroidery down the front "lapels" almost to the waist. But its characteristic feature—what made a girl from the Mariovo uplands instantly recognizable—is a veritable mane of long red fringes of hard-spun wool over the armholes at the shoulders as well as protruding from the side seams. Yet more fringes could be added by pulling extra sleeve-ends on over the forearm like bracelets, tucking the top ends under the medium-length sleeves of the chemise.

Over the *saja* is tied an apron (*pregač*). This apron, too, woven mainly of red wool in two narrow panels, has a thick red fringe at the bottom that climbs part way up the sides. It is usually further ornamented with a zigzag of gold braid across the bottom, some sequins, and a few coins. A wide, red, band-woven sash (*pojas*) is wound around the waist. The sashes on some Macedonian costumes can be sixteen feet long. If the girl is wealthy, she may display some of her dowry by hanging the coins as thickly as possible along her belt (see fig. 1.61a) as well as on her chest. Or she might wear eye-shaped, silver belt buckles (*pafti*) of a type found in many parts of the Balkan peninsula. These buckles may be ornamented with jingly chains and occasionally gemstones. Sometimes they were quite enormous—in order, it was said, that the occupying Turks would be unable to distinguish who among the Christian women was pregnant and who was not, thereby deflecting punitive raids.

The socks (*čorapi, bukajkite*), too, are mainly red, with tiny patterns knitted into them in black, dark red, yellow, and white. The shoes (*opanci, opintsi*) are very comfortable and durable sandals of pigskin or cowhide with a pointed toe and wide straps across the instep—the typical Macedonian style (see fig. 1.61b).

1.61A Woman's ensemble
Mariovo, southwestern Macedonia, twentieth century
FOWLER MUSEUM X97.27.1A–E; BEQUEST OF MARSHA LIPMAN. X96.6.23E–H (SCARF, DICKIE, STOCKINGS), X96.6.36A,B (SHOES); GIFT OF PROFESSOR ELSIE IVANCICH DUNIN. PRIVATE COLLECTION (UBRUS, COIN BELT, SILVER BUCKLE) (*See Appendix for full details.*)

The costume consists of a white chemise with red and black wool embroidery on the sleeves, collar, neck placket, and hem; a white cotton dickie ornamented with embroidery and/or glass beads; a white sleeveless coat or vest with red and black wool embroidery and heavy red wool fringes hanging from the shoulders, side seams, and neck opening; a red apron decorated with heavy red fringe, gold rickrack in a conventional pattern, and coins (here, Greek, Turkish, and Bulgarian); a red belt or sash, often covered with coins (as in this case) and serving as visible dowry and a private bank; a very long black belt-cord of braided rope; tall red knitted socks; leather moccasins with cross-straps and turned-up toes; and two very different head scarves, often worn at the same time.

1.61B Knitted socks and leather moccasins that accompany the ensemble shown in figure 1.61a.

Crowning all this are not one but two headdresses, which may be worn individually or together. One consists of a square white scarf edged with large pompoms, some always red (telling us that these, too, are a "fringey" reflex of the sacred strings), others perhaps blue and/or white (see fig. 1.61g). The second, very archaic headdress (*ubrus*) is a long strip of homemade linen with embroidered edges and a wide band of thick red and black woolen embroidery at each end, tipped by tremendously long fringes of combed, spun, and plied red wool yarn (see fig. 1.61f). In both shape and decoration this embroidered linen strip bears a remarkable resemblance to the headcloth used by non-Slavic, non-Indo-European Chuvash women in the area between Moscow and the Urals.[13] This forms yet another Balkan tie directly to the Eurasian interior, along with the vestigial sleeves.

On some occasions, the girl may wear just the scarf, tied around her head in such a way that the pompoms frame her face. At other times, she might wear just the long strip, tied in one of several traditional ways, but always so that some of the fringes hang down in front and/or in back or frame her face. Given all the other fringes she is wearing, this mode typically envelopes her in red fringes. The third option is to twist the two headdresses together and wrap them turban-like around her head, with fringes and pompoms sprouting everywhere and one tasseled end of the *ubrus* hanging far down her back.

OPPOSITE, TOP

1.61C Detail of sleeve of figure 1.61a.

OPPOSITE, BOTTOM

1.61D Detail of apron of from figure 1.61a. Aprons from this village always have three golden triangles delineated across the bottom, although a girl with less wealth might make them with yellow thread rather than gold. The girl also sews on whatever spare coins she possesses, whether current or of centuries past and from other regimes. The coins on this apron date from 1926 to 1940.

ABOVE

1.61E Detail of figure 1.61a.

This entire outfit, with its jewelry and extra "bridal" showpieces (such as more jewelry, and thick black fringes simulating hair), could weigh upward of 130 pounds (60 kilos; more than the girl herself!).[14] It represents an enormous amount of handwork, starting with spinning all the thread, weaving all the cloth, and then fringing and embroidering everything. Furthermore, it all had to be done before the girl reached puberty. In some areas of eastern and southeastern Europe, the girl did everything; in other cases some work was done by her mother and other female relatives, but always at least certain pieces had to be produced by the girl herself. As noted earlier, a woman won her husband by the elaborateness and beauty of her holiday dress, and she had to show by her outfit that she was both skillful and industrious.

1.61F,G Head covers for the ensemble seen in figure 1.61a. One head cover is traditionally a long rectangle of heavy linen, embroidered in red, with long red woolen fringes at both ends. It may be wound around the head and neck with the fringes covering the chest and/or back (cf. figure 1.19b). The other is a square of lighter-weight cotton edged with colored pompoms. It may be worn alone, folded into a triangle, or it may be twisted together with the other headpiece, being wound around the head like an enormous turban, fringes hanging in back.

1.61H Back view of figure 1.61a. Note the vertical panels of
embroidery climbing up from the back hemline (cf. fig. 1.48e).

Where people would see her was in the line of dancers in the village square on Sundays after church, so everything was geared to displaying the outfit to best advantage there. Dances, too, were tweaked to make the outfits show off well. A girl was not allowed to join the dance until she reached puberty—that is, was ready for marriage and childbearing; then she had to appear at her very best. If she attracted the attention of a young man (figs. 1.62–1.64), he might begin to test her physical strength and endurance for future farmwork by learning how she danced. In several areas of southeastern Europe, antique "bride-testing" dances have survived in which the men pull down hard on the women or make them jump high or spin fast to test their hardiness and agility.

It wasn't just the young men looking, either: future mothers-in-law were busy scanning the crowd for likely prospects for their sons. Since the bride would move into her husband's extended household and take over many of the mother's chores (not to mention those of the household's daughters who were marrying out), the mother actually stood to gain or lose the most in the choice of a bride. She could recognize good or shoddy textile work because she had made such things herself; she could also gauge the industriousness of the girl by her handwork. The young woman's costume was critical and each village had its own required forms (figs. 1.65–1.71).

OPPOSITE

1.62 Man's ensemble
Mariovo, southwestern Macedonia, early to mid-twentieth century
FOWLER MUSEUM X99.34.32A–D; GIFT OF ROBERT LEIBMAN
(See Appendix for full details.)

The Mariovo man's clothes were plain compared to the woman's.
The elaborate pleated white "kilt" (*vustan, fustan, foustanella*) worn
as a separate garment by men in parts of Macedonia, Albania, and
Greece betrays its origin as elaborated shirttails by its use over trousers (unlike the Scottish kilt). These calf-length trousers are rather
looser than is usual.

ABOVE

1.63 Man's ensemble
Skopje, northern Macedonia, twentieth century
FOWLER MUSEUM X99.34.27A–E; GIFT OF ROBERT LEIBMAN
(See Appendix for full details.)

This entire outfit was made from heavy felted wool, even the shirt—
although it is a slightly lighter plain weave, whereas the coat and
leggings (the "pant legs" are not sewn into trousers) are of heavier
twill. A faggoting stitch has been used for the seams of the leggings
and to attach the fancy knitted cuffs to the shirt.

1.64 Man's ensemble
Skopje, northern Macedonia, twentieth century
FOWLER MUSEUM X99.34.25A–D; GIFT OF ROBERT LEIBMAN
(See Appendix for full details.)

A specialty of Skopje, this very durable striped material of combed
and tightly spun wool was used for the vests of both men and women
from Skopje (see fig. 1.66a,b). The tails of the shirt, protruding from
under the all-important red sash, show us what developed into the
fustan seen in figures 1.37, 1.38, and 1.62. The worsted (combed wool)
twill sash sports a coin dated 1751 from Germany.

1.65 Woman's ensemble
Debar, western Macedonia, twentieth century
FOWLER MUSEUM X99.34.6A–H; GIFT OF ROBERT LEIBMAN
(*See Appendix for full details.*)

Dress in the larger regional town of Debar became slightly "modernized." The silhouette remains the same, but the apron is mostly woven, with minimal fringing, while the long fringes necessary for a bride are provided by a commercially made silk scarf tied around the waist. The sleeve-ends, too, are of commercial velvet. Only the white head scarf, with its pink embroidery and tassels (similar to those in fig. 1.67), and the color scheme of the jacket still look archaic. Note the exquisitely made silver filigree "buttons."

1.66A Woman's ensemble
Skopje, northern Macedonia, twentieth century
FOWLER MUSEUM X96.6.41A,C,D; GIFT OF PROFESSOR ELSIE IVANCICH DUNIN.
X69.108; MUSEUM PURCHASE
(*See Appendix for full details.*)

One can instantly recognize a costume from Skopje because of the
distinctive dark-red striped fabric in the vests of both sexes (see fig.
1.64). The woman's vest also has peculiar triangular panels sticking
out like wings on either side (like those on the padded vest from
Titov Veles, a town a little to the south of Skopje; see fig. 1.50).

1.66B Back view of figure 1.66a.

1.67A Woman's ensemble
Debarski Drimkol, western Macedonia, twentieth century
FOWLER MUSEUM X99.34.1A–G,J; GIFT OF ROBERT LEIBMAN
(See Appendix for full details.)

This costume from Drimkol, like examples from Drenok and other little villages in the Debar region along the current Albanian border, preserves the red fringes by placing them both on the apron (the rickrack of which is carefully placed to frame the pubic region, when worn), on the side seams of the jacket, and on the ends of a tremendously long black or red sash (fig. 1.67c). When worn, this sash is wrapped tightly around the waist several times, over the top of the apron, with the fringed ends carefully placed over the buttocks in back. With the addition of the headcloth and its long red tassels, the girl is entirely surrounded by the protective and fertility-bringing fringes, which swish as she walks or dances.

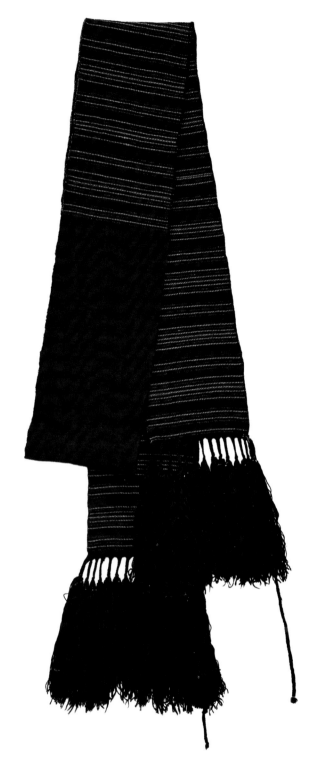

1.67B Head scarf that accompanies figure 1.67a.

1.67C Tasseled sash
Smiljevo, western Macedonia, twentieth century
*Black wool twill with weft stripes; plied and plaited tassels;
braided wool ties*
Woven segment: 158 x 20 cm; tassels at each end: 27 cm
FOWLER MUSEUM X99.34.8G; GIFT OF ROBERT LEIBMAN

1.68a Woman's ensemble
Bitola, southwestern Macedonia, twentieth century
FOWLER MUSEUM X99.34.19A–G; GIFT OF ROBERT LEIBMAN
(*See Appendix for full details.*)

As usual in this part of Macedonia, thick embroidery has been lavished on the hem of the chemise and the sleeve-ends, and the apron consists of two horizontal pieces of cloth sewn together. The only trace of fringe, however, is in the long white tassels on the head scarf (see fig. 1.68c). The eight-pointed star on the sleeves, interestingly, is the same geometrically constructed pattern as that on the Ukrainian back apron in figure 1.22.

1.68b Detail of figure 1.68a. The linen dickie visible under the ornate lapels of the sleeveless coat is heavily ornamented with glass beads, sequins, commercial braid, shirred silk flowers, one plastic button, and several coins dated 1906.

1.68c Head scarf and socks that accompany the ensemble shown in figure 1.68a.

1.69A Woman's ensemble
Ohrid, western Macedonia, twentieth century
FOWLER MUSEUM X2010.9.1A,B–5A,B; PURCHASED WITH FOWLER MUSEUM
TEXTILE COUNCIL FUNDS FROM THE COLLECTION OF MARGARET HEMPSTEAD
(*See Appendix for full details.*)

The hem of the chemise has been lavishly ornamented with embroidery, including quite tall vertical panels up the back (typical of the

Ohrid-Bitola area in the southwest), as well as with masses of glass beads and sequins, and even a few little metal bells. Set at regular intervals, the coins come from many lands: Turkey, Greece, Yugoslavia, Hungary, and even Denmark. The head scarf is similar to that of Bitola, having elaborately worked white tassels at its corner, this time with black embroidery and wrapping (see fig. 1.69c).

1.69B Detail of figure 1.69a.

1.69c Back view of figure 1.69a.

1.70 Woman's ensemble
Skopje, northern Macedonia, mid-twentieth century
FOWLER MUSEUM X96.6.19A–D,F,G; GIFT OF PROFESSOR ELSIE IVANCICH DUNIN
(See Appendix for full details.)

This woman's vest, heavily padded for winter, has the traditional
Skopje "wings" and two-paneled apron. The amount of gold braid
and ribbon on it suggests the wearer was not poor, as does her belt,
ornamented with metallic ribbon and hooked with round silver
buckles called *pafti*, which in some parts of the Balkan Peninsula
reached enormous proportions.

I.7A Woman's ensemble
Gostivar, northwestern Macedonia, twentieth century
FOWLER MUSEUM X99.34.5A–C,G–I; GIFT OF ROBERT LEIBMAN
(See Appendix for full details.)

Coming from a slightly larger town, this costume shows many
subtle changes from the attire of the more conservative villages
around it. The skirt of the chemise is much fuller, requiring more
fabric; the sash is woven in a plaid twill; the dominant colors are
black and yellow (not red); and the top is of commercial velvet,
decorated with professionally couched gold thread and Ottoman-
style ball-shaped buttons.

I.7IB Detail of front of figure 1.71a.

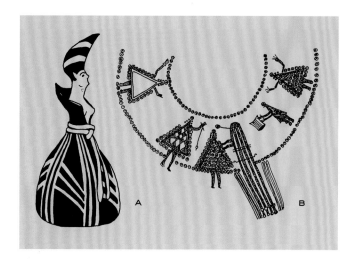

1.72A,B New full-skirted silhouettes for European women began to appear in the Bronze Age. Earliest is the Minoan clay statuette seen in figure 1.72a (arms missing), from Petsofa, Crete, circa 1900 BCE (drawn after reconstructive drawing by R. Dawkins, in Myers 1902–1903, pl. VIII), while the figurines from Cîrna, Romania (see figs. 1.25a–c), show that the new clothing style soon spread north. By circa 800 BCE, incised images on urns of the Hallstatt culture demonstrate its progress into the heart of central Europe. The designs in figure 1.72b, on an urn from Sopron, Hungary, show women spinning, weaving, and dancing (after Barber 1991, fig. 13.3). Their peculiar silhouette is remarkably close to that of Hungarian girls only fifty years ago (see figure 1.73).

1.73 Hungarian village girls wear full skirts and multiple petticoats (as they chat over a fence), which create a triangular silhouette remarkably like that seen on pottery found in Hungary from the Bronze Age (see fig. 1.72b). Drawn after an anonymous travel photo, circa 1950.

GATHERING SKIRTS AND BLOUSES

While the "layered look" was developing in much of the Balkan Peninsula, a rather different approach to women's clothing was evolving to the northwest. The watershed between the two types of costume, like that between couple and non-couple folk dances, matches fairly well the dividing line between those areas Christianized from Rome and those Christianized from Constantinople (present-day Istanbul), as well as the similar but not identical line encompassing the parts of southern Europe held for centuries by the Ottoman Empire (see fig. 2.1). The white linen chemise or shirt still formed the foundation, but the basic outerwear was a gathered skirt, so that the woman's silhouette became more hourglass-like than columnar. This shape was not new: we find it already in the Bronze Age (fig. 1.72a), but it developed differently in different regions.

In some areas, for instance, the top and bottom halves of the chemise became separate garments: a blouse above, a skirt below. In others, a separate skirt, usually quite full, covered the chemise from the waist down, so the bottom half of the chemise, still attached, came to function as a petticoat, while the top part—often half-covered by a bodice—functioned as a blouse. All sorts of variants of these basic principles occurred as well.

Croatian women's dresses, especially those from the Pannonian Plain (along the Sava River from Zagreb to the Danube), figure among the most magnificent costumes of southeastern Europe.[15] The long, full skirts and aprons, as well as the blouses and caps, are often covered with large satin-stitched flowers, sometimes all in one color (including occasionally all white, as in fig. 1.74) but more often in glorious polychrome (figs. 1.75a,b–1.79a,b). Occasionally, as in figures 1.78, 1.81, the designs are more geometrical. One of the favorite types of dance in Croatia, the *drmeš*, includes steps that make the tight circle of dancers spin quickly, which causes these beautiful, tightly gathered or pleated skirts to billow out like opening flowers. In contrast to all the color worn by women, men typically wore white shirts, wide-legged white trousers, and dark vests (fig. 1.83). In colder climates men's and women's vests were sometimes lined with woolen fleece (fig. 1.84).

I.74 Woman's ensemble
Trebovec village, Posavina, Croatia, circa 1900–1920
FOWLER MUSEUM X83.273A–C; GIFT OF PROFESSOR ELSIE IVANCICH DUNIN
(See Appendix for full details.)

Women's clothing from the Sava River valley (Posavina) typically has large sleeves and very full gathered skirts. The white-on-white floral pattern on the blouse and apron was created using supplementary weft.

1.75A Woman's ensemble
Croatia, twentieth century
FOWLER MUSEUM X70.1592A–D; GIFT OF MIA SLAVENSKA
(See Appendix for full details.)

The masses of predominantly red embroidery on ample white
ground are usual for the heart of Croatia, yet each outfit shows
the individual tastes and design talents of the girl who made it for
herself. These garments are made of fine white linen with red roses
embroidered in woolen yarn.

1.75B Back view of figure 1.75a. Note the handsome embroidery on
the shawl, and how far around the apron goes. Aprons are typically
very wide in this region.

OPPOSITE
1.76a Woman's ensemble
Posavina, Croatia, twentieth century
FOWLER MUSEUM X99.39.1A–C; GIFT OF HELEN, JAMES, JERRY,
AND NICHOLAS MAROTT
(See Appendix for full details.)

In addition to huge, colorful, eye-catching flowers, these
garments display subtler features, such as vertical tucks
and white silk cutwork on the front of the blouse, as well
as hemstitching and white embroidery on the white netting
on the skirt.

1.76b Back view of figure 1.76a.

1.77 Woman's ensemble
Bonovina, Posavina, Croatia, twentieth century
FOWLER MUSEUM X99.39.2A–C; GIFT OF HELEN, JAMES, JERRY,
AND NICHOLAS MAROTT
(See Appendix for full details.)

The massing of embroidery on this outfit, mostly in satin-stitch,
makes it almost the epitome of Croatian dress in the broad river
valleys. It has been finished off with lace around the apron and
hemstitching at the bottom of the skirt.

I.78 Woman's ensemble
Posavina, Croatia, twentieth century
FOWLER MUSEUM X99.34.10A–B; GIFT OF ROBERT LEIBMAN.
X93.14.5 (APRON); GIFT OF DOROTHY DAW
(See Appendix for full details.)

Some outfits have very geometric embroidery. The floral motifs
on this example are reserved for the elaborate pink cutwork on the
collar, cuffs, and tails of the blouse. The designs on the blouse and
apron are embroidered, not inwoven.

1.79a Back view of figure 1.79b.

1.79B Woman's ensemble
Posavina, Croatia, twentieth century
FOWLER MUSEUM X2008.4.1 (BLOUSE), X2008.4.2 (APRON), X2008.3.2 (SKIRT);
GIFT OF JEAN AND GARY CONCOFF
(See Appendix for full details.)

The apron is satin-stitched with massive flowers and edged with handmade bobbin lace. The flowers on the blouse front have been satin-stitched onto colored silk ribbons so they can be easily removed when the garment needs cleaning.

1.80A Woman's ensemble
Donja Bebrina area, Baranja, Croatia, twentieth century
FOWLER MUSEUM X69.29 (DRESS), X69.30 (APRON), X69.986 (CAP);
GIFT OF ANTHONY SHAY.
(See Appendix for full details.)

Instead of a separate skirt and blouse, this outfit consists of a one-piece dress. It is sewn from strips of cloth woven with weft-float patterning, alternating with wide and narrow strips of white lace, everything being heavily ornamented with sequins, glass beads, metallic thread, commercial silk ribbon, and colored lace. The dress is finished off with wide white lace of different styles.

1.80B Detail of figure 1.80a.

1.80c Back view of figure 1.80a.

1.81A Woman's ensemble
Baranja, Croatia, twentieth century
FOWLER MUSEUM X72.186A–E; GIFT OF VILMA MACHETTE
(See Appendix for full details.)

These pieces were made from commercial cotton instead of homespun linen, and they were embroidered with thick chenille-like looping. Note the trousers worn Ottoman-style under the skirt (see fig. 1.81b). The apron, decorated with slit tapestry and a large fringe, is usually worn at a rakish angle.

1.81B Pants worn under figure 1.81a.

1.81C Detail of apron shown in figure 1.81a.

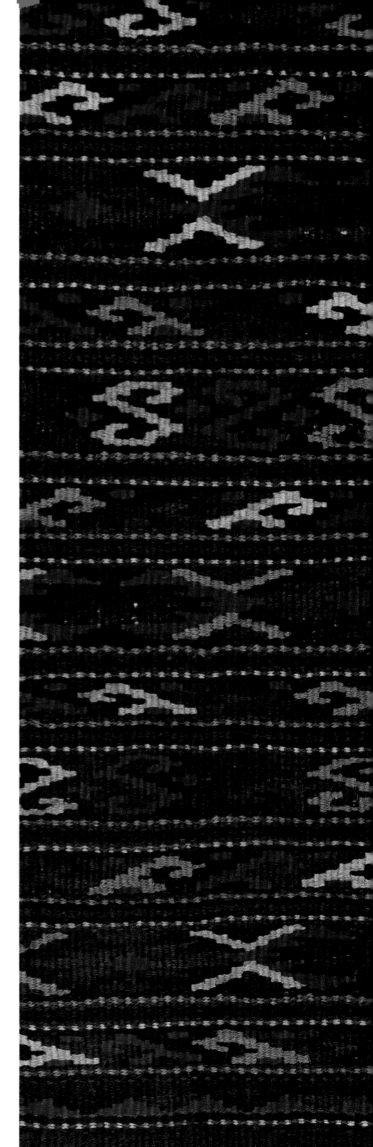

1.81D Back view of figure 1.81a.

1.82A Women's ensemble
Baranja, Croatia, probably ethnic Hungarian; early twentieth century
FOWLER MUSEUM, X97.27.6A–F; GIFT OF MARSHA LIPMAN
(See Appendix for full details)

This outfit is as remarkable for the riches it covers up as for those that catch the eye. The large, satin-stitched, chintz-style flowers of the apron virtually cover a handsome red silk brocade (of large white tulips and roses on a red ground, much like the brocade of the shawl in figure 1.87), while those on the skirt and cap cover black velvet, and those on the sleeves cover white damask. White flowers of similar design have also been embroidered onto white netting to form sleeve panels. All these flowers resemble Hungarian designs, whereas the geometric embroidery around groups of sequins and the narrow panel extending under the arm from body to sleeve are typical of Croatian costumes in Baranja. Metallic ornamentation also abounds: gold and silver lace and rickrack trim each garment, while the belt has been embroidered with flat strips of metal set off by rows of black and sometimes red stitching and more silver braid.

1.83 Man's ensemble
Lika area, Dalmatia, southern Croatia, twentieth century
FOWLER MUSEUM X72.187A–F,I,J; GIFT OF VILMA MACHETTE
(*See Appendix for full details.*)

White linen could be grown, spun, and woven at home, as well as being very durable and easy to wash. For that reason, in large areas of Dalmatia and Croatia the basic attire of men and sometimes women consisted largely of white linen. The long vest of fine black wool is lined with a handsome and striped commercial cotton and subtly decorated with black machine stitching. Note the red pillbox cap—not a fez—which has been traditional in this area for millennia. Its sides are covered with black embroidery, and it carries a long black tassel, often of silk, over the man's left ear. The uppers of the turned-up-toe leather moccasins are woven of leather thongs.

1.84A Woman's ensemble
Posavina, Croatia, twentieth century
FOWLER MUSEUM X95.50.2A,D,F,G,K,L; GIFT OF PROFESSOR ELSIE DUNIN
(See Appendix for full details.)

Like the shirt and pants illustrated in figure 1.85, the blouse, dress, and apron in this outfit are examples of clothing made without cutting into the cloth. The wearable form is achieved by sewing the original uncut edges to each other and into tubes, and then gathering some of the fabric together at the cuffs and waist, in this case with tight smocking and mini-pleats. In this way, no precious cloth is wasted. Except for the smocked and cross-stitched cuffs, the largely red decoration is woven (weft-faced). The sheepskin vest is decorated with intricate cutouts of thin dyed leather, woolen tassels, and thread-covered buttons.

1.84c Front panel of the blouse hidden under the vest in figure 1.84a.

1.85A Man's ensemble
Posavina, Croatia, twentieth century
FOWLER MUSEUM X95.50.1A–D; GIFT OF PROFESSOR ELSIE IVANCICH DUNIN
(See Appendix for full details.)

Although the front and cuffs of the shirt are covered with cross-stitched and woven designs, the eye is drawn to the tight vest, which is so covered with embroidery, couched red cords, and metal studs that one can scarcely see that its base fabric is black. (Note that it has a collar and lapels, seldom found south of Croatia.) The black fiber-felt hat sports matching trim.

Back detail view of vest in figure 1.85a.

1.85C Front panel of shirt hidden under the vest in figure 1.85a.

1.86 Spurs
Hungary, twentieth century
Iron, leather
Each: 10.1 x 8.8 x 2.7 cm
FOWLER MUSEUM X68.225A–B; GIFT OF JAMES KRIS

Spurs like these were used in Hungary, Romania, and northwestern Bulgaria for men's dances, especially (in older times) for ritual dances in which the noise of the metal was intended to ward off evil.

Up near the Hungarian border, women sometimes mixed Croation and Hungarian traditions. Thus the costume in figure 1.82 has a white blouse with paneling and sleeves typical of Croatia, whereas the skirt and apron are respectively of velvet and brocade (fabrics favored in Hungary), and all of them are covered with typically Hungarian-style embroidered flowers.

Costumes in Slovenia and Hungary, just north of Croatia, look even more like those familiar to us from western Europe. Hungarian women's costumes typically consist of a short- to medium-sleeved blouse ornamented with embroidery and/or cutwork, held in by a tight sleeveless bodice, below which spreads a full skirt topped by a showy apron tied with a big bow. In most areas, the skirt was tightly pleated and puffed out by as many petticoats as possible, the number of which indicated how rich the family was (see fig. 1.73). In fact, girls considered it the height of elegance to wear so many petticoats at the Sunday dance that they couldn't sit down but had to subside into a squatting position surrounded by a great wheel of fabric, which they referred to as "a cheese." Girls also favored dance steps that made the skirts swish and fly as much as possible. Unlike people in most of the Balkan Peninsula, who traditionally wore the absolutely flat-soled pigskin moccasins known as *opanci*, Hungarians typically wore high leather boots with a slight heel. Again, the dances evolved to show this handsome footwear to its best advantage, the women rocking and twisting on their boot heels (a motion that also makes suitably short skirts fly), while the men rhythmically slapped their bootlegs and clicked their spurs (fig. 1.86).

Quite unlike the traditional clothing of the Balkan Peninsula, Hungarian dress in recent centuries was constructed from purchased cloth as opposed to homemade fabric (although this was not true for outerwear, like coats, or for the white cloth used for shirts and petticoats). The same was true in parts of Slovakia to the north. Extremely popular during the last two centuries was bicolor satin brocade with large flowers. It was used for pleated skirts and often for matching shawls and/or jackets (fig. 1.87). Wide silk brocade ribbons with polychrome flowers were also purchased to make wide bows for the hair (fig. 1.88) and to enhance aprons and bodices.

In many places, however, the principal form of decoration consisted of embroidery. Two Hungarian locales are remarkable in this regard. One is the northern town of Mezőkövesd, where long black aprons, worn by both women and men, displayed long, intricately tied black silk fringes and polychrome flowers worked in satin stitch (fig. 1.89). The other is the town of Kalocsa, where the women covered almost every inch of their bodices, headgear, and aprons, as well as the shirtfronts of their men, with brightly colored satin-stitched flowers embroidered on white fabric (fig. 1.90a,b). Both the caps of married women (who, in most of Europe, were required of old to cover their hair, where their fertility was thought to reside) and the tiara-shaped strips worn by unmarried girls carried this embroidery.

OPPOSITE
1.87 Shawl (detail)
Šestine, Croatia, twentieth century
Silk brocade
76 x 76 cm
FOWLER MUSEUM X95.50.2H; GIFT OF PROFESSOR ELSIE IVANCICH DUNIN

Commercial silk brocade with a pattern of large flowers (usually white on a contrasting color) was one of the most popular fabrics in Hungary for skirts, vests, and jackets. This piece, however, happens to be a shawl from Croatia.

ABOVE
1.88 Hair ribbon and tiara-shaped diadem
Hungary, twentieth century
Silk brocade, velvet, synthetic pearls, gold braid
44 x 33 cm
FOWLER MUSEUM X79.465F; GIFT OF MRS. HELEN WHARTON

Commercially produced, polychrome silk brocade ribbons were extremely popular throughout much of central Europe for use in finishing off festive apparel. In Hungary and Slovakia, such ribbons were often worn, as this one was, in a wide bow at the back of the neck, with the tails fluttering down behind. The peaked diadem fastened it to the head. The reverse side of the brocade can be seen on the tail at the right

1.89A Detail of apron shown in figure 1.89b.

1.8B Man's ensemble
Mezőkövesd, northern Hungary, twentieth century
FOWLER MUSEUM X68.218–222; GIFT OF JAMES KRIS
(See Appendix for full details.)

The heavily gathered white shirtsleeves and pant legs of men's cloth-ing in Mezőkövesd are almost as distinctive as the characteristic long black apron with dense floral embroidery and tied silk fringe. Women, too, wore similar, though slightly smaller, embroidered black aprons, a specialty of the local Matyó people.

1.90A Woman's ensemble
Kalocsa, central Hungary, twentieth century
FOWLER MUSEUM X69.979A,B,E–G; GIFT OF DR. MARIJA GIMBUTAS.
X68.248 (FLORAL CAP); GIFT OF DR. JUANA DE LATAN
(See Appendix for full details.)

The town of Kalocsa is widely known for its bright floral patterns, copiously embroidered in satin stitch on aprons, bodices, women's blouses and headgear, men's shirts, and all manner of household linens. They are also painted on walls (see fig. 3.13) and pottery. Another specialty is cutwork, seen here especially on the sleeves and apron. Married women covered their hair with a cap, whereas girls wore a tiara and ribbons.

1.90B Back view of figure 1.90a. As in most of Hungary, the woman's skirt is tightly pleated and calf length (rather than ankle length, which is usual farther south), so that it swishes wonderfully when she dances.

Although sometimes a bodice might be worked in a single color, originally they were polychrome, in imitation of the East Indian chintzes imported into Europe by the English. These cheap, shiny cottons printed with brightly colored flowers sprouting from a vase (patterns that Indian cloth makers copied from imported English crewel pattern books) became so popular that they were ruining the European cloth industry, and in 1686 and 1700 respectively, France and England outlawed chintzes in self-defense. Not to be denied, women from Hungary to Mexico copied the attractive Indian chintz flowers in embroidery (cf. fig. 1.28a).[16] And that is why American folk dancers can substitute Mexican blouses for Hungarian ones in their cobbled-together costumes and almost get away with it.

Slovakian women's attire generally resembles Hungarian examples in silhouette, being composed of a very full skirt and a short-sleeved blouse held in with a form-fitting bodice. All these more western-looking modes of dressing were heavily influenced by upper-class Renaissance and Baroque fashions,[17] just as the traditional outfit in parts of Brittany picked up and perpetuated the Elizabethan-style starched lace ruff and triangular stomacher (cf. Corbett, this volume). The upper-class use of gold and silk embroidery and appliqués, reminiscent of both Catholic ecclesiastical robes and western court dress, is particularly noticeable in some of the Croatian outfits of both sexes (figs. 1.91–1.93). In Slovakia, however, if the family wasn't rich enough to use actual gold, the elaborate cutwork decoration, most prominent on the sleeves, was carried out in golden yellow thread (see figs. 3.3, 3.5, 3.6),[18] just as in Macedonia.

Southeastern Europe, cut off from western developments by Ottoman subjugation, absorbed instead the fashions of Middle Eastern potentates (see fig. 3.6), especially long sleeveless coats or vests. Countries in the middle, most especially Hungary, could pick and choose from both sides.

For married women throughout Europe, the most important part of their costume was the cap. Called *cepec* in Slovak (see fig. 3.6), the marital cap "deterred evil spirits and brought fertility to the wearer."[19] The point at which a woman was considered married was the moment when a cap was set over her hair. As with married women in most of Europe, she then kept her hair covered with a cap the rest of her life. Such traditions, which once existed in England too, seem to have spawned our idiom about a girl "setting her cap" for someone, meaning that her goal is to marry him.

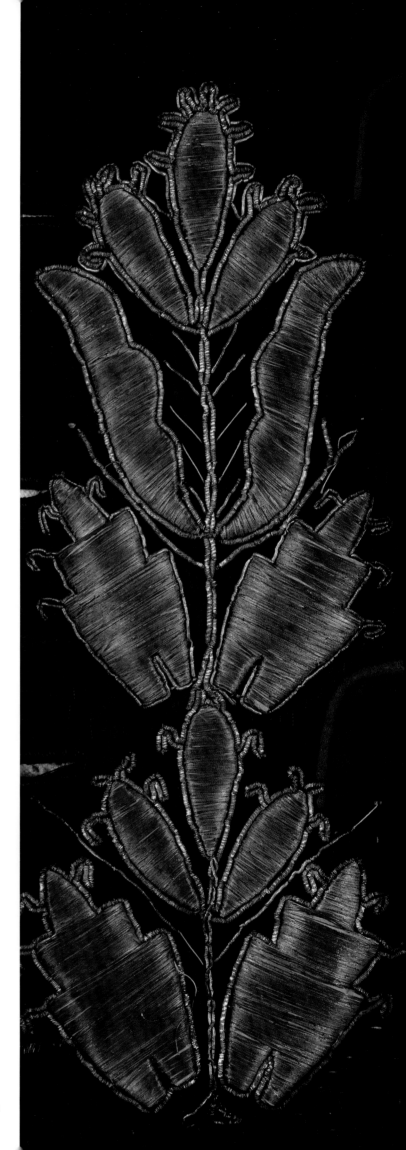

1.91A Detail of vest in figure 1.91b.

1.91B Man's ensemble
Northern Croatia, twentieth century
FOWLER MUSEUM X71.881A,D–F; GIFT OF MIA SLAVENSKA
(See Appendix for full details.)

Gold and silver metallic thread was introduced into Croatia from Turkey in the mid-nineteenth century. As in this vest, the fine metallic thread was often sewn over a paper pattern, creating a relief-like decoration. Such gold embroidery was sometimes executed on separate bands of woven cloth that could be removed when the garment had to be cleaned.

OPPOSITE
1.92A Woman's ensemble
Slavonia, Croatia, twentieth century
FOWLER MUSEUM X93.14.6A–E; GIFT OF DOROTHY DAW
(See Appendix for full details.)

In addition to metallic thread, lace has been used as a form of textile ornamentation in Croatia since the Middle Ages. This blouse and skirt contain fine examples of a net-like needle lace called *reticella*, as well as fine examples of cutwork and drawnwork on the skirt, and beautiful gold work.

1.92B Back view of figure 1.92a.

OPPOSITE

1.93A Woman's ensemble
Slavonia/Croatia, twentieth century
FOWLER MUSEUM 2010.26.1.1 (DRESS), X2010.26.1.2 (APRON),
X2010.26.1.3 (HEAD COVER), X2010.26.1.4 (SHAWL); GIFT OF PROFESSOR
ELSIE IVANCICH DUNIN
(See Appendix for full details.)

Gold thread (*zlato*) was initially used on the head covers of married women. It quickly gained popularity, however, for use as decoration on women's skirts, blouses, aprons, and shawls, as well as men's shirts, pants, and vests.

1.93B Back view of head cover in figure 1.93a.

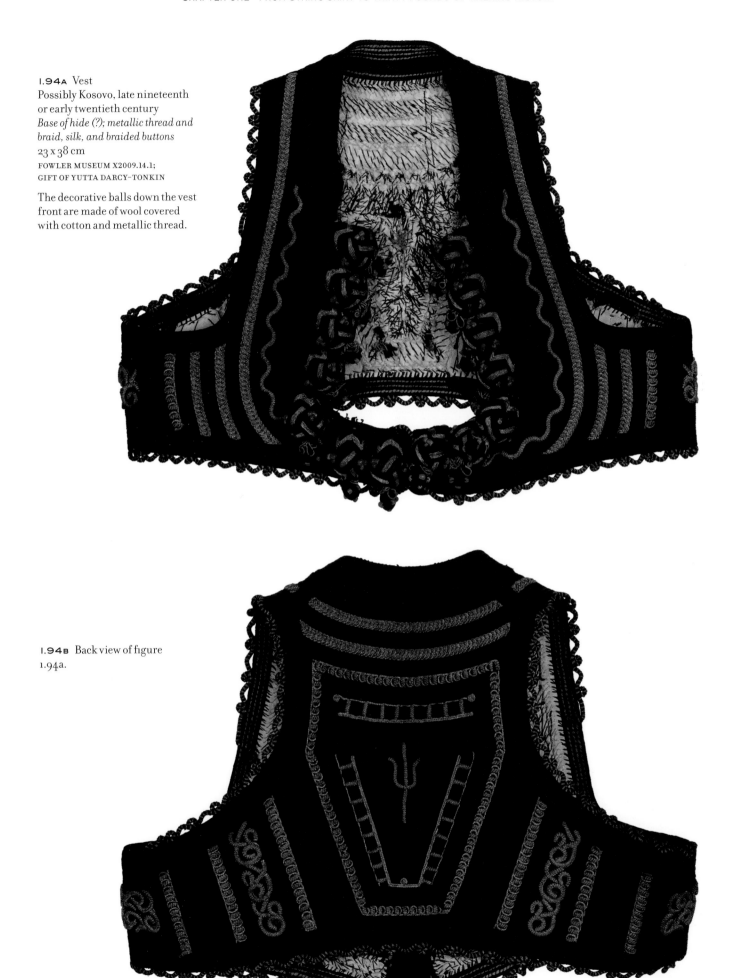

1.94A Vest
Possibly Kosovo, late nineteenth
or early twentieth century
*Base of hide (?); metallic thread and
braid, silk, and braided buttons*
23 x 38 cm
FOWLER MUSEUM X2009.14.1;
GIFT OF YUTTA DARCY-TONKIN

The decorative balls down the vest
front are made of wool covered
with cotton and metallic thread.

1.94B Back view of figure
1.94a.

PANTS FOR WOMEN

The Turkish conquest of southeastern Europe in the late fourteenth to the sixteenth century brought with it new ideas about clothing that had been developing among Turkic and other Middle Eastern peoples. The most noticeable is the use of long, roomy pants by women, worn with or without an overskirt. These trousers (South Slavic *šalvari*, from Turkish *şalvar*, ultimately from Persian; often nicknamed "harem pants" in English) are especially prevalent where the local people converted to Islam, but others wore them as well (see Jirousek, Dunin, this volume).

Another prominent trait seen in the areas once dominated by the Turks is the use of metallic braids couched in ornate patterns on the layers of sleeved and sleeveless coats and vests worn by both men and women over the basic pants and blouse or shirt. Couching is a technique in which the decorative thread lies entirely on the surface of the cloth, being held down by largely invisible stitches that fasten the pattern thread to the base cloth (see, e.g., figs. 1.47a,b, 1.51a,b). Normally in embroidery the pattern thread itself pierces the base cloth and can be seen on both sides of the fabric; this means the thread must be slender enough to be pulled through. Any kind of thick thread may be couched, but "metal thread" in particular is difficult to pull through the cloth intact, since it often consists of braided wire or a fine strip of metal foil wrapped around a plant-fiber core. The thin thread used for couching is visible inside the vest in figures 1.94a,b, since the vest is not lined. People in the central and southern Balkan Peninsula also picked up the Turkish fondness for long rows of ball-shaped buttons worn down the front, whether these were confected from silk or plant-fiber yarn or from metallic thread (e.g., figs. 1.94, 1.95; and see Jirousek, this volume).

1.94c Back detail view of figure 1.94a.

1.95A Vest
Probably Kosovo, late nineteenth or early
twentieth century
Velvet, metallic rope and braid, braided buttons,
coral beads, braided silk
31 x 41 cm
FOWLER MUSEUM X75.76; GIFT OF GUSTAVE PABST III

Little vests heavily covered with metallic trim
were particular favorites of the Albanian
population of the area.

1.95B Back view of figure 1.95a.

1.96 Pillbox caps with a long tassel down the left side have been found in the graves of people of the Iapodian tribe, living in the uplands southeast of modern Trieste in the mid-first century BCE. Instead of using thread for the tassels and embroidery around the side of the cap, as is done today (see figs. 1.83, 1.97), they made these ornaments of little metal chains, which have survived. RECONSTRUCTIVE DRAWING BY KELVIN WILSON, ROTTERDAM.

1.97 Tasseled hat
Lika, Dalmatia (Croatia), twentieth century
Red felt, black silk embroidery, black silk tassels
Hat: 20L x 18W x 7H cm: tassel: 29 cm
FOWLER MUSEUM X72.187D; GIFT OF VILMA MACHETTE

Compare the design of this hat to the hat from 2,700 years earlier illustrated in figure 1.96.

Yet another trait we associate with Turkish dress is the hat we call a fez. Felted of wool dyed dark red with madder, the fez spread among the Turks during the nineteenth century (see Jirousek, this volume) and from them to their Balkan subjects. In Croatia, Dalmatia, and northwestern Bosnia, however, a rather flatter pillbox-shaped hat, red on top and black around the sides, with a long black fringe hanging down beside one ear (see fig. 1.83), has a much longer local history. Caps with half a dozen long thin metal chains forming an identically shaped and positioned "fringe" have been excavated in graves attributed to an ancient Illyrian tribe, the Iapodians, who lived in northwestern Croatia in the mid-first millennium BCE (fig. 1.96).

Among the groups who absorbed Turkic styles of dress, probably even before they reached Europe, were the Roms (formerly known in English as Gypsies). Speakers of an Indo-European language closely related to Hindi, this group had migrated slowly from northern India westward across the Middle East, arriving in Greece in the fourteenth century. The Greeks thought these newcomers had come from Egypt, so they (misleadingly) called them *(E-)Gyptiano-* (whence Spanish *gitano* and also English *Gypsy*); but the group itself prefers the name *Rom*, from Indic *Dōm* "untouchable." (Greek *a-thingan-* "untouchable" seems to have produced the other common European name for this group, as in French *tzigane*, German *Zigeuner*.) As the garments show, Romani women in Macedonia not only adopted the *šalvari* but continue to wear it today for their most festive occasions (see Dunin, this volume). Always fond of bright colors, however, the Roms have updated their apparel by enthusiastically shifting to sewing it from colorful modern store-bought nylon and polyester fabrics. Interestingly, the Turkic peoples still living in Central Asia today—Kazakhs and Uyghurs, for example—also now choose to make their traditional-style clothes from the brightest polyesters they can obtain. And why not? Synthetics can be beautiful too. ∞

2

Ottoman Influence
in Balkan Dress

Charlotte Jirousek

The Balkan Peninsula was a land bridge traversed and settled by many peoples over a lengthy period. The mountainous geography of the Balkans, however, always protected older settlers from newer invaders. This contributed to the retention of the ethnic diversity resulting from various layers of invasion occurring over time. While isolation encouraged linguistic and cultural differences, not to mention variations in dress, blendings and borrowings also occurred among conquerors, subjects, and neighbors.

The Turkic factor in the mix predates the emergence of the Ottoman Empire by nearly a thousand years. A number of invasions by nomadic Turkic peoples occurred beginning with the Avars in the sixth century, followed by the Bulgars in the seventh century, Pechenegs in the eleventh century, and Cumans in the eleventh and twelfth centuries.[1]

The Turkic Avars, possibly of the Oghur tribe, encountered the Slavs around the borders of the Byzantine Empire in the sixth century and established a nomadic empire north of the Danube that extended from the Black Sea through parts of what is now Hungary and Austria. Avar incursions into the Balkans apparently also facilitated Slavic invasion and settlement in this period. During the seventh century, the Avars established a presence in the Balkans as far south as Macedonia and participated in a failed siege of Constantinople itself. After this period their influence subsided, but Avar communities remained in the western Balkans.[2]

The earliest Bulgars were a Turkic tribe that may have been present on the steppes north of the Black Sea as early as the second century, when they were apparently swept up in the Hunnic invasions of central Europe. After this they dispersed throughout eastern and southeastern Europe. They controlled a substantial region between the Danube and the northern Black Sea in the seventh century, and in this period established a presence in what is now known as Bulgaria.[3]

The Pechenegs appear in history in the eighth or ninth century in the Crimea and north of the Black Sea. By the tenth century they had established a substantial area of control. In the eleventh century a breakaway group received permission from the Byzantine Empire to settle south of the Danube. Subsequently, however, their relations with the Byzantines soured, and eventually they were defeated by the Byzantines with the help of the Turkish Cumans. Following this, the Pechenegs were mostly assimilated by their Magyar and Bulgar neighbors. They also remained, however, as nomads in the Balkan highlands, where they eventually converted to Islam.[4]

The Cumans, who together with the Kipchak Turks had established a sizeable confederation that ranged from the northern Balkans to Kazakhstan in the twelfth century, subsequently settled and mingled with other populations throughout the Balkans. The Byzantine emperor invited them to aid him in turning back Pecheneg invasions, including an assault on Constantinople. Nonetheless, as the Mongol conquests pushed the Cumans out of their Central Asian lands in the thirteenth century, they too invaded Byzantine territory. Although they were defeated, many were settled in the Balkans along the borders of Byzantium as a defensive buffer against other invaders.[5]

Thus these various groups invaded, conquered, and subsequently blended into settled communities where they might retain their religious or ethnic identities to a greater or lesser degree (fig. 2.2).[6] No Turkic peoples, however, retained long-lasting control over the whole Balkan region before the arrival of the Ottoman Turks.

OPPOSITE
Detail of figure 2.11.

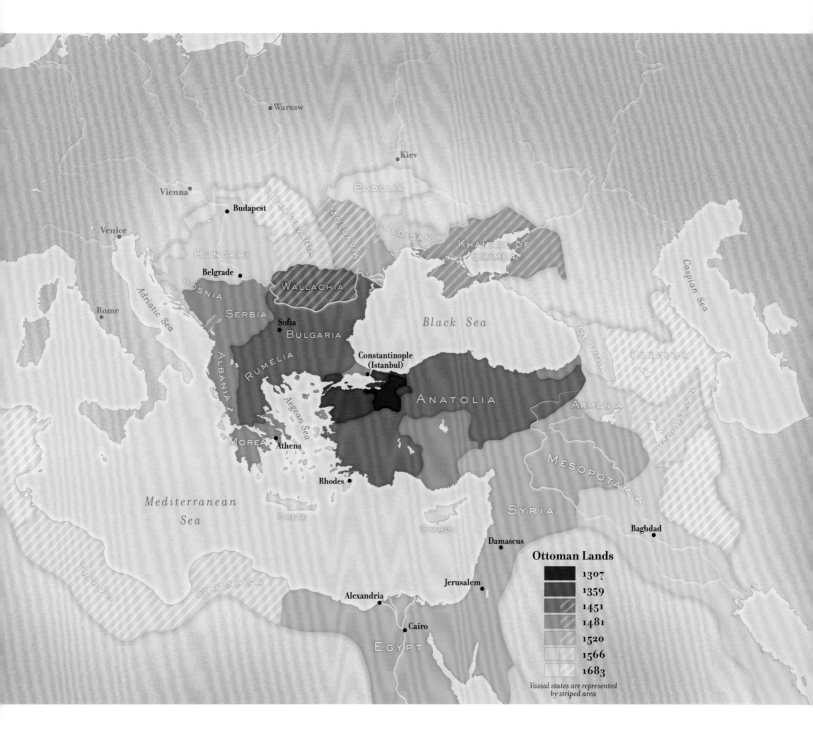

Ottoman Lands

■	1307
■	1359
▨	1451
■	1481
■	1520
■	1566
▨	1683

*Vassal states are represented
by striped area*

2.1 This map illustrates the progress of the Ottoman invasion
of southeastern Europe.

ARRIVAL OF THE OTTOMANS

The term "Ottoman" is a European translation of the Turkish
term "Osmanlı," or "descendant of the house of Osman,"
the founder of a dynasty that emerged in the thirteenth
century (fig. 2.1). The Osmanlı/Ottoman state grew until
by the sixteenth century it encompassed much of what had
been the Eastern Roman Empire (as the Byzantine Empire
was also known).

The Turks had first invaded the Byzantine Empire
from the east in the eleventh century. (The earlier attempts
at invasion by Turkic tribes, as outlined above, had been
made through the Balkan Peninsula to the north and west

of the Byzantine lands.) The tribe known as the Seljuk Turks established an empire in Anatolia in the eleventh century with their capital at Konya. This empire, which included much of Persia, was demolished by the Mongol invasions of the thirteenth century, pushing many Turkish tribes into western Anatolia. Following the end of Mongol rule in the region, Turks remained in Anatolia with various clans establishing regional rule. The clan of Osman established itself in northwestern Anatolia, at the frontier of what remained of the Byzantine Empire. Since Islamic law forbade wars of conquest against fellow Muslims, many Turkish clans flocked to the standard of Osman, and the rule of the Ottomans expanded north and west at the expense of the Byzantine Empire. In 1352 the Ottomans crossed the Dardanelles into Europe, ostensibly at the invitation of the Byzantine rulers who were fighting Bulgars and Serbs in Thrace. Taking advantage of a weakened Byzantine authority and local conflicts within the Balkans, the Ottomans systematically conquered the region, bringing in Turkish nomads and also establishing Turkish settlements and communities. By 1389 and the epic Battle of Kosovo, substantial resistance to Ottoman dominance was at an end.

Ottoman rule, unlike that of Orthodox Christian Byzantium or the Catholic rulers of Europe, was tolerant of religious difference, giving considerable autonomy to the various religious and ethnic communities, providing that allegiance was given and taxes were paid. This communal autonomy preserved the variety of ethnic distinctions in the Balkans (and elsewhere in the Ottoman Empire) and encouraged many communities to accept Ottoman rule initially.[7]

By the eighteenth century, however, the preservation of ethnic and religious diversity would also permit the emergence of militant nationalism, as economic and social conditions changed.[8] This tolerance, therefore, would paradoxically contribute to the eventual downfall of the Ottoman Empire. In the interim, Ottoman rule and the transfer of Turkish populations to the Balkans created a consistent Turkish cultural presence that would leave its marks on dress and culture.

Most of the Balkan peninsular region was able to achieve independence from Ottoman rule by the 1870s, before the final dissolution of the Ottoman Empire. Following Ottoman defeat in World War I, the Treaty of Lausanne (1923) and subsequent agreements divided the empire into a new set of nations, most of which had never before existed as independent entities within their new boundaries, including Greece and Bulgaria, not to mention Syria, Iraq, Lebanon, Palestine, Egypt, Sudan, Yemen, Saudi Arabia, and the new Republic of Turkey. Many ethnic Turks left the Balkans for the new Turkish Republic in the years before World War II, but many remained in the places where their ancestors had lived for the previous five centuries.

2.2 This shepherd and village woman are from the Malesi district of the Shkodar region of Albania, a mountainous region that was a likely refuge for early Turkic nomadic immigrants in the western Balkans. The garments worn by the couple are typical of nomadic horse cultures, adapted to harsh mountain winters but retaining a trousered, layered aesthetic. The man's costume resembles that of mountain Turks living along the Black Sea, except that the garments there would be black rather than white. PHOTOGRAPH REPRODUCED FROM HAMDI BEY AND DE LAUNAY (1873). COURTESY OF THE LIBRARY OF CONGRESS PRINTS AND PHOTOGRAPHS DIVISION, WASHINGTON, D.C., LC-USZC4-11728.

OTTOMAN RULE AND THE REGULATION OF DRESS

The Ottoman administrative system permitted ethnic/religious groups within the empire to maintain their own rule, including their own courts of law, for domestic purposes. These groups were referred to as *millets*. As noted earlier, the rights of these groups were protected, providing that they paid their taxes and obeyed Ottoman laws governing commerce and other broader imperial concerns. The Ottomans therefore saw marking ethnic distinctions through dress as an important matter in that it reflected rights and responsibilities. Sumptuary law was established beginning in the fifteenth century with a major codification occurring under Sultan Suleyman in the sixteenth century. These laws were apparently accepted and followed at least through the seventeenth century, presumably because the distinctions they described conformed with the general social expectations of the citizenry. They remained in force until the major reforms of the early nineteenth century.

In the eighteenth century, however, there was a sudden flurry of new decrees reemphasizing the previously existing sumptuary regulations. This new activity implies that these laws were not being followed, and so they required reinforcement. This happened at the same time that the Ottoman system in general began to show signs of trouble—economic problems, military defeats, and growing restiveness among the general population and particularly among the minorities. It is in this period that nationalism began to emerge. Adoption of European forms of dress apparently came to be seen as a sign that Christian Ottoman citizens were increasingly identifying with the resident European trading communities found in Ottoman ports, and this was perceived as a challenge to the status quo.[9]

Sumptuary law defined particular materials and colors that were to be reserved to different minority groups within the Ottoman Empire. In addition to very specific stipulations concerning headgear, the style and color of garments, and footwear for the various ranks within the imperial hierarchy, distinctions in materials and colors were made for the various religious/ethnic communities under Ottoman rule. Footwear was specifically defined according to color: black and purple were only for Jews and Armenians; red for Greeks (meaning Greek Orthodox Christians of whatever ethnicity); yellow for Muslims. Non-Muslim males were expected to wear outercoats of gray broadcloth—with a small sash of a specific silk and cotton mixture—of no more than a designated value. For women the outercoat was to be of brightly colored "Bursa cloth" with specified head coverings and blue trousers.[10] The style of turbans was also prescribed in minute detail for different minority groups. A decree of 1729 denounced turban makers who had created a new style that could be confused with that worn by Jews, thereby causing embarrassment and insult to Muslim wearers.

2.3 The woman's dress in this photograph of a Bulgarian couple from Sofia includes the skirted forms typical of European dress, although modestly worn under a long unfitted coat. The man, however, wears clothes typical of later nineteenth-century official dress as worn by an Ottoman dragoman, guard, or similar official service. The couched silk threadwork seen on both the jacket and *šalvari* (trousers) is typical Ottoman embellishment; compare with figure 2.4. PHOTOGRAPH REPRODUCED FROM HAMDI BEY AND DE LAUNAY (1873). COURTESY OF THE LIBRARY OF CONGRESS PRINTS AND PHOTOGRAPHS DIVISION, WASHINGTON, D.C., LC–USZC4–11743.

In 1784 another decree pointed out that "some subjects in the Balkans have started to dress like soldiers and officials without holding any official posts; they should be notified that such acts are prohibited."[11] Limitations were also placed on the use of gold-thread embroidery as embellishment for dress and accessories. Sumptuary law dating back to the reign of Mehmet II in the fifteenth century had specified the types and quantities of gold and silk embroidery that could be employed as a feature of official attire.[12] To the Ottoman authorities, dressing as if to cross social boundaries was a threat to the structure of the state. The attractions of the rich and powerful, even if they are despised, as models for dress and appearance are, however, notoriously seductive and difficult to resist on the one hand or suppress on the other. Following the significant government reforms instituted by Sultan Mahmud II in 1826, major dress reform was decreed for all in government service, generally along western lines (fig. 2.3).[13] After this time, the old sumptuary laws were generally not enforced, although the traditional forms continued in use.

FEATURES OF OTTOMAN DRESS AND THEIR INFLUENCE ON BALKAN DRESS

The complex history, narrated in brief above, makes it very difficult to trace specific features of a particular Balkan garment to any one source. The characteristic features of nomadic horse-rider dress, however, can be identified as a common element for all of these groups. The wearing of trousers is a fundamental habit of both men and women in horse cultures, as trousers protect the legs from chafing while on horseback. Over the trousers, a set of open-fronted shirts, vests, coats, and/or jackets is worn. The advantages of such an ensemble for an equestrian are that coats and jackets can be donned or doffed as needed depending on the weather and that this can be accomplished while riding on horseback; whereas pulling a tunic off over the head would be impractical and potentially dangerous. Tunics and gowns seem to be associated with the more settled cultures of farmers and so represent a different cultural origin in which closed garments were customary.

Over the course of time, the advantages—or the look—of these differing vestimentary systems would have been noted, and so elements of each system might be borrowed. Thus today we may see trousers worn under closed tunics or dresses with vests or jackets worn over them. In spite of this, certain forms of dress retain dominant features that reflect their origins.

Jackets, vests, and longer coats were all common features of Ottoman Turkish dress. The layering of these garments could be done for warmth but was also a sign of formality in dress. Persons of elevated status were more likely to wear a long coat; and highly formal dress might involve jackets, vests, and long coats. Imperial dress usually involved two long coats, one with narrow sleeves, and an outer coat which allowed the narrow inner sleeve to show, either by the use of a short, wide sleeve or a partially attached sleeve that was allowed to hang to the back (see Barber, this volume).

2.4 Examples of layered Ottoman Turkish dress with hanging sleeves are visible in this photograph depicting Muslims of Bursa in the Ottoman province of Hudavendigar in northwestern Anatolia. Bursa was the capital of the Ottoman Empire before the taking of Constantinople in 1453. PHOTOGRAPH REPRODUCED FROM HAMDI BEY AND DE LAUNAY (1873). COURTESY OF THE LIBRARY OF CONGRESS PRINTS AND PHOTOGRAPHS DIVISION, WASHINGTON, D.C., LC-USZC4-11736.

The hanging sleeve was a very common characteristic in Turkish dress and could be seen in short jackets worn either over long coats or over other jackets. The sleeve could in some cases be fully buttoned to the edge of the armhole and along the arm so that it could function as a sleeve if warmth was desired. The hanging sleeve, however, lent motion to a man's ensemble that added a certain dash and swagger, or, in the case of the long sleeve-ends of a woman's coat, an element of grace in movement (fig. 2.4).

Headgear was famously important among Turkic peoples, dating all the way back to their origins in Central Asia. Various kinds of hats were worn, including the *kalpak*, a short brimless cap made of curly sheared karakul sheepskin. Turbans became essential after Turks began to convert to Islam in the tenth century. They were wound in various

ways but usually over a supporting hat of varying height and shape. After the sixteenth century, sultans marked their accession by changes in the form of their headgear. The wearing of correct headgear was a particularly important point in Ottoman sumptuary law, so important that a man's tombstone was carved in the form of the headgear he was entitled to wear.

The fez was a late introduction, part of the military and governmental reforms of the early nineteenth century (fig. 2.5). Originating in Morocco, it was adopted by Mehmet Ali in Egypt as part of the uniform of his modernized army. Subsequently, it was employed by Sultan Mahmud II as part of his reformed army uniform and also for bureaucratic dress; it was even worn by the sultan himself. Since Ottoman soldiers everywhere in the empire wore this new hat, it was widely adopted as well by non-Turks throughout the Ottoman lands in the course of the nineteenth century. The wide distribution of the fez may also be related to the fact that after the reforms, military and government service was no longer restricted to Muslims. Thus many a young man would have returned home with his uniform and hat and may have continued to wear them. The fez, in slightly varying forms with and without tassels, seems to be a widespread feature of Balkan dress, seen in many historic photographs and in the Fowler Museum collection (see fig. 2.5).

The use of gold-thread couched embroidery as an embellishment on garments of wool, velvet, or silk was a highly developed craft, and specific craftsmen's guilds were authorized to practice this art. Once restricted to certain classes of citizens, such embellishment not surprisingly became a major feature of dress among those who could afford it. Woven gilt-thread tapes and braids were also produced as less labor-intensive ways of achieving the desired effect. For those who could not afford gold, a similar look could be achieved with silk cord or braid, or even coarser materials, as seen in the embellishment of the shepherd's costume in figure 2.2. A particularly spectacular use of such embroidery can be seen in the dress of a wealthy Muslim Albanian family from Yanya (Ioánnina; fig. 2.6), where the man appears to be wearing at least two vests and a jacket entirely encrusted in gold thread, while the woman wears a dress and full-skirted outercoat also heavily embellished with gold embroidery. The Fowler Museum collection includes several spectacular examples of this kind of embroidery (figs. 2.7a,b–2.13). The vest in figure 2.7a,b appears to be the type worn by the Albanian man and his son in figure 2.6, but the vest in figure 2.8a,b and the jacket in figure 2.9a,b may be for women, based on the open deep neckline. The vest resembles one worn by an Albanian woman of Prizren (in present-day Kosovo) under her long coat (fig. 2.14). The type of long coat we see in figure 2.14 is distinct from Ottoman Turkish coats worn by either women or men because of its fitted top and full semicircular skirt, designed to accommodate or emulate the full skirts of European-style garments.

2.6 This photograph records the dress of a wealthy late nineteenth-century Muslim Albanian couple and their son from Yanya (Ioánnina). COURTESY OF THE LIBRARY OF CONGRESS PRINTS AND PHOTOGRAPHS DIVISION, WASHINGTON, D.C., LC-USZC4-11733.

OPPOSITE
2.5 Man's ensemble
Sarajevo, Bosnia-Herzegovina, mid-twentieth century
FOWLER MUSEUM X93.23.1B–D,F–H; GIFT OF PROFESSOR ELSIE IVANCICH DUNIN
(See Appendix for full details)

The bands across the shoulders and side seams of the jacket in this ensemble are tablet woven, and the handwoven cotton lining of the jacket is provided with a pocket. A fez would be worn with this ensemble. Madder root was usually used as a dye to produce its characteristic purplish red color.

2.7A Woman's vest
Bosnia-Herzegovina, early
twentieth century
*Heavy felted wool; silk and
metallic ribbon; couched with
silk cord, metallic braid, and fine
and thick cords of metal strips
wrapped around fiber core*
30 x 36 cm
FOWLER MUSEUM X93.23.4; GIFT OF
PROFESSOR ELSIE IVANCICH DUNIN

2.7B Back view of figure 2.7a.

2.8A Vest
Serbia, twentieth century
*Velvet; metallic ribbon, sequins;
couched with metallic cord, braid,
and ribbon, cotton braid; oval
buttons with metallic thread,
glass beads; cotton lining, metal
hooks and eyes*
29 x 37 cm
FOWLER MUSEUM X2011.4.69; GIFT
OF DR. JOEL MARTIN HALPERN

2.8B Back view of figure 2.8a.

2.9a Jacket
Balkan Peninsula, early twentieth century
Velvet; couched with metallic cord, braid; oval buttons with metallic
braid, coral beads; filigree metal balls; striped cotton and silk lining,
metal hooks and eyes
29 x 144 cm
FOWLER MUSEUM X2008.30.6; GIFT OF ANTHONY SHAY

The sleeves of on this type of jacket are purely for show, since they
are left flat (not sewn into arm tubes), although on this particular
jacket a heavy hook and eye are available to hold the sleeve around
the arm at about the elbow.

2.9b Detail of sleeve in figure 2.9a.

2.10 Jacket
Kraljeva Sutiska, Bosnia-Herzegovina, mid-twentieth century
Woven wool; metallic rope, braid; sequins; woven cotton lining
43 x 143 cm
FOWLER MUSEUM X68.3573; GIFT OF MARIJA GIMBUTAS

2.11A Sleeveless coat
Prizren, Kosovo, twentieth
century
*Woven wool; sequins, metallic
cord, braid, and ribbon; printed
cotton lining*
112 X 117 cm
FOWLER MUSEUM X2008.30.3;
GIFT OF ANTHONY SHAY

The coat, known as a *dolama*,
has a scalloped hem of golden
braid and a cotton-print lining.

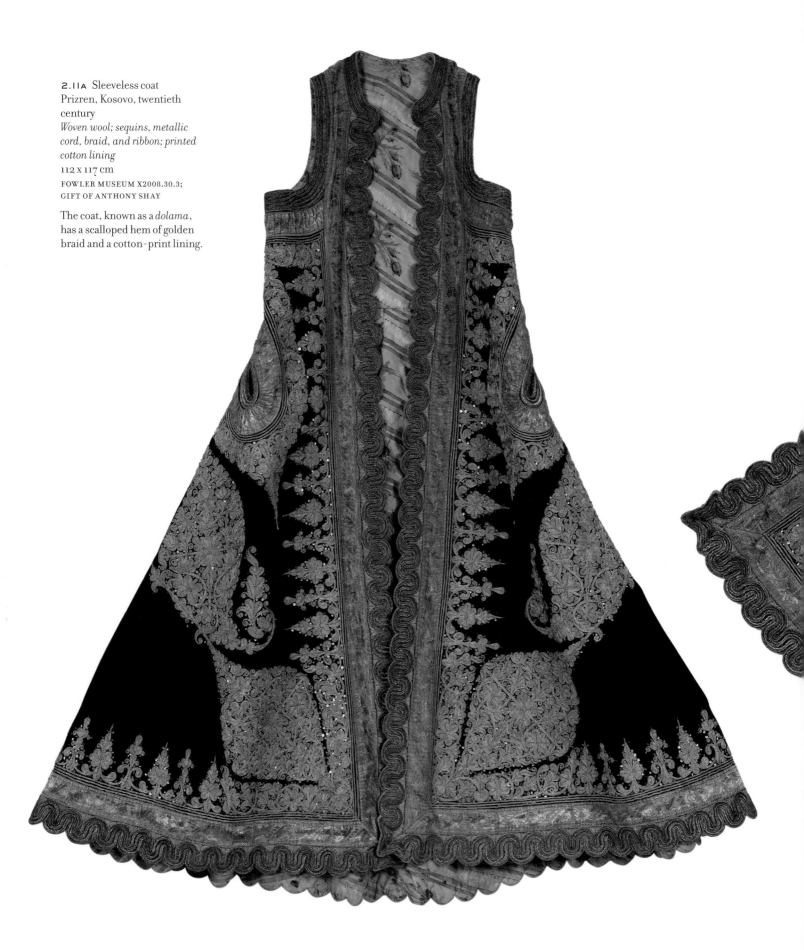

2.11B Back view of figure 2.11a.

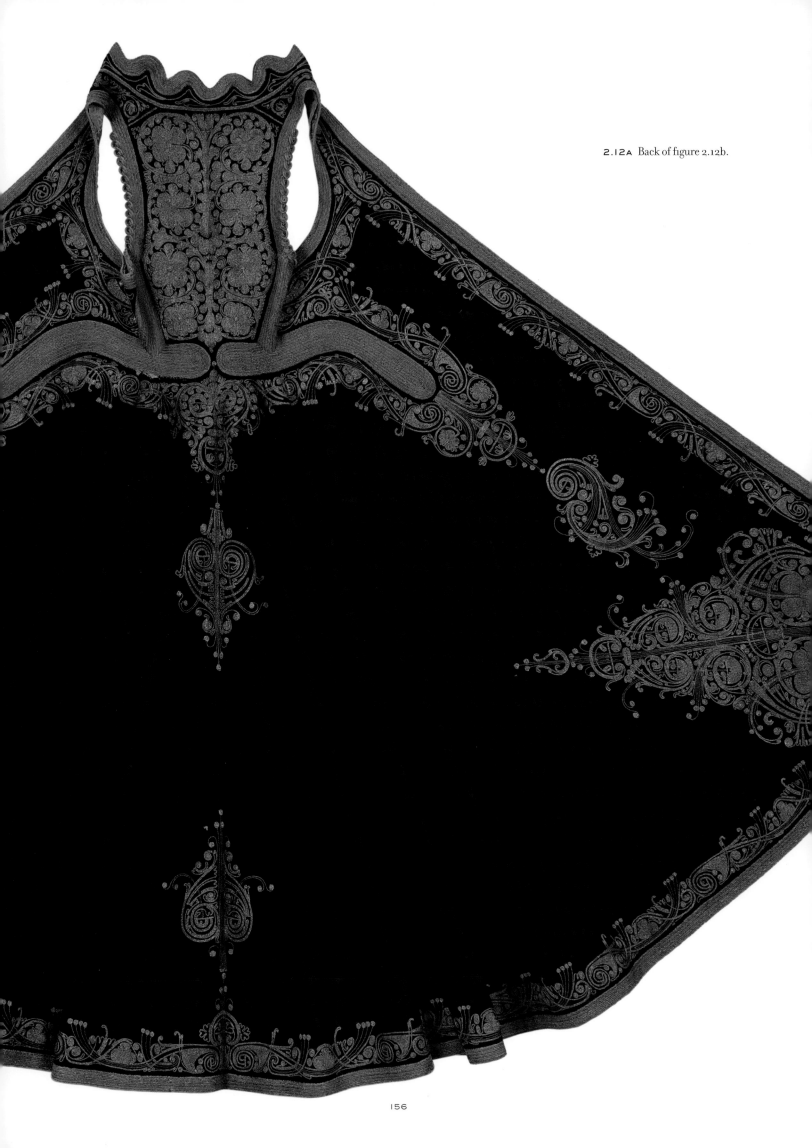

2.12a Back of figure 2.12b.

2.12B Sleeveless coat
Prizren, Kosovo, twentieth
century
*Woven wool; metal-wrapped
fiber-core thread and braid;
printed cotton lining*
115 x 170 cm
FOWLER MUSEUM X2008.30.2;
GIFT OF ANTHONY SHAY

Two cotton print fabrics were
used to create the lining of this
coat (*dolama*), which because
of its fullness would swing open
to show the attractive colors
inside.

2.13A Sleeveless coat
Albania, twentieth century
Woven wool stiffened with thin cardboard backing; couched with black silk cord and braid; metallic ribbon; printed cotton lining
98 x 145 cm
FOWLER MUSEUM X2007.17.1;
GIFT OF HARRIET WERNER

Coats were often ornamented with black thread when a family could not afford gold or silver thread.

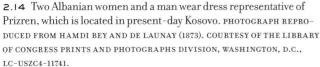

2.14 Two Albanian women and a man wear dress representative of Prizren, which is located in present-day Kosovo. PHOTOGRAPH REPRODUCED FROM HAMDI BEY AND DE LAUNAY (1873). COURTESY OF THE LIBRARY OF CONGRESS PRINTS AND PHOTOGRAPHS DIVISION, WASHINGTON, D.C., LC–USZC4–11741.

The jacket shown in figure 2.15 appears to be the cut of a standard men's jacket commonly worn by Ottoman Turks of middle station in life, and a type commonly seen in the southern Balkans. A simpler example is shown in figure 2.5. The embellishment on the jacket illustrated in figure 2.16a,b, however, suggests higher status or more formal dress, as in wedding clothing.

The wearing of trousers, known in Turkish as *şalvar*, is universal for both men and women in traditional Turkish dress. For women, these trousers are often barely seen and are sometimes considered to be underwear (*don*). Styles of cut for *şalvar* vary according to region and clan/tribal affiliation across Turkey. In some cases they are extremely full with a crotch that is as low as the leg openings, essentially a flat double rectangle of fabric with leg openings at the corners and a drawstring waist. In other types there is a separate structure for each leg, which may be quite full and gathered at the bottom or may be narrow. They can also be quite short, ending above the knee among the Turks of southwestern Turkey; others are full to the knee but are finished with separate leggings that reach the ankle. Examples of these leggings can be seen on the men of Bursa shown in figure 2.4, and also in figure 2.17. These leggings match the jacket seen in figure 2.15.

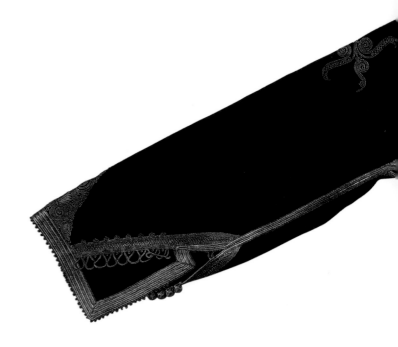

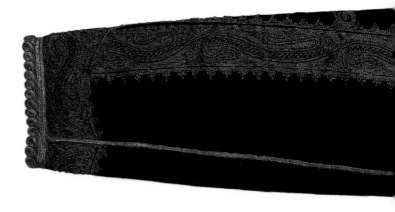

2.16A Man's jacket
Serbia, early twentieth century
Velvet; couched with metallic rope, braid; printed cotton lining, plastic and metal button
33 x 151 cm
FOWLER MUSEUM X96.6.5; GIFT OF PROFESSOR ELSIE IVANCICH DUNIN

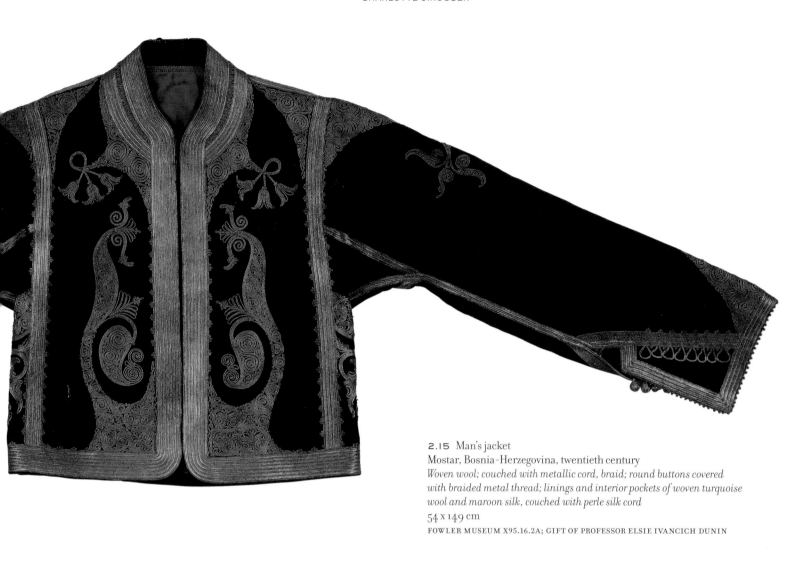

2.15 Man's jacket
Mostar, Bosnia-Herzegovina, twentieth century
*Woven wool; couched with metallic cord, braid; round buttons covered
with braided metal thread; linings and interior pockets of woven turquoise
wool and maroon silk, couched with perle silk cord*
54 x 149 cm
FOWLER MUSEUM X95.16.2A; GIFT OF PROFESSOR ELSIE IVANCICH DUNIN

OPPOSITE
2.16B Detail of back view of
figure 2.16a.

2.17 Pair of man's leggings
Mostar, Bosnia-Herzegovina,
twentieth century
*Woven wool; couched with metallic
cord, braid; metal hooks and eyes;
lining of woven wool and cotton*
41 x 19 cm
FOWLER MUSEUM X95.16.2B,C;
GIFT OF PROFESSOR ELSIE
IVANCICH DUNIN

These leggings were worn
with the jacket illustrated in
figure 2.15. They would have
been worn with knee-length
trousers (*şalvar*).

The longer and closer-fitting varieties seem to be associated with the cold climate of the northern mountain regions
of Turkey. Some of these types of Turkish *şalvar* resemble
those found in the Balkans. On the whole, the men's *şalvar*
types seen in the Balkans have a fitted lower leg attached to
the fuller upper part of the trousers, using a drawstring waist
and leaving fullness in the crotch for ease of movement. The
fitted lower leg would provide greater protection and warmth
in a rugged landscape subject to severe winters. Several types
can be seen in the Fowler Museum collection, notably as part
of the Sarajevo ensemble, which shows a very deep (to the
knee) crotch with fitted lower legs attached (see figure 2.5b).
Another *şalvar* example, also from Sarajevo, seems to have
an even deeper crotch with attached lower legs that are wider
(fig. 2.18). Other examples can be seen in figures 2.2 and 2.3.

Frequently among Ottoman women the *şalvar* or *don*
are of softer materials, usually cotton but perhaps silk.
Generally the upper part of the *şalvar* is covered by other
garments, which may include a chemise, long coat, and/or
aprons. This may not be the case in parts of central Anatolia, where the *şalvar* was worn on a daily basis with only
a short blouse and jacket. The cut is usually quite full at
the top but may taper to a moderately narrow leg opening.
Alternatively, the legs may remain very full and be gathered
at the leg opening. Again, length may vary, with the gathers
occurring anywhere from below the knee to the ankle, and
the shorter length more likely in warmer climates.

The Fowler Museum collection includes an example
with a tapered leg (fig. 2.19a,b) and an example that is gathered at the leg opening (fig. 2.20). An interesting feature of
the example with the tapered leg is that the upper part of the
garment is made of a plain white fabric, but the lower part
of the legs is made from a colored material. This is also not
unusual in Turkish women's *şalvar,* since only the lower part
of the garment will be visible. *Şalvar* of this type can be seen
in figure 2.4 (center).

2.18 Man's ensemble
Bosnia-Herzegovina, twentieth century
FOWLER MUSEUM X66.1061A–K; MUSEUM PURCHASE
(*See Appendix for full details*)

2.19A Woman's ensemble
Kosovo, late nineteenth century
FOWLER MUSEUM X83.259A–F, H–J, L–Q; MUSEUM PURCHASE
(*See Appendix for full details*)

2.19c This hip harness would have been worn with the ensemble shown in in 2.19a,b. It offered additional support when the wearer carried heavy loads.

2.19b Back of figure 2.19a.

2.20 Woman's ensemble
Bosnia-Herzegovina, twentieth century
FOWLER MUSEUM X93.23.16A–G, X69.103 (METAL BELT); GIFTS OF PROFESSOR
ELSIE IVANCICH DUNIN
(*See Appendix for full details*)

Aprons are a well-known and very ancient feature of the dress of European women who have reached marriageable age, particularly noted in eastern Europe.[14] They are also a feature of Turkish traditional dress that seems to be quite universal. The materials, colors, and techniques of embellishment vary and identify specific localities. A front-apron is most common, but attention is also paid to the back of the ensemble as well. In many cases this is done by lifting and tucking the front corners of the outermost coat into the sash at the back. In addition, card-woven bands may be wrapped over the sash, with the elaborately tasseled ends of the bands allowed to fall and swing in the back. Card weaving was once a very widespread craft, practiced in every household as a means of making straps for tent support, animal harnesses, and accessories for dress. Examples of card weaving also appear in the Fowler Museum collection in connection with Bosnian dress ensembles (figs. 2.21a,b).

It is also common among the Turks of Anatolia, however, to wear a back apron, usually in the form of a triangularly folded shawl with deep fringe (fig. 2.22). Figure 2.23 shows Turkish villagers wearing aprons in the Azdavay region of Kastamonu, a mountain district near the Black Sea. Although today the rest of their dress is made from industrially produced fabrics, it is interesting that these aprons continue to be handwoven by the wearers and their families, evidence of their importance.

Turkish socks have been the subject of several monographs and a minor craze among western knitters. The form and construction of the Turkish sock is distinctive: a flattened tube with an inserted triangular heel and no easing around the turn of the foot, while the toe tapers to a flat symmetrical triangle. They were elaborately patterned, and the patterns traditionally carried meanings and messages. Socks played an important role in the exchanges of gifts during courtship and betrothal and were traditionally given as invitations to wedding guests (unless shoes were given instead). Turkish-style sock making was practiced in the Balkans as well, and elaborate socks sometimes appear in Balkan costume. One pair is part of an ensemble from Bosnia-Herzegovina identified as Serbian (see fig. 2.21b), patterned and constructed like classic Turkish socks but with embroidered cuffs. A second pair, identified as being from Bosnia-Herzegovina, is plain white (see fig. 2.20), but the basic construction follows the Turkish sock form.

A pair of shoes (see fig. 2.21b) that is part of an ensemble from Bosnia-Herzegovina would have been worn with the patterned socks. These shoes are identical to a pair in the Cornell University Costume and Textile Collection that were acquired in Merzifon, south of Trabzon toward the eastern end of the Black Sea. They are also identical to pairs acquired by the author in Ankara from a traditional shoemaker in the 1960s. It is noteworthy that these shoes are red, a color which in the old Ottoman sumptuary tradition would have been reserved for Christians. Other styles and construction methods for shoes are seen in eastern Turkey.

OPPOSITE
2.21A Back detail view of the vest shown in figure 2.21b.

ABOVE
2.21B Woman's ensemble
Bosnia-Herzegovina, twentieth century
FOWLER MUSEUM X66.1062A–G; MUSEUM PURCHASE. X93.23.17C,E,F
(HEAD COVER, APRON, SASH); GIFTS OF PROFESSOR ELSIE IVANCICH DUNIN
(See Appendix for full details)

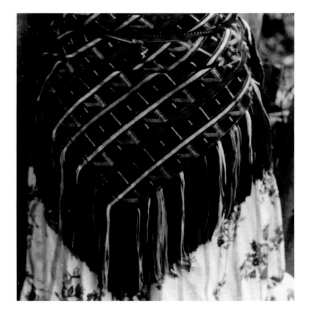

2.22 This photograph shows a back apron in the form of a triangularly folded shawl with a deep fringe. PHOTOGRAPH BY CHARLOTTE JIROUSEK, AZDAVAY REGION OF KASTAMONU, TURKEY, 1998.

2.23 Turkish villagers in the Azdavay region of Kastamonu, a mountain district near the Black Sea, wear front and back aprons. PHOTOGRAPH BY CHARLOTTE JIROUSEK, TURKEY, 1998.

Vests are a fundamental element of the layered system of clothing common to all of the horse-culture nomads, where the more layers worn, the more formal and rich the dress. Even when the vests are not attributed to men or women in the surviving records, their shapes often serve to assign them by gender. Those with deeply curved necklines, which fit snugly at the waist but also support and frame the bust, were generally worn by women, and those with high necklines by men. The few examples actually identified by gender support this assumption (fig. 2.24). The type of vest with deeply V-shaped straight, diagonal front edges differs, however, from the other examples of deep necklines and could be worn by either males or females. For example, the type of small red vest in figure 2.25 is shown worn by a woman from Ulcinj in a photograph published in *National Geographic* (1931), although it could possibly have belonged to a boy. Ottoman sleeved jackets with this sort of opening and cut were commonly worn by both men and women.

Two of the vests with a high neckline identified as men's garments have a center front opening (figs. 2.26a,b, 2.27a,b). Neither could actually be buttoned up, but each has large and elaborate decorative "buttons" on each side of the opening. Such vests were common for men's dress throughout the Ottoman Empire. Another vest in the collection, said to come from Peć, in Kosovo, has an asymmetrical, overlapping closure (fig. 2.28). Vests of this type formed part of urban costume—a similar one, pictured in

Osman Hamdi Bey's *Elbise-yi Osmaniyye* (1873), was worn by the Bulgarian man of Sophia (see fig. 2.3) and another by the Albanian from Ioánnina (see fig. 2.6). Similar vests are recorded in Ottoman Turkish dress, from various parts of the Empire, dating to 1873 and earlier.

Elaborately worked buttons, a widespread feature of Ottoman dress, are particularly prominent on many vests and jackets. These buttons consist of a core of cotton or wool over which either silk or metallic thread is woven with a needle until the core is covered. In some instances (see figs. 1.94, 1.95, 2.26) small coral beads have been worked into the button. The buttons can be as small as one-quarter inch in diameter, and as large as one to two inches. The larger examples are decorative and not intended as closures for the vest. In Ottoman Turkish garments, however, the buttons intended actually to close a garment were typically of the small size seen on figure 1.56; such buttons may have been removed from the similar vest illustrated in figure 2.29a,b. Both have gold cord loops for buttons, but also hooks and eyes to supplement them.

For five centuries the Balkans comprised a series of provinces within the Ottoman Empire, and during all those centuries there was extensive movement of population and trade between that region and Ottoman Anatolia, traffic that continues to this day in spite of the creation of national borders. This long relationship is made visible in the shared forms of dress that are part of the complex and varied cultural landscape of the Balkan Peninsula. ∞

2.24 Woman's vest
Sarajevo, Bosnia-Herzegovina,
twentieth century
*Velvet, couched with metallic
thread on fiber core; silk braid,
sequins; silk twill lining*
33 x 49 cm
FOWLER MUSEUM X93.23.6;
GIFT OF PROFESSOR ELSIE
IVANCICH DUNIN

2.25 Boy's or woman's vest
Albania, twentieth century
*Woven cotton, woven and felted
wool, couched with perle silk,
metallic cord, metallic ribbon,
sequins; cotton lining*
23 x 31 cm
FOWLER MUSEUM X69.982;
MUSEUM PURCHASE

2.26A Man's vest
Pristina, Macedonia, twentieth
century
Velvet; metallic rope, braid, and
ribbon; sequins, oval buttons with
metallic rope, glass beads; printed
cotton lining; areas stiffened with
thick paper
33 x 39 cm
FOWLER MUSEUM X67.2425;
GIFT OF MR. AND MRS. THEODORE
LOWENSTEIN

Ottoman influence on the
trimming of this vest includes
not only the elaborate designs
done in applied metallic thread
but also the little round buttons
crowding down the front.

2.26B Back view of figure
2.26a.

2.27A Man's vest
Ulcinj, Montenegro, probably
Albanian, twentieth century
*Woven cotton or linen; couched
with perle silk cord, metallic
thread; sequins, braided buttons;
printed cotton lining*
31 x 41 cm
FOWLER MUSEUM X69.983;
MUSEUM PURCHASE

Although chiefly dark brown,
this vest is so covered with orna-
mental cording that the base
cloth can scarcely be seen. The
extra-large, decorative buttons
on this vest have fabric centers
that are covered with thread.

2.27B Back view of figure
2.27a.

2.28 Man's vest
Peć, Kosovo, early twentieth
century
*Velvet, woven wool; metallic cord,
braid, and ribbon; silk braid frogs*
134 x 36 cm
FOWLER MUSEUM X69.984;
MUSEUM PURCHASE

Although this vest is said to
have been made in Peć in
present-day Kosovo, it was
purchased at the Ulcinj market
in Montenegro.

2.29A Vest
Serbia, early twentieth century
*Velvet; sequins, couched with
metallic wire, rope, braid; metal
hooks and eyes, striped cotton
lining*
140 x 42 cm
FOWLER MUSEUM X2011.4.72; GIFT
OF DR. JOEL MARTIN HALPERN

2.29B Back view of figure 2.29a.

Thread
and Living Tradtions

THE EMBROIDERER'S ART IN CENTRAL
AND SOUTHEASTERN EUROPE

Joyce Corbett

The gradual development of local forms of dress and the associated styles of embroidery in the Czech Republic, Slovakia, Hungary, Romania, and the Balkan Peninsula is as complex and varied as the history of those countries. Today's borders—drawn for political expediency in the aftermath of World War I—do not even begin to suggest the diversity of the extraordinary and varied cultures existing within them. Furthermore, these territories have had the distinction of acting as a bridge between two significant cultural forces: western Europe and Ottoman Turkey.

The Turks entered central Europe following the Battle of Mohács in the south of Hungary in 1526. Louis II, King of Bohemia and Hungary, was killed in the battle. Even today, Hungarians will console themselves in moments of bad luck with the reflection "*Több is veszett Mohácsnál*" (We lost more at Mohács). Louis was succeeded in part by his brother-in-law Ferdinand I, Archduke of Austria—a Habsburg and brother to Charles V of Spain. Ferdinand, who at this point assumed the title of King of Bohemia and Hungary (he would later become Holy Roman Emperor), ruled over the northern and western parts of Hungary, which were known as Royal Hungary, while yet another monarch, John I, secured the Eastern Hungarian Kingdom. The central and southern portions of Hungary ultimately fell under the rule of the Ottoman Empire following the Turkish triumph at Mohács and other victories (see Jirousek, this volume).

The result of this was that a significant part of central Europe became a divided territory. The Habsburgs dominated the western regions and the Ottomans the eastern, while Transylvania became a suzerainty under the Turks. The domination of the Ottomans ended after they were defeated at the Battle of Vienna in 1683, and by the year 1689, when the map in figure 3.1 was made, the territory of the Kingdom of Hungary extended from Poland in the north, to the Balkans in the south, Austria on the west, and east into Transylvania, Moldavia, and Wallachia (areas belonging to present-day Romania). The relative openness of the region allowed migrations and cross-cultural contacts that would cease to exist in later times. The influence of the courts of western European countries, including France, Spain, and Germany, reached the region, as did the religious and social upheavals of the sixteenth to the eighteenth century.

Political and religious implications aside, the interface between two seemingly different entities, western European and Ottoman, resulted in creative expressions in the textile arts that are artistically unique and vibrant. Every region, down to the village level, had its own fluid and dynamic ways of integrating the meeting of the two spheres, solutions that are still part of the living tradition in parts o f central and southeastern Europe.

It is clear that there was a thriving textile and embroidery industry during the period of Turkish rule. A flourishing trade in linens, wool, gems, lace, and leather existed in both directions. At the same time fine linen and embroidery thread were supplied from Vienna to the eastern parts of the Hungarian Kingdom. During the sixteenth century, the styles of the Spanish court, through the Habsburg monarch Charles V, set the fashion across Europe.

Turkish embroideries became enormously popular in the court of the Hungarian Kingdom, along with other eastern styles. Written evidence points to the creation of these embroideries by the ladies of the court. The traditional custom of presenting finely embroidered kerchiefs for special occasions, such as weddings, is still practiced in villages today. Clothing was not the only focus of embellishment, however; dowry items, household linens, and ecclesiastical textiles also required the expertise of skilled needle workers.

OPPOSITE
Detail of figure 3.19.

3.1 This map, a colored etching made by S. Sanson in 1689, was created subsequent to the victory over the Ottomans at the Battle of Vienna (1683). The yellow line indicates the extent of the Kingdom of Hungary at the time. REPRODUCED FROM MAGYAR NEMZETI MÚZEUM (2001, 6).

3.2 The costume depicted in this portrait of Borbála Wesselenyi (unknown artist, oil on canvas, 1662) reveals a mixture of European and Ottoman traits. REPRODUCED FROM MAGYAR NEMZETI MÚZEUM (2001, 64).

Portraits dating from the sixteenth and seventeenth centuries create a window onto the garments worn at the court in the past. In the portrait of Borbála Wesselenyi of 1662 (fig. 3.2), we can see elements of her costume clearly showing both western and Ottoman influences. The Balkan shape of her vest, the Turkish pomegranate pattern decorating her full sleeves, and the non-western motifs exquisitely embroidered on her gloves contrast with the western style of her beaded crown, fur cuffs, and elaborately embellished collar. These are all elements still existing in the village clothing of central Europe.

The remainder of this chapter will examine examples of embroidery drawn from the Fowler collection, starting in the north with Slovakia, Moravia, and Hungary, then moving south through Romania and Serbia to Bosnia-Herzegovina—that is, moving from those areas with the greatest western influence to an area of particularly heavy Ottoman influence.

3.3 Woman's ensemble
Čičmany, Zilina, Slovakia, circa 1918
FOWLER MUSEUM X66.1863–65; MUSEUM PURCHASE
(See Appendix for full details)

This costume is embroidered with a variety of standard techniques using cotton thread on linen and cotton. Smocking, pulled thread, drawnwork, cutwork, straight stitches, herringbone, and small cross-stitches are sewn in various combinations, while the unusual peacock motifs are embroidered in satin stitch. In addition, bobbin lace is attached to the apron hem and blouse cuffs and collar.

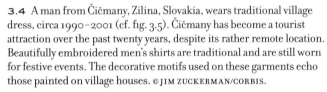

3.4 A man from Čičmany, Zilina, Slovakia, wears traditional village dress, circa 1990–2001 (cf. fig. 3.5). Čičmany has become a tourist attraction over the past twenty years, despite its rather remote location. Beautifully embroidered men's shirts are traditional and are still worn for festive events. The decorative motifs used on these garments echo those painted on village houses. © JIM ZUCKERMAN/CORBIS.

3.5 Embroidered panel and sleeve trim for a man's shirt
Čičmany, Zilina, Slovakia, twentieth century
Satin-stitch embroidery, cutwork, drawnwork, hemstitching, and needle lace, on cotton
Panel: 137 x 20 cm; sleeve trim: 47 x 4 cm
FOWLER MUSEUM X66.1867, 1868; MUSEUM PURCHASE

These magnificent little panels of dense ornamentation were typically completed separately, then sewn onto the garment. Thus they could be carried around easily while being made, as well as removed easily for cleaning the base garment or for tranferring to a new garment when the old one wore out.

SLOVAKIA AND MORAVIA
ČIČMANY, SLOVAKIA

The village of Čičmany lies in a mountainous region of northern Slovakia. The remoteness of the area doubtless contributes to the unique and archaic quality of its arts. The village is famed for its houses, which are decorated with symbols in geometric arrangements. These are painted in white lead and evoke ancient runes. The same designs—crosses, spirals, suns, hearts, and peacocks—are also found in the embroidery work done on clothing from the area. Earlier examples from this region were embroidered with silk thread on linen. The style of garments worn in the area is unique in central Europe, and there is local anecdotal information claiming that Čičmany and neighboring villages were populated in the fifteenth century by Slavic peoples migrating from the Balkans.

Čičmany village dress is archaic in style in that it employed uncut linen, just as it came from the loom, for its elements (figs. 3.3–3.5). People who had to produce their thread and cloth entirely by hand naturally tended to avoid wasting any of it by cutting. Both the gathered skirt and the blouse in figure 3.3 are finely pleated by hand using traditional methods. The unique headdress that usually accompanies such a costume is not fitted but is assembled from several cloth components bound with an embroidered band.

PIEŠŤANY, SLOVAKIA

Piešťany is located in western Slovakia. The mineral springs there have been known and visited for their salutary effects since Roman times. The Piešťany costume is the best-known and most iconic Slovak dress. It represents one of the more spectacular variants of Slovak regional embroidery and has a rich, glowing, opulent quality. In the late nineteenth and early twentieth century, visitors to the mineral springs,

particularly those from the Czech territories, bought and exported these costumes in quantity.

Piešťany embroidery reflects a significant development in the promulgation of needlework in Slovakia, the founding of the Izabella Society in Bratislava in 1895. The goal of the group was to preserve and promote the art of embroidery. The society's workshops in various locations around the country employed up to fifteen hundred people at one time. It created fashion and ecclesiastical designs as well as preserving historical techniques. The Izabella Society was awarded the Grand Prix at the prestigious World Exposition in Paris in 1900.

International exhibitions, such as those held in Paris, were organized across Europe around the turn of the century with the aim of showcasing national superiority in the manufacture of artistic goods. Exhibition pavilions included displays of regional "folk crafts," often in replicated village settings. This succeeded in bringing the awareness of village culture to urban dwellers for the first time. The textiles, costumes, and objects displayed in these exhibitions appealed to musicians, writers, private collectors, and the museum community, stimulating the collection and preservation of an enormous amount of material culture.

The cotton blouses from Piešťany illustrated in figures 3.6, 3.7 follow the basic construction characteristic in central Europe, being gathered at the neck and wrist. Satin stitches are usually used for the vines and leaves. The designs often consist of floral sprigs within solar-motif roundels surrounded by leaves and tendrils. Brocade ribbon, gold metallic lace, and bobbin lace are used to embellish the collar, which is a descendant of the seventeenth-century ruff. The accompanying fitted bodice (see fig. 3.7) was traditionally made of silk brocade trimmed with brocade ribbon.

3.6 Woman's partial ensemble
Piešťany, Slovakia, twentieth century
FOWLER MUSEUM X70.1225A,B; GIFT OF ERIC BARKER
(See Appendix for full details)

The blouse and its cap are worked in eyelet technique, in which tiny patches of the base fabric are cut out and the raw edges of the hole bound with very fine stitches. The predominantly gold color range favored here may be related to the use of gold embroidery in court fashions of earlier times.

3.7 This commercially printed postcard demonstrates the romantic image of traditional dress and life that was cultivated in the early twentieth century. The ornate and beautiful Piešťany embroidered costume was widely illustrated before World War II (cf. fig. 3.6). COLLECTION OF CAROL BOWDOIN GIL.

3.8 Woman's ensemble
Hel'pa, Gemer County, Slovakia, twentieth century
FOWLER MUSEUM X2006.11.3A–D; GIFT OF MS. MARTHA ADAMS
(*See Appendix for full details*)

A small vest of wine-red wool challis—a much-loved fabric in central Europe—is worn over a full-sleeved blouse with dense red embroidery and completed with a lace ruff. The printed cotton skirt is ornamented with ribbons, lace, and white stitchery. It is tightly pleated so that it will swing and swish when its wearer dances.

HEĽPA, SLOVAKIA

Situated in central Slovakia, the village of Hel'pa is the site of a large regional folk festival lasting for three days each year. The women's costume of the village has an appealing, cheerful, and exuberant quality. In recent years the embellished sections of the clothing have become larger and more ornate. It is anecdotally reported that immigrants to the United States from the Hel'pa region sent bright pink and red factory-made ribbons and lace trimmings back to their relatives at home, contributing to the clothing's colorful appearance. The use of commercially made materials in combination with labor-intensive hand needlework has produced a costume that is now at a transitional stage between the past and the present.

The blouse and vest follow the typical central European form, as does the full pleated skirt with a vertical front apron (figs. 3.8, 3.9). The upper sleeve and cuff of the blouse and the large flowers in the apron are worked in a densely embroidered satin stitch. The stitches worked in this frequently used form imitate earlier woven decoration. The skirt and vest, however, are of commercially made floral challis, and the knife-pleated skirt is overlaid and stitched with commercially made ribbon and lace. The lacy collar, cloth tape edging, and ribbon are all factory made. There are running stitches throughout in contrasting colors.

MORAVIA

Moravia is located within the borders of the present-day Czech Republic, which adjoins Slovakia. It has a rich culture and is celebrated for its beautiful traditional dress. During the summers, annual folk festivals attract crowds of tourists, and village dance groups are an important feature of these celebrations. The festivals have stimulated a huge revival in the wearing of regional dress. The dress ensemble of Ratíškovice is renowned for its elaborate and beautifully embroidered elements.

One of the most remarkable components of this costume is the dark blue apron (see figs. 6.24a,b), first dyed with a subtle vertical tie-dye pattern, then embroidered with colorful floral bouquets of pomegranates, carnations, tulips, and village garden flowers. A distinctive addition to this type of apron comes from the handmade bobbin-lace edging along the bottom. This lace was traditionally made in Vamberk, a historic center for the handicraft. The white band dividing the floral design is needle woven. There is a triangular "wolves' teeth" needlework connector stitch, an ancient protective symbol, in the places where the lace attaches to the apron.

Booklets produced in the early 1900s by D. M. C. Mulhouse, the French manufacturer of colorfast embroidery thread and materials (fig. 3.10) are relevant to the needlework of this region. These booklets were widely distributed across Europe. They were valuable tools for educating women in needlework patterns and techniques, but they also they fostered appreciation of regional styles of embroidery. Titles were published on "Czecho-Slovakian," "Yugoslavian," "Turkish," and "Bulgarian" styles of embroidery. The booklets featured illustrated texts, color plates, and patterns.

3.9 Three women wear their festive attire at an event in Hel'pa, Slovakia. PHOTOGRAPH BY HELENE BAINE CINCEBEAUX, 2012.

3.10 The D. M. C. Mulhouse needlework booklets were produced from the late 1800s through the twentieth century and were internationally distributed in French, German, English, and other languages. The series was edited by the iconic Therese de Dillmont, author of the *Encyclopedia of Needlework* (1886), which is considered the Bible of embroidery and is still in print today. PRIVATE COLLECTION.

Primarily intended for the instruction of a general audience in towns and cities, these publications also likely found their way into village households, making it possible to revive traditional techniques that had been lost. It was fashionable in the Czech Republic, as early as the mid-nineteenth century, to adopt "folk" costume as a symbol of national identity. Fashion journals regularly featured "Slavonic" versions of costumes. The Moravian mode of dress was particularly popular.

The general style of Moravian costume is western European and shows stylistic affinity with seventeenth-century court dress. This is seen in the fitted vest, square collar, ballooned upper sleeves of the blouse, and the full gathered skirt (fig. 3.11 and see figs. 6.24a,b). The black-thread stitching relates stylistically to early German needlework. The Moravian blouses with their square collars and graphic black-thread stitchery are notable for their charming embroidered hearts, pomegranates, tulips, and rose motifs. Additionally, there are adaptations of ancient solar and spiral symbols. The apron echoes Turkish sources in its floral motifs. The ornate beaded cap with its metallic decoration also shows influence from Turkey and the Balkans.

The embroidery on the upper sleeves and cuffs of the blouse is mainly satin stitch, the flowers and leaves being connected by stem stitch. The leaves are sewn with fern stitches. There is fine cutwork and drawnwork on the collar and cuffs, which are edged in black bobbin lace. The vest is brocade, bordered with ribbons and cockades, all purchased from Czech manufacturers. The dark blue apron is festooned with garden flowers embroidered in stem and satin stitch.

HUNGARY

MEZŐKÖVESD

Mezőkövesd is one of three villages in northern Hungary (Mezőkövesd, Szentistván, Tard) populated by the Matyó people, who were once itinerant workers. The form of dress they evolved used embellishment to signify status and wealth. Both stylistically and in terms of surface ornamentation, Matyó clothing is unique in Hungary. Quite atypically, the man's clothing for festivals and weddings is more ornate than the woman's; in fact, the Matyó man's ensemble is the most dramatic dress in Hungary (figs. 3.12a,b). The woman's costume is also stylistically unique, with a narrow, bell-shaped silhouette and a headdress decorated with large pompoms. The woman's apron is similar to the man's but less flamboyant. The floral designs on the aprons are strongly related to Turkish prototypes, no doubt influenced by the Ottoman occupation of the region in the sixteenth century.

The Matyó villages, particularly Mezőkövesd, were developed as tourist destinations in the early 1900s. The chief cottage industry of these market towns was making their handmade and embroidered decorative household goods. City dwellers sent clothing to the villages to be embroidered. Matyó women also sold their embroideries in other locations. Many of these items found their way to homes and collections in western Europe and the United States where they were regarded as treasured works of village textile art.

3.11 This man and woman from Vacenovice, Moravia, are serving as bridal attendants. The attendant couple has special status and is charged with the ceremonial role of managing the wedding, as symbolized by the carrying of wine jugs. The beautiful embroidered garments and headgear are the very best festive wear the couple owns. The embroidery is unique to their village. PHOTOGRAPH BY HELENE BAINE CINCEBEAUX, KYJOV, MORAVIA, CZECH REPUBLIC, 2011.

In the 1920s an infamous event occurred in Mezőkövesd. The Catholic Church declared that the local people were spending too much of their earnings on expensive and ostentatious clothing and ordered the villagers to surrender these garments. Irreplaceable textiles were destroyed in a bonfire held on Ash Wednesday of 1924. In spite of this tragedy, the unique traditions of Mezőkövesd survived and continued to appeal to the popular imagination. During the 1930s and 1940s, colorful advertising graphics often depicted adorable children dressed in Mezőkövesd costume. Mezőkövesd remains a popular tourist destination today, with its folkloric sites and festivals.

Figure 1.89 illustrates a remarkable mans' ensemble from Mezőkövesd. The shirt has characteristic elongated sleeves, which would cover the hands, an embroidered front apron, and wide gathered trousers (*gatya*) patterned in an archaic style. The vest and the typical tall, jaunty, bowler-style hat are adaptations of European fashions.

Older women, known as "writing women," drew the embroidery patterns, which were then filled in with densely stitched embroidery. The red flowers and leaves on the man's shirt, as well as the yellow "net" pattern, are worked in satin stitch with curved stem stitch forming connecting vines and tendrils. The man's large apron, sporting ties of brocade ribbon, is heavily satin stitched in horizontal bands on a black cotton ground—the effect from the massed floral forms is silky and brilliant. At the bottom, the apron is finished off with an intricately tied black silk fringe long enough to swing elegantly. The showiest men's outfits featured several bands of gold metallic lace as well.

3.12A Matyó men from northern Hungary wear festival dress that is atypical in that it is more ornate than that worn by the region's women for weddings and festive occasions. The flamboyant ornamentation of the men's clothing is a signifier of wealth and status. CORBIS, HU050701.

3.12B Detail of the Matyó man's apron in figure 1.89.

3.13A Two young married women from Kalocsa, Hungary, paint interior walls with motifs resembling those embroidered on their attire, a twentieth-century development. REPRODUCED FROM SNOWDEN (1979, 23).

3.13B Detail of the bodice from Kalocsa in figure 1.90.

3.14 A Moldavian couple wears the sheepskin vests characteristic of the region. The diagonal embroidered designs on the sleeves of the woman's blouse are related to similar designs seen in votive paintings from the Byzantine era. The man's outfit includes a high fur cap, long shirt, and pleated legging bottoms that can be seen in church frescoes dating from the sixteenth century. REPRODUCED FROM BANATCEANU (1977), PHOTOGRAPH BY ELENA ZLOTEA.

KALOCSA

On the Danube River south of Budapest, the town of Kalocsa is located in the heart of paprika-raising country. Kalocsa was invaded by the Turks in 1529, and during the lengthy period of Turkish rule, it remained decimated and depopulated, only managing to recover later in the eighteenth century. The colorful costume worn by village women developed as a result of the skilled needlework for which the area is known. Embroideries designed by local women took on bright colors and began to represent delightful gardens, including many kinds of flowers, peppers, and other vegetation. The commercial availability of brilliantly colored thread contributed to this development.

Kalocsa embroidery is not limited to women's dress. Household textiles, such as tablecloths, pillow covers, and small table linens, are an important part of the local needlework output; men's shirts are similarly embroidered. Furthermore, local women also paint the interior walls of buildings in the town with floral motifs echoing those on the textiles (figs. 3.13a,b).

Some of the costume elements have interesting historic roots. A type of backless slipper, known by the Turkish name *papucs*, is always worn with this costume, as are hose embellished with pompoms. The small hair bows worn earlier became larger and now function as headdresses. The central and main floral motif on the aprons follows a format that is reminiscent of the Renaissance vase-of-flowers design. The Kalocsa style is compatible with contemporary taste in fashion and décor, and the embroideries have become enormously successful as souvenirs in Hungary. One unhappy result of this popularity is the proliferation in the marketplace of Chinese machine-made reproductions.

A recent adaptation of an older style of traditional Hungarian village dress is illustrated in chapter 1 (see fig. 1.90). The heavily embroidered sleeves, blouse front, and vest evolved from a less complex white ensemble. The embroideries are worked in satin stitch, and the elegant white "lace" is cutwork. The finely pleated skirt—whether plain (as in this example) or of two-color brocade—has applied machine-made lace.

3.15 Man's Vest
Rădăuți, Moldavia, Romania,
twentieth century
*Sheepskin with fleece turned
inside; leather appliqué, wool
braid, silk cords and tassels,
beads; embroidered with cotton*
63 x 54 cm
FOWLER MUSEUM X2003.14.1;
GIFT OF PATRICIA REIFF ANAWALT

This vest is embroidered with
multicolored floral sprigs and
garlands. The flowers, leaves,
and bouquets are worked in
satin stitch with perle cotton,
and the small branches are
worked in straight stitches.
Bands of twisted black wool
form the outer borders and
narrow inner strips, and are
trimmed with jet beading.
Herringbone stitches define
the inner border and the two
small pockets. The natural
sheep's wool of the garment
comprises the lining of the
inside of the vest, and the front
opening features red cording
with tassels.

ROMANIA

MOLDAVIA

"Moldavia" used here refers to the northeast region of
Romania and should not be mistaken for the neighboring
country of Moldova. To further confuse things, the contiguous
territory that is now the Republic of Moldova was formerly a
part of Romania; it was annexed by the Soviets in the 1940s
and declared an independent nation in 1991.

Embroidered sheepskin vests are worn by both men
and women in the Moldavian region (figs. 3.14, 3.15). The
most beautifully embellished examples are worn for festive
occasions, whereas those worn for daily activities are plain
or sparingly ornamented. Sheepskin vests are an important
part of traditional dress, being warm, practical, attractive,
and serving as outward expressions of regional identity. They
are made by skilled craftsmen, whose number is decreasing

rapidly as a result of the diminishing number of those who
seek to become apprentices and the ready availability of
commercially made garments.

The careful placement of symmetrical designs gives
the vests of this region an elegant quality. The motifs are
located on traditionally significant areas of the body, as
in t|he case of many archaic garments. Each color in the
embroidered flowers—red, blue, yellow, green, brown, and
purple—is stitched in several subtly changing shades. There
is no doubt that the court costumes in Moldavia of the nineteenth century, which combined both Ottoman and French
fashion elements and were influenced by the carpet-weaving
centers of the region, contributed greatly to the style of
these garments.

3.16 Young men and women from Bistriţa-Năsăud wear festive dress while participating in a regional folk festival. PHOTOGRAPH COURTESY OF THE BISTRIŢA-NĂSĂUD WEB SITE: HTTP://WWW.VISITBN.RO/ENGLEZA/TRADITIONS.HTML.

3.17 This remarkable man's hat, unique to Năsăud in Romania, is decorated with a semicircular arrangement of peacock feathers. REPRODUCED FROM BANATCEANU (1977), PHOTOGRAPH BY ELENA ZLOTEA.

3.18 Woman's vest
Năsăud, Transylvania, Romania,
twentieth century
*Sheepskin with fleece turned
inside, velvet, silk embroidery,
leather appliqué and buttons,
wool braid*
41.5 x 46 cm
FOWLER MUSEUM X84.1220;
GIFT OF MARY KAHLENBERG

Embroidering the outsides of
sheepskin vests and cloaks was
a favorite way of decorating the
heavy clothing necessary for
the cold winters. The style of
polychrome flowered embroidery is the same as that used on
aprons and other lighter wear all
along the Carpathian Mountains,
whether in Transylvania, Hungary, or Slovakia.

NĂSĂUD

The county of Bistriţa-Năsăud in northern Transylvania
has long been a bridge between the western and Ottoman
worlds. Until the twentieth century it was part of the Austro-
Hungarian Empire, and the southern part of the county is
still home to many ethnic Hungarians who dwell side-by-side
with Romanians.

The traditional dress of the town of Năsăud and its
neighboring villages is considered to be the most spectacular
in Romania. The man's hat is fantastically decorated with a
large wheel composed entirely of peacock feathers (fig. 3.17).
The corresponding women's small headdress is called the
"peahen" and has a decorated headband with cockades worn
over each ear.

The woman's vest (figs. 3.16, 3.18) functions as an outer
garment. Motifs with multicolored tulips and other flowers
show distinct Hungarian influence, being stylistically similar
to the traditional floral motif embroideries found in northern
Hungary and to types of Turkish-influenced embroideries
found throughout Transylvania. While the woman's vest is
short and has a side fastening, the man's vest opens in

the front and has a very different ornamentation, making
Nasaud an interesting example of a region in which the
sheepskin vests worn by men and women are very dissimilar.
The embroidery on the woman's vest shown here is multicolored cotton in satin stitch, worked on dark brown sheepskin.
Black velvet bands were used as edging for the neck, sleeve
openings, and bottom borders.

During the past twenty years, the style of the women's
vest has undergone a major change. It is no longer made from
sheepskin but rather of brown or black velvet. While the
stylized floral bouquets of the embroidery retain the balanced
composition used in the older vests, the motifs are western
European in style and are hardly recognizable when compared
to their predecessors. While the style of the Năsăud vest has
recently evolved, it should be noted that other costume elements, including the man's costume, have remained virtually
the same. This may be the result of the dying out of the artisans
who made sheepskin vests and coats, and it also may be due
to the gradual assimilation of traditional Hungarian-style arts
into the dominant Romanian culture.

3.19A Man's vest
Banat, Romania, twentieth century
*Woven felted wool with damask linen (?) backing; velvet; silk embroidery,
couched wool cord and braid; leather buttons, cutout flaps, and braided
cords; pattern-woven coarse wool*
65 x 102 cm
FOWLER MUSEUM X86.2959; GIFT OF MR. AND MRS. VICTOR P. GARWOOD

Machine stitching anchors the decorative soutache braid to the felted
wool on this vest. The decorative appliqués and embroidered areas
are in satin stitch. There are two appliquéd leather back-flaps, as well
as leather cords, and decorative "buttons," while strips of woven red
wool border the garment's edges.

3.19B Back view of figure 3.19a.

BANAT (ROMANIA)

The Banat region is located principally in southwestern
Romania, although part of it falls within the eastern portion
of present-day Serbia. (The region also shares a border with
Hungary.) The inhabitants of Banat on both sides of the Danube
are nonetheless mostly Romanian in language and culture.

The costume of the region shows distinct Balkan
influence in its materials and embellishment. Long, com-
paratively fitted vests, such as the one illustrated in figure
3.19a,b, derive much of their ornamentation from Hussar
uniforms of the Austro-Hungarian era, and they sometimes
have vestigial lapels and leather components reminiscent
of equestrian costume.

The lines of cording separating the decorative elements
on such vests relate to the structural features of tailored
garments. The extensive felted wool surfaces of the vest also
allow for elaborate and densely applied patterns of braid—
spirals, loops, tree forms, and so on. Black braid is used
exclusively in some parts of the Banat, whereas other locales
feature blue braid, in addition to other colors. Vests are
further embellished with contrasting colored appliqués and
stitchery in leaf or other vegetal forms to yield an overall effect
that is rich and visually exciting. This vest-type is still worn
on festive occasions in the Banat region, and the basic style of
ornamentation, although now simplified, has been preserved.

BANAT (SERBIA)

Following borders drawn at the close of World War I, part of the Banat region falls within present-day Serbia. This part of eastern Serbia is known as the Vojvodina, and it continues to be home to Romanian enclaves. They have preserved much of their culture, and their traditional dress has survived in an archaic form. The embroidered sheepskin vests of this region are similar in style to those still found over the border in Romania, yet they are unique in their beautiful ornamentation

    The sheepskin vest illustrated in figure 3.20 is embroidered in satin stitch using cotton thread. It has leather pockets, leather back-flaps and interlaced cording, wool pompoms, and brown lambswool borders. The black ground fabric is barely visible under the colorful embroidered designs.

3.20 Woman's vest
Vicinity of Uzdin, Banat, Vojvodina Province, eastern Serbia, twentieth century
White-wooled sheepskin with fleece turned inside; gray, chocolate-colored, and black sheepskin pieced both inside and out; leather appliqué, leather cutwork; braided and woven leather cords, edgings, and pompoms; silk embroidery
35 x 48 cm
FOWLER MUSEUM X97.27.4; BEQUEST OF MARSHA LIPMAN

The motifs used here are characteristic of those used in archaic types of embroidered vests. They include rams' horns, snake-like forms, trees of life, rainbows, solar wheels, stars, and floral buds. The two small leather pockets feature ram's horn motifs. Interlaced leather cording and connecting pompoms are draped at the top and bottom. Three leather "tags" with their pompoms are attached at the center base of the back and at the front closures, and an interwoven leather border surrounds the wool at the bottom of the vest. Note the fine cutwork patterns on some of the leather. Cutwork leather is an ancient art, found among the archaeological remains from eastern Europe back at least twenty-five hundred years.

3.21A Woman's long vest (*zubun*)
Sarajevo, Bosnia-Herzegovina, twentieth century
Woven wool, with embroidered, couched, and appliquéd decoration
51 x 52 cm
FOWLER MUSEUM X2011.4.73; GIFT OF DR. JOEL MARTIN HALPERN

BOSNIA-HERZEGOVINA

Bosnia-Herzegovina was particularly heavily influenced by
the Muslim Turks during the Ottoman era. This influence
extended to both religion and clothing styles. The sleeveless
long vest, or *zubun*, was worn extensively throughout the
Balkans during the nineteenth and early twentieth century
(figs. 3.21a,b). It is typically, but not exclusively, worn by
women. There is a longer, sleeved version of this garment that
serves as an overcoat and is worn by both men and women.
Although found in numerous stylistic and ornamented variants
all over the Balkan Peninsula, it is the most celebrated and
representative form of the traditional dress of Serbia.

This open-fronted vest is of heavy black felted wool.
The curved front edge at the bottom is characteristic in
garments of Eurasian origin, likely brought to the Balkans
during the Ottoman occupation, and examples of this garment were described in accounts as early as the fourteenth
century. It has been worn in some areas until the present.
The extreme longevity of this garment-type is a consequence
of its simple, archaic style in combination with powerful
symbolic embellishment.

The embroidered motifs are executed in a variety of
multicolored stitches, including split, running, buttonhole,
satin, and herringbone. The "Algerian eye" stitch centers
radiate gold and blue "stars" alternating with gold sequins
along the bottom border. Arches, narrow and wide strips,
and wedges of red, white, and green felted wool are applied
and embroidered. There is a thin red, white, and black
twined cording running along the blue wool soutache edging
outlining all of the vest openings.

The beautiful graphic quality of the embellishment
of the *zubun* embodies a vigorous and joyful energy. The
embroidered motifs are placed in specific locations on the
garment and are beautifully realized. Magical symbols of
many kinds are used—for example, the snake, the eye, the
spiral, and the zig-zag or protective "wolves' teeth." Radiating
solar wheels and stars appear in a several versions. Stylized
vegetal motifs include the tree of life, flowers, leaves, spiral-
ing tendrils and the symmetrical branched floral form often
called the "goddess" figure. A stitched pair of Orthodox
crosses ornaments the upper front panels. The presence
of so many talismans on a single garment ensures that the
owner will prosper and avoid harm. ∞

3.21B Back view of figure 3.21a

4

After the Ashes of War

CONTINUITY AND CHANGE IN THE COSTUME, MUSIC, AND DANCE OF A CROATIAN VILLAGE

Elsie Ivancich Dunin

In 1984 the Fowler Museum mounted the exhibition *Dance Occasions and Festive Dress in Yugoslavia*, and I was invited to write the text for its accompanying publication.[1] One of my chapters included a description of a dance and music performance I had witnessed in 1977 in the village of Čilipi, located in the Konavle region of Croatia near the famed walled city of Dubrovnik.[2]

Čilipi, the largest village in Konavle,[3] consists of seven hamlets, and centered among them is the impressive Saint Nicholas church, originally built in the fifteenth century. Wide stairs in front of the church offer ample seating for an audience looking out toward a flat stone terrace used for performances. Economic assistance provided before World War I by emigrant relatives (many living in California)[4] enabled the renovation of some of the old structures, such as the church, and the construction of some of the larger stone buildings in the village center. In 1977 the economy of the village was essentially tourist based, and three important components of its appeal were its dance and music program (fig. 4.1), regional museum, and the embroidery and other goods made and sold by village women (fig. 4.2). My impressions of my visit in 1977 follow:

> The weekly folklore program takes place immediately after Sunday mass in the open area in front of the church. Twelve to fifteen busloads of tourists from Dubrovnik hotels are driven over twenty kilometers to the village for the eleven o'clock performance. A nominal admission fee is charged.

Early arrivals may stroll amidst booths where traditionally clad women offer local handicrafts for sale (embroidery, dolls dressed in Konavle costume, handmade cloth, and wood carvings), as well as postcards and slides of Čilipi and recordings of the tamburitza orchestra. Adjacent to the church square is a village museum exhibiting historic costumes and artifacts from the recent past.

> …[B]oth villagers and tourists [attend church mass]. Afterwards, the performance site is readied and spectators are directed to the front of the church. A young woman in costume welcomes the audience and introduces the program in five languages: Croatian, English, French, German, and Italian.… [O]ver 700 people [attended] one performance.…

> The village profits from admission fees to the program, and Čilipi women earn money from the sale of their handiwork. Tourists enjoy seeing an "authentic" village with people dressed in festive "folk costumes," hearing the music, and watching the dances. A pleasant and colorful dimension is added to their Dubrovnik visit.… The popularity of the Sunday Čilipi Folklore Program testifies to the attraction of the quaint, the exotic, and the old. From the villagers' perspective, these "folklore" performances are entertaining, profitable, and a source of community pride.[5]

OPPOSITE
Detail of chemise in figure 4.5a.

4.1 In 2009, more than thirty years after my visit of 1977, dancers continued to perform the Potkolo dance. PHOTOGRAPH BY ELSIE IVANCICH DUNIN, ČILIPI.

4.2 Katica Stanković wears her black wool winter-season outfit (*modrina*) in 2011. Her white starched headpiece is of the type traditionally worn on Sundays and holidays by married women. She sells her handmade geometrical Konavle style embroideries on Sundays. Stanković has also performed in the Čilipi dance program since 1967 (see fig. 4.13). PHOTOGRAPH BY ELSIE IVANCICH DUNIN.

THE DEVELOPMENT OF ČILIPI
AS A CENTER OF CULTURAL TOURISM

With funding from the World Bank, a major effort was made in the 1960s to establish the historic walled city of Dubrovnik as a center of tourism.[6] This entailed the building of an international airport near Čilipi; bringing electricity to rural village areas in 1964; completing a paved Adriatic highway in 1965; constructing twenty large-capacity hotels in close proximity to the city;[7] and establishing the Dubrovnik-based Atlas Travel Agency. The new infrastructure provided employment, at least for the villagers who lived near the highway, airport, and new hotel complexes, and Čilipi fell within this realm. Both Dubrovnik and Čilipi were approached by the Atlas Travel Agency to support organized performances incorporating "traditional" dance, music, and costume for visitors.

DANCE IN ČILIPI

Dancing for an audience was not new to the residents of Čilipi, as "*folklor*" performances had been organized in regional programs during the 1930s and in the 1940s following World War II.[8] A Čilipi group was formed to perform the dance known as Potkolo in a documentary film made in 1948,[9] and the dancers were later invited to perform at the first Dubrovnik Summer Festival in 1950, as well as at a program for the International Folk Music Council meeting in 1951.[10]

The Čilipi village-based performance group that Atlas had approached presented its first village tourist program in 1967, directed by Stijepo Vezelič Mijovov.[11] Vezelič was a local musician familiar with the dance music and repertoire of the Konavle region. He had also participated in and organized the group for earlier programs. While the pre-1967 performances had consisted of only one or two dances, Potkolo (accompanied by bagpipe) and Poskočica (accompanied by *lijerica*, a three-string, bowed instrument), the expanded Čilipi dance program of 1967 added the Čičak, Namiguša (fig. 4.3), Seljančica, and waltz (*valcer*), accompanied by *tamburitza* orchestra (see below). In the same year Vezelič became the first director of the KUD Čilipi (an acronym for Kulturno Umjetničko Društvo, or Cultural and Artistic Association).[12]

In the mid-twentieth century Croatia's pioneer ethnochoreologist, Ivan Ivančan, who was based in Zagreb, traveled to villages throughout Croatia to collect information about dances and to interview dancers. He visited the Konavle villages during research trips in 1951 and 1961. He was therefore in the region before Čilipi developed into a tourist center. In his essay of 1966, "Konavle's Folk Dances," Ivančan lists Vezelič as one of the renowned dancers in Čilipi. Several dances are described and notated in his article, including Potkolo, Poskočica, and Čičak, which formed part of the Čilipi program. Seljančica is not described, but Ivančan states that it is danced just as it is elsewhere in Croatia and sung with familiar lyrics.[13]

4.3 In 2007 the dancers of KUD Čilipi continued to perform Namiguša, the winking dance, which was added to the dance program in 1967. PHOTOGRAPH BY ELSIE IVANCICH DUNIN.

KUD ČILIPI MUSIC

Čilipi school teacher Niko Skurič is credited with forming the first *tamburitza* group in 1912.[14] The *tamburitza* is a plucked steel-string instrument, and a group composed of three or more will utilize different sizes, which may be mandolin- or guitar-like in shape. Vezelič, who was born in 1907, was therefore exposed to this type of music as a young boy and became the main proponent of integrating this style of musical accompaniment into the dancing for the tourist program. The earliest performances of Potkolo and Poskočica, shortly after World War II, had been accompanied by bagpipe or *lijerica*, but by the 1960s the dances were accompanied by *tamburitza* musicians. With the exception of the use of the *lijerica* in the Lindjo dance, which would be introduced into the repertoire much later (see below), the dance and singing (*klapa*) program was accompanied by *tamburitza* musicians.

The *klapa*, a male a cappella singing group, was formed in 1984 and also became a part of the KUD Čilipi. Its repertoire consists mainly of Dalmatian-style songs, sung without or with *tamburitza* accompaniment. The group sings weekly in the Sunday programs and is also engaged to sing in Cavtat and Dubrovnik restaurants and for hotel programs. The *klapa* represents an addition to the 1977 program that I recorded.

4.4 During the Sunday performances, village women demonstrate their needlework and sell examples of their embroidery. PHOTOGRAPH BY ELSIE IVANCICH DUNIN, ČILIPI, 2011.

OPPOSITE

4.5A Woman's ensemble
Čilipi, Konavle, twentieth century
FOWLER MUSEUM X2010.26.2.1–4, 6, 7, 11, 13A,B; GIFT OF PROFESSOR
ELSIE IVANCICH DUNIN
(*See Appendix for full details*)

This ensemble was exhibited in the Fowler Museum's exhibition *Dance Occasions and Festive Dress in Yugoslavia* (1984). It is also presented in the exhibition that accompanies this volume. It has become more precious in view of the destruction that Čilipi suffered in the intervening years and the consequent loss of much of its textile heritage.

The overall impression given by most Konavle costumes is of much white cotton ornamented with a bit of colored trim. That trim, however, is executed in minute detail. Removable strips of very fine counted-thread embroidery have been attached around the collar and cuffs, while many slim horizontal stripes of colored wool have been woven into the twill cotton cloth adorning the bottom of the apron. The black wool vest is also a fine-grained twill edged with black silk cords. The tightly woven black belt is ornamented with a few gold silk threads, whereas the thin cotton sash is plain-weave with tiny stripes in four colors. Gold-colored silk tassels finish off the collar, cuffs, and little embroidered bag.

KONAVLE EMBROIDERY

Tangible cultural heritage in the form of embroidery from Konavle had been shown abroad as early as the beginning of the twentieth century. Local school teacher Nike Balarin prepared an album entitled *Konavoski vezovi* (Konavle embroidery) for the Paris Exposition in 1900, showing samples of old and modern Konavle needlework, along with photographs of Konavle brides, girls, and young women in costume.[15] In 1906, Jelka Miš, another school teacher in Konavle, sent examples of embroideries made by her students to a London exposition as a part of the Austrian exhibition, and in 1907 to a display titled *Das Kind* (The Child) in Vienna at an exhibition of *Hausindustrie* (cottage industry). A photograph of the latter shows two young women wearing the Konavle costume in front of the Dalmatian pavilion.[16] Miš also sent a fully embroidered Konavle-style twelve-person tablecloth, titled *Freedom*, to President Woodrow Wilson in 1919. A thank-you note from the president sent to Miš states, "your great gift…will be an eternal memory of your friendship, whose work sprung from the nation we hold great interest in."[17] The significance of the gift and note is that through peace negotiations held in 1919, President Wilson assisted in the formation of Yugoslavia at the end of World War I.

Hundreds of examples of embroideries were collected at the turn of the century by Nike Balarin, Marija Lovrič, and Jelka Miš. However, it is the analysis of the embroideries by Miš, her teachings, and her organizing of an embroidery school in Cavtat and an embroiderers' guild in Dubrovnik (1922–1946), that are significant for the history and continuity of the Konavle needlework tradition. Her hundreds of samples of needlework are the mainstay of the Konavle and Dubrovnik museum textile collections and serve as models for current textile designs (fig. 4.4).

4.6 This commercial postcard, probably dating to the 1970s, shows the type of woman's ensemble illustrated in figure 4.5. The starched white headdress was worn by married women on holidays, and the red cap by those who were unmarried.

4.5B Detail of sleeve embroidery in figure 4.5a.

Miš recorded that in the past villagers planted flax and hemp; combed, dyed, and spun wool; and bred silkworms for threads. The dyes used were native to the area. A girl would weave, sew, and embroider her entire outfit. The most decorated part of a woman's attire was on the long shirt (*košulja*), with an embroidered bib (*poprsnica*), narrow collar (*ogrob*), and bottom edges (*ošva*) of the long sleeves (figs. 4.5a,b, 4.6). The embroidery pieces for the female costume and other household articles (tableclothes, curtains, pillows) demonstrate the meticulous and demanding practice of counted-thread stitching, which does not allow for any mistake on the front or the back side of the decoration.

By the end of the nineteenth century, the white base fabric for the long dress was no longer woven at home. Instead, industrially made Czech cloth[18] was imported to shops in Cavtat and Dubrovnik, where Konavle women purchased it. According to a fabric store shopkeeper I spoke with in Dubrovnik in 2011, fabrics with mixed synthetic fibers used in the former Yugoslavia between 1944 and 1991 came from Macedonian and Slovenian textile producers, and now in the twenty-first century, they are once again produced by and imported from the same factories.

At the beginning of the twentieth century, silk embroidery threads were still produced and dyed at home. Because the dyes sometimes bled when washed, the embroidery was not done directly on the chemise, but on separate pieces of sturdier cloth stitched temporarily to the front of the dress and the ends of the sleeves. At each washing, these silk-embroidered pieces were removed. By the 1930s, however, factory-made DMC silk threads could be purchased in colors comparable to the original natural dyes, and today various commercial threads are used.[19]

4.7 The regional museum of Čilipi was destroyed in 1991–1992. Reproduced from Desin (1993, 74).

THE REGIONAL MUSEUM

In 1974, seven years after the KUD Čilipi began their Sunday performances for tourists, a Konavle regional museum house (*zavičajna kuća Konavala*) was established in a two-story stone building near the church and performance site. Organized by local volunteers, who provided artifacts drawn from their own homes, the local museum typified a village house with an open-fireplace cooking area and a well opening to an underground water cistern carved out of stone.[20] Among the items exhibited in the small volunteer museum were women's and men's costumes, embroidered and woven textiles, jewelry, weapons, musical instruments, and household utensils. Processes including silkworm production, the dyeing of threads for embroidery, and the production of wool for weaving on a large wooden loom were also illustrated. Ten years after its founding under the aegis of the KUD Čilipi, Marina Desin, a professionally trained conservator, was hired to manage and guide the ethnocultural collection.[21]

THE DESTRUCTION OF ČILIPI, 1991–1995

In October of 1991 the JNA (Yugoslav National Army) invaded and demolished most of Konavle in a horrific offensive.[22] The highway from the border of Montenegro passes through Čilipi and nearby village hamlets, leading to the Dubrovnik airport and onward to the city of Dubrovnik itself. These settlements were especially targeted. Following immediate evacuation procedures, villagers fled to hotels in Cavtat (five kilometers away) or to Dubrovnik (twenty kilometers away), while the attacking army plundered and burned whatever it could. Those villagers who remained behind were captured and assassinated or interned. Their experience—as with that of other refugees within the former Yugoslavia—is perhaps best summed up in the oft-heard lament, "All that we had, all that we were, reduced to memories."[23]

The major part of the Čilipi regional museum's movable collection of textiles, costumes, smaller artifacts, and some literature were hidden in the ancient carved stone cistern under the building, and therefore saved from the flames. The museum building, however, was completely burned with only its stone walls left standing (fig. 4.7).

Although most of the damage took place in 1991–1992 and the occupation was lifted by fall of 1992, newly constituted Croatian forces arrived bent on revenge. Furthermore, Serbian forces in Bosnia unpredictably shelled across the mountain border into the Dubrovnik coastal strip until the day of the signing of the Dayton Peace Agreement in November 1995. Most Čilipi villagers (and other Dubrovnik-area villagers whose homes had been destroyed) were forced to live as displaced families in hotel rooms in Cavtat and Dubrovnik.

RECLAIMING IDENTITY

Following the war, decisions about the future of the village could have taken a number of directions, ranging from its abandonment (as occurred in many other areas), to reconstruction following modern global models, to the rebuilding of the village as it had been before the war. It was the latter decision that was supported by the surviving villagers who were determined to prove to their aggressors that they could not be moved. For those who lived through the devastation of Čilipi, the overriding decision to continue their lives in their village came from a deep-seated emotional need to reclaim their cultural identity through their "*folklor*" program, their museum, and their needlework tradition.

In 1993 I spoke with Vezelič, and during the first decade after the millennium, I was able to speak with three performers[24] from the KUD Čilipi about their wartime experiences and the losses that they had endured. They explained that along with other performers, they decided to present their regular

4.8 The museum in Čilipi was rebuilt on the same site and reopened on May 18, 2007, International Museum Day (cf. fig. 4.7). PHOTOGRAPH BY ELSIE IVANCICH DUNIN, 2011.

peformance on Palm Sunday, April 4, 1993,[25] whether or not they had an audience. The performers themselves helped to clear the rubble in front of the church so they would have an ample area in which to dance. Those who had lost their costumes—typically passed from generation to generation—to fire borrowed from others who had been more fortunate or managed to escape with their personal textile treasures. The *tamburitza* instruments were another casualty of the war, and all had to be replaced in time to perform in the 1993 programs.

Although in 1993, as noted above, enemy forces were no longer occupying Konavle, battles were still fought along other border areas of Croatia and within adjacent Bosnia-Herzegovina. Nevertheless, both KUD Čilipi (under the leadership of Luko Novak[26]) and the museum's director, Marina Desin,[27] were invited to the 27th International Folklore Festival held in Croatia's capital of Zagreb, an event that lent moral support to the displaced people of Konavle and their threatened culture.[28] Selected Konavle textiles from the saved museum collection were exhibited for a week, and the dance/music group performed in costume for the public.

With initial postwar support provided by ARCH (Arts Restoration for Cultural Heritage), a Lugano-based foundation, and continuing aid from the Ministry of Culture of Croatia, the regional museum was rebuilt with the same façade on the same site (fig. 4.8). Some old furniture pieces that had survived in Konavle homes were donated to the reconstructed museum (including the loom seen in fig. 4.9). The museum was reopened on International Museum Day, May 18, 2007. Marina Desin continues to oversee the collection and interfaces with visitors each Sunday, occasionally entertaining special guests such as President Ivo Josipović of Croatia (fig. 4.10).

Some changes were made to the dance program following the war, although as my photographs attest (figs. 4.11, 4.12), there were no major differences in the program as I saw it in 1977 and again in 2011, thirty-four years after—and twenty

years since the village was invaded. The initial dance of the program, the two-part Potkolo, is now accompanied by singing in the first part, whereas in 1977 both parts were performed only with *tamburitza* accompaniment. Performances, even of traditional dances, are never completely static, however, and we can also observe change between the dance as performed in 1948 without singing but accompanied by a bagpipe and the performance of 1977 accompanied by *tamburitza* music.

The absence of a solo *gusla* singer of epic poetry in the program also marks a change. In 1977 the singer, Pavo Martinović was already elderly, and no younger man assumed his role. Although epic singing was common in the rural areas of Dubrovnik and throughout much of the Dinaric mountain region, the form tended to be associated primarily with Montenegro, and therefore its continuation was not encouraged in the postwar Konavle program. A short Konavle wedding scene replaced the *gusla* segment of the program. This made it possible for two members from the first generation of performers in 1967, who no longer danced, to continue to participate in the program. A bride with an ornate floral headress and the groom walk as a threesome with the bride's mother-in-law (played by Katica Stanković) who assists with the tossing of wrapped candies backward over their heads into the audience (fig. 4.13). When they reach the end of their walk, the second long-term performer, Luko Novak, proceeds with a shortened drinking toast to good health (*zdravica*) that is still a part of wedding feasts in the Konavle area (fig. 4.14).

The postwar program also replaced the dance known as Seljančica Kolo, an open circle dance, with the Lindjo, a couple's dance. Luko Novak explained that the *kolo* was too much like the dances performed in the interior of the former Yugoslavia, and it was therefore replaced with a dance from the Dubrovnik area, even though it was not originally performed in Konavle as a social dance.

4.9 This loom, which survived the invasion and the war years, was donated to the museum after its rebuilding. PHOTOGRAPH BY ELSIE IVANCICH DUNIN, 2007.

4.10 Marina Desin, the curator of the regional museum in Čilipi, shows President Ivo Josipovič of Croatia part of the collection. PHOTOGRAPH BY NEDA MATIČ, 2011.

4.11 Dancers in Čilipi perform the Poskočica in 1977. This photograph was published in the Fowler Museum's catalog *Dance Occasions and Festive Dress in Yugoslavia* (1984, 32). PHOTOGRAPH BY ELSIE IVANCICH DUNIN.

4.12 Nearly twenty years after the destruction of Čilipi, the performance of Poskočica in 2011 appears nearly identical to that of 1977 (see fig. 4.11). PHOTOGRAPH BY ELSIE IVANCICH DUNIN, 2011.

4.13 The wedding promenade in the current program replaces the *gusla* epic singing of the 1977 program. Here villager Katica Stankovič (see fig. 4.2) takes the role of the mother-in-law with other performers assuming the roles of bride and groom. PHOTOGRAPH BY ELSIE IVANCICH DUNIN, 2011.

4.14 Villager Luko Novak offers a toast to good health (*zdravica*) in the wedding scene that forms part of the performance. PHOTOGRAPH BY ELSIE IVANCICH DUNIN, 2007.

4.15 This painting by Miho Šiša Konavljanin was donated by the artist to the reconstructed museum for its opening in May 2007. His earlier painting at the museum, also featuring a dance scene, musicians, and costume, was destroyed by the military assault in 1991.

RISING FROM THE ASHES

The KUD Čilipi continues to be a vital community organization, representing the village and Konavle as an attraction to the outside world, but it is just as important, if not more so, to the social cohesion of the village community. Earnings from the KUD Čilipi performances have continued to enhance the museum site, as well as to improve the infrastructure of the village and assist it in its humanitarian projects.

One painting that graces the museum walls was donated in time for the reopening of the museum in May 2007. Miho Šiša Konavljanin, a local artist, painted a new picture to replace one of his that had burned in the museum during the war (fig. 4.15). The large new painting shows villagers in various roles on Sunday: performers of the Poskočica dance; musicians playing on *tamburitza*, *lijerica*, and bagpipe; part of a wedding scene; mothers carrying babies; children playing in the foreground on newly laid stone; and an old instrument being passed to a child. In the background is the museum building on the left, the bell tower and church in the center, and other renovated stone buildings on the right, all with new red tile roofs replacing those destroyed in 1991.

Although parents and grandparents may continue to feel a collective sense of resentment against their invaders, young dance performers born after the 1991 invasion continue the tourist program that is deemed their rightful heritage. Costumes are inherited from family members for the performance or for participating in other aspects of the Čilipi Sunday program, such as collecting tickets, selling textiles at family stands, working as security guards at the museum, or demonstrating crafts.

Today the dances and music are learned for the tourist performances, rather than as a means to socialize on Sundays, holidays, or during other free time in the center of the village, as they were a century ago. The costumes are no longer worn or passed on as social identifiers of age, marriage, or widowhood, but to be displayed to the outside world in performance. And the continuation of needlework with motifs from the past is part of a family's economic support system rather than for making outfits to be worn at different stages of life and on holidays. Dress, dance, and music continue to be a mainstay of life but in a markedly changed context.

5

CHAPTER
FIVE

Festive Dress and Dance Events in the Romani Community of Skopje, Republic of Macedonia, 1967 and 2011

Elsie Ivancich Dunin

Migrating, probably no earlier than the eleventh century, from present-day northwestern India and Pakistan, the Roms (formerly referred to as Gypsies)[1] began to settle in southeastern Europe before the Ottoman conquests of the late fourteenth century.[2] Early twenty-first-century population profiles, based on census statistics from southeastern European countries, show that the Roms presently constitute the third or fourth largest population groups in Bulgaria, Greece, Macedonia, Serbia, Kosovo, and Albania.[3] These Romani groups are sedentary, with their own homes, unlike their nomadic counterparts. The Roms further identify themselves according to subgroups,[4] they speak their own dialects of the Romani language, and they do not intermarry with nomadic groups.

In 1963 an earthquake devastated the Macedonian city of Skopje.[5] Prior to that time the Roms had lived there for generations in neighborhoods or enclaves (Turkish: *mahala*) located for the most part near the ancient fortress (*kale*) on a bluff overlooking the Vardar River.[6] Topaana (or Tophana), one of these Romani *mahala*, was adjacent to a larger group of Turkish Muslim neighborhoods. After the earthquake, the city was rebuilt, and most of the Romani families resettled in the new suburb of Šuto Orizari (nicknamed Šutka), northwest of the city. A shrunken Topaana with crowded makeshift homes and narrow streets still stands, but modern high-rise apartment buildings surround the small Romani houses, and in 2009 the newly built United States Embassy opened on an adjacent hill.

Šuto Orizari is the only municipality in history to have acknowledged the Romani language and has a bilingual (Romani/Slavic Macedonian) charter. The 2002 census showed 13,342 residents (out of a total 22,017) to be of Romani ethnicity.[7] They follow either Islam or Christianity, though Romani religious practices differ from those of the rest of the groups in Macedonia.

OPPOSITE
Detail of *čintiani* in figure 1.1.

The situation of the Roms in Skopje today—where they have been recognized as an official minority population since 1991 by the Republic of Macedonia—differs substantially from what I observed in 1967[8] when I began my dance ethnology recordings and analysis at festive occasions with the Cigani, the derogatory term by which the Roms were then known. The Romani appellation was changed from Turski Cigani (Turkish Gypsies) to Roma at the time of the First World Romani Congress held near London in 1971.[9]

ROMANI DRESS AND IDENTITY IN SKOPJE

The Fowler Museum's preservation of two sets of women's pantaloon outfits—one collected in 1967 and the other in 2011—from the same Romani community in Skopje is perhaps unique among museum holdings. Coming from the very same place, these costumes provide a tangible basis from which to compare lifestyle continuities and changes. The outfits consist of two major components: *čintiani* (pantaloons) and *mintan*[10] (a short jacket or vest).

Čintiani are made of about ten meters of fabric sewn into a kind of bag with two ankle holes at the outer bottom corners; the upper end of the bag is gathered at the waist by a drawstring and secured with a separate metal belt. The *čintiani* legs are formed by the wearer who lifts the excess fabric from between her ankles up in front of her and then tucks it in at the sides of her waist. This lifting and tucking forms a crotch and a large "pocket" below the waist. This manner of forming "legs" for the pantaloons distinguishes them from the way that their Turkish Muslim and Slavic Bosnian counterparts (*šalvare* and *dimje*, respectively) are worn.

The *mintan* may be a sleeveless vest or a short jacket with full puffy sleeves. In 1967 the *mintan* neckline was adorned with a pleated collar (fig. 5.1). The style of the outfit from 2011 (fig. 5.2) continues to accent the neckline but with an extended collar. The *mintan* is fitted so that it is open at the front and reveals a camisole, slip, or cotton T-shirt of any color underneath.

5.1 Woman's ensemble
Skopje, Macedonia, 1960s
FOWLER MUSEUM X69.100A,B–103; GIFT OF PROFESSOR ELSIE IVANCICH DUNIN
(*See Appendix for full details*)

The flowered *čintiani* (pantaloons) in this outfit are made of nylon
with a full 280 cm (9 ft.) of fabric between the ankles. This excess
fabric is lifted by the wearer and tucked in at the sides of her waist
to form legs. The matching *mintan* (jacket) boasts a pleated ruff, and
the blouse collar and scarf (*šamija*) are decorated with multicolored
tatting. The metal belt placed over the drawstring waist of the pants
is of intricate filigree wire work.

5.2 Woman's ensemble
Skopje, Macedonia, 2011
FOWLER MUSEUM X2011.33.1A–9; GIFT OF PATRICIA ANAWALT
(See Appendix for full details)

Almost fifty years after the pantaloon outfit in figure 5.1 was collected, Romani women had switched to festive ensembles requiring less fabric. The pants (*kuli*) now have two actual fixed pant legs, and the fabric has been sewn into flat pleats around the waist. The jacket now has short sleeves and a fuller three-layer ruff. Accessories include a heavy metal belt, as well as a white puff and hankies, all decorated with sequins and used for the lead in various dance lines. This ensemble also includes a flower-decorated flour sifter covered with red fabric, as well as a pair of sequined red net covers to protect henna designs on the hands and a red scarf to cover the henna bowl at the henna ceremony during the wedding cycle. At the top left are hair ornaments attached to combs.

5.3 These Romani women have tied their head scarves (*šamija*) in the manner typical for married women between the 1960s and 1980s. They also wear the customary red cotton apron with white stripes. PHOTOGRAPH BY ELSIE IVANCICH DUNIN, SKOPJE, MACEDONIA, 1987.

In 1967 the pantaloon outfit was used by Romani women for everyday wear as well as festive dress. It was accompanied by a square scarf (*šamija*), made of a thin cotton edged with tatting. This was folded into a triangle with the two ends crossed at the nape of the neck and tied on or near the top of the head (fig. 5.3). In contrast Bosnian, Albanian, and Turkish women covered their hair and ears in public by tying their larger scarves under the chin or at the back of the head under the triangular flap. In the years between 1967 and the 1980s, Romani women also wore an apron of red cotton fabric woven with white stripes, which was wrapped around the torso at the waist and overlapped at the back (see fig. 5.3).

Today Romani women can no longer be distinguished from the mainstream urban population of Skopje by their daily attire.[11] The type of outfit acquired by the Fowler in 2011 is now usually restricted to wear during wedding cycles and in those performance contexts that emphasize a distinct Romani dress code and identity. The dance repertoire similarly is no longer featured in community events as it was in 1967, but it persists in the wedding cycles of 2011. The permutations of the Romani festive dress and dance repertoire in Skopje can therefore be documented over three generations.

Within the ten-year span following my visit of 1967, many Roms had gone from living in small houses where familial activity was essentially confined to a single room with carpets and cushions on the floor, to occupying bigger spaces with tables and chairs in the suburbanz houses of Šuto Orizari. In 1967 the "new" nylon fabric used in the earlier outfit (see fig. 5.1) could be easily washed, dried, stored in a small packet, and refreshed without wrinkles. It was well suited to the relatively scarce storage space of its day.

By 1977 the everyday use of the pantaloon outfit had become less common, and storage space for additional clothing and household goods had increased. *Čintiani* might be worn for special holidays, such as the fifth day of the Saint George's celebration, also known as Erdelezi (fig. 5.4), but by 1987 they were restricted to special occasions such as weddings (*svadba-nevesta*) and circumcisions (*svadba-sunet*), as well as for use by dance performance groups. The Fowler's pantaloon outfit of 2011 is made of colorful, attractive fabric, but it is not practical to wash. If an outfit becomes soiled, the economic resources of the Romani have increased to the point where it can simply be replaced with another, perhaps in a newer style, for the next family wedding.

It is definitely at weddings that pantaloon outfits are most visible today. Most Romani weddings, which are expensive, multi-day events, take place during the "wedding season" of July and August, when family members living in other European countries are able to visit Skopje. The streets of Šuto Orizari fill with cars bearing license plates from Germany, Belgium, the Netherlands, Italy, and France.[12] These visiting relatives, who usually enjoy higher incomes, generally assist with family expenses in Skopje, and weddings have become increasingly extravagant affairs. Every bride has at least three outfits: a white formal wedding gown, and two differently colored *čintiani* outfits. All the other women in the wedding party own at least one elaborate pantaloon outfit. A recently married woman maintains her identity as a *nevesta* (bride) for a period of one to three years after her own marriage ceremony whenever she is in attendance at the marriage of another family member. She wears *čintiani* and a white veil on the back of her head to mark this status.

Romani "weddings"[13] were especially numerous in the second half of July 2011, a year in which the month-long Muslim holiday of Ramadan began on the first of August. Every day several wedding parties danced in the streets of Šutka. The bride being married in each of these ceremonies could be easily identified by the strands of body-length tinsel hanging from her hair (fig. 5.5), and women in the bride's extended family dressed in shiny *čintiani* making for an extremely colorful event. The men of the family do not dress in special garments at weddings, and they generally congregate around the men's *švedski stol* (Swedish buffet) of bottled beverages and appetizers—cold cuts, cheeses, sausages, grilled *čevapčiči* (sausage-shaped ground meat), cut vegetables, and bread. Except for the groom and the fathers of the couple, the men tend not to dance with the women; they do, however, generously pay the singer or musician who plays in the center of the women's open circle dance (fig. 5.6).

5.4 The woman holding a hankie leads a dance line during the fifth day of the Saint George's Day (Erdelezi) holiday. The dance participants wear *ćintiani* (pantaloons). PHOTOGRAPH BY ELSIE IVANCICH DUNIN, SKOPJE, MACEDONIA, 1977.

5.5 A bride can be recognized by the long strands of tinsel that hang from the sides of her hair. Here she dances with the women of her family in the street outside of her home. PHOTOGRAPH BY ELSIE IVANCICH DUNIN, SKOPJE, MACEDONIA, 2011.

Around 2007 a variant of the *čintiani*, known as the *kuli*, began to appear, which had an actual waistband, as opposed to a drawstring. The photograph in figure 5.7, which was taken in 2011, shows both *čintiani* and *kuli* at a festive occasion. Although both styles continue to be made and worn, *kuli* appear to be increasingly popular, because they are easier to wear (the drawstring doesn't have to be readjusted), and they use less of the expensive fabric. In July 2011, a Romani seamstress with her own shop near the center of Šutka had only *kuli* on display, although she would sew *čintiani* on request.

The fabrics used for *čintiani* and *kuli* in 2011 were imported from Dubai in the United Arab Emirates and were readily available in the old market center of Skopje in fabric shops catering to Muslim clientele (including Roms, Turks, and Albanians). Finished outfits in styles appropriate to each group were also sold to this diverse clientele. Roms living outside of Skopje and Macedonia (in Croatia and Germany, for example) travel to Skopje to purchase these festive outfits in large numbers for weddings in their own diasporic communities.

5.6 Men in everyday summer outfits pay the clarinetist who plays for the dances led by the woman with the *sito* (flour sifter) at the far left. Each man pays the musicians to play for the women in his family when they lead the dance. PHOTOGRAPH BY ELSIE IVANCICH DUNIN, SKOPJE, MACEDONIA, 2011.

Čintiani and *kuli* outfits are sold with a matching *marama* (hankie), which is held in the right hand while leading a dance (see figs. 5.2, 5.4). During the wedding cycle, every woman in the bride's or groom's family leads a dance. Depending upon the sequence of dances, she may hold a hankie or a decorated flour sifter in her right hand. In 2011 hankies of various fabrics were about 26 centimeters square with an added edging, often tipped with large sequins, making a 30-centimeter square (26–30 cm are equivalent to approximately 10–12 in.). The fabric of these hankies ranges from polyester, rayon, or light cotton to netted fabric (see fig. 5.2). Another item for leading a dance looks like a white puff, made of stiffly wound thread that is tipped with shiny sequins (see fig. 5.2). Known as *bojraki marama*, this puff is held in the palm of the bride's right hand, rather than dangling from

the fingers. Both the puff and the hankie, however, are fitted with thread rings that can slip over a finger.

The *sito* is a flour sifter, a wooden frame holding a wire screen, which may also be held by a dance leader and is said to symbolize the chastity of the bride. In 1967 the *sito* was held by the mother-in-law of the bride to announce, through her dance lead, that the bride had indeed been a virgin on her wedding night (fig. 5.9). The bride's mother-in-law (*svekrva*) would lead a round of dance holding the *sito* and then pass it to her own mother-in-law, the *baba* (grandmother) in the household. If one of these women was not able to be present, then the *sito* was given to the oldest woman in the groom's household (most likely a paternal aunt).

By 2011 the dance lead with the *sito* had an expanded role that included the women of the bride's family at her household, and the women of the groom's family at his household. A *sito,* wrapped in red fabric, was held by the bride's mother in the dancing that took place in the street in front of her house (fig. 5.8). The mother symbolically uses the *sito* to show that her daughter is chaste, but the other members of the bride's family who lead dances with the *sito* do so to wish the

5.7 Women in this dance line wear both types of pantaloons, the *čintiani*, which have a drawstring waist, and the *kuli,* which have a sewn waistband (see the woman in green, second from right). All the women wear the *mintan*, which may take the form of a puffy-sleeved jacket or a sleeveless vest. PHOTOGRAPH BY ELSIE IVANCICH DUNIN, SKOPJE, MACEDONIA, 2011.

bride good health and fertility. Later, at the groom's household, the bride's mother-in-law leads with the *sito* when the dancing takes place in the street in front of that home.

On the first day after the bride is brought to the groom's family home, the hierarchy of the women in the household is plainly demonstrated to the bride through the order of the dancing. The first dance with the *sito* is led by the bride's mother-in-law, and then by the groom's *baba*, and so on. After all the women in the groom's family have been acknowledged, the *sito* is taken away, and the dancing and music commence with the hankie used to lead the next dance.

In 1967, there were no hairstylists in Topaana or in the new suburb. A woman regularly wore a scarf covering her hair, often worn in long braids, and a headdress during festive occasions. Bathing and shampooing tended to

5.8 In 2011 the mother of the bride leads the first dance with a decorated flour sifter (cf. fig. 5.9). PHOTOGRAPH BY ELSIE IVANCICH DUNIN, SKOPJE, MACEDONIA.

5.9 The bride's mother-in-law (*svekrva*) leads a dance with an undecorated flour sifter (sito) in 1967. PHOTOGRAPH BY ELSIE IVANCICH DUNIN, SKOPJE, MACEDONIA.

take place in an Ottoman Turkish public *amam* (steam bath) near the old Topaana neighborhood.[14] By 2011 hairstyles and headwear had changed, and most women now have their hair professionally styled for weddings. The preferred hairstyle is called *Turska moda* (Turkish style) and has been a favorite for several years (see fig. 5.8). Hundreds of Romani women wear this elaborate hairstyle when they are dressed in festive pantaloons and also when dressed in full-length evening gowns in restaurants (another part of the wedding cycle). There are now at least five fully equipped hair salons in Šutka, and several women who independently style hair in their homes. All are fully engaged during the summer wedding season.

As recorded in 1967, and for at least another decade, the women invited to a wedding received *apušme*—decorations cut out of paper into various shapes accented with glued-on sequins, beads, fake coins, or strands of metallic thread (fig. 5.10).[15] These were pasted on their cheeks with sugar-water and saliva or secured to their foreheads with a couple strands of tinsel tied at the back of the head. Every *apušme* was unique but also fragile, wearable through only a single wedding cycle. By the mid-1980s gold pieces purchased for a bride from jewelry shops in central Skopje were used as *apušme*. These were smaller in size than the home-made *apušme* but were more durable and could be worn at subsequent wedding events. The *apušme* were discontinued in the twenty-first century and have been replaced by large hair ornaments attached by combs (see fig. 5.2). These hair ornaments are sold in the "women's market" (*ženski pijac*) within Skopje's central market.

In the 1960s makeup was limited to lipstick, considered a luxury item and shared among the women in a family. By the 1980s, makeup was readily available, and in current weddings, nearly every young woman wears elaborate eye shadow, liner, mascara, false eyelashes, foundation, and blush (fig. 5.11). In addition, many women wear fashionable acrylic fingernails, and pedicured toes peek through their high-heeled sandals.

ROMANI DRESS AND DANCE FROM 1967 TO 2011

In the 1960s the community-wide five-day celebration of seasonal change, which was held May 5–9, was expressed with the wearing of festive *čintiani* and communal dancing.[16] Over the last nearly fifty years, however, younger generations have gradually adopted more global fashion, and the pantaloon outfits of the past are no longer worn on a daily basis or to celebrate the passing of the seasons. Today's young Roms nonetheless continue to express their identity at weddings and circumcisions, and through the strong connections of their extended paternal families, which are evidenced through leadership in dancing. The dancing with a *sito* lead especially demonstrates the kinship of a Romani family. The wearing of pantaloons during the wedding cycle is an expression of family cohesion not only through dress but also through the repetitive and unified dancing in a moving line, since the high volume of the music in the street or in restaurants does not allow verbal exchanges. The cohesive movement in the dancing, the recognition of the dance leadership, and the visual beauty of the fabric and color worn by the dancing women provide positive reinforcement of Romani cultural identity that is unique in Skopje.

5.10 A young bride and a family member wear delicate, homemade *apušme* decorations on their foreheads in 1967. These were later replaced by more durable gold ornaments. In the twenty-first century, however, they are no longer used, and elaborate hair ornaments seem to have taken their place. PHOTOGRAPH BY ELSIE IVANCICH DUNIN, SKOPJE, MACEDONIA.

5.11 Women in Skopje today attend festive events with their hair professionally styled and wearing make-up. PHOTOGRAPH BY ELSIE IVANCICH DUNIN, SKOPJE, MACEDONIA, 2011.

6

CHAPTER
SIX

the Stories behind the Clothes

Barbara Belle Sloan

If the textiles in the Fowler Museum's collections could talk, they would have some very interesting tales to reveal to us, and none more so than the traditional costumes of south-eastern Europe. The following four stories, each unique yet not atypical, ensure that some of the memories of the past survive and give insight into the preservation of textiles that, though still resplendent, are now separated from their early histories and homelands.

EMILY BLACKSTONE CAMP IN ALBANIA

Well into the twentieth century in rural areas of Albania, men and women wore traditional forms of dress on a daily basis (fig. 6.1), and some still do even today. Men attired themselves in embroidered jackets with white wool trousers and caps. Women dressed in long, black, bell-shaped skirts

made of heavy homespun wool and necklaces of old silver coins that clinked against their wide, nail-studded metal belts.[1] By the early twentieth century, however, changes had already begun to take place in Albania that would lead to a move away from these garments as everyday wear in more urban and less remote contexts.

Following Albanian independence from Ottoman rule in 1912, a struggle for power arose between conservative landowners who wanted to perpetuate old ways of life and those who wanted to modernize the country. The winner in this struggle was Ahmed Bey Zogolli (1895–1961). Born in Mati, a small village in mountainous northern Albania, Ahmed was the second son of a powerful tribal chief, the head of the Mati clan. He was therefore raised in the center of power, watching his father settle all disputes—large or

6.1 An Albanian man and woman wearing everyday dress walk down a street in Kavajë, circa 1928. The seams of the man's white wool trousers are decorated with dark braid, and the woman wears a head cover indicating that she is married.
EMILY BLACKSTONE CAMP ARCHIVE, FOWLER MUSEUM.

OPPOSITE
Detail of figure 6.8.

6.2 Immaculately attired, King Zog I of Albania stands in front of a portrait of his mother, Sadije, March 16, 1938. ASSOCIATED PRESS, NO. 3803160252.

6.3 Starting at the left of this photograph are King Zog's sister Nafije, his mother Sadije, the king, his sisters Ruhije and Senije. The family poses wearing traditional dress circa 1934. HULTON ROYALS COLLECTION, HULTON ARCHIVE. GETTY IMAGES, NO. 3426897.

OPPOSITE

6.4 King Zog's sisters appear dressed in fur coats and the latest fashions, circa 1929. EMILY BLACKSTONE CAMP ARCHIVE, FOWLER MUSEUM.

6.5 Emily Blackstone Camp reads while seated in an armchair at Samarcand Manor in North Carolina, where she worked as a farm manager at the State Home and Industrial School for Girls the 1920s. Like C. T. Erickson, who recruited her, Emily wanted to help promote education in Albania. EMILY BLACKSTONE CAMP ARCHIVE, FOWLER MUSEUM.

small, military or civil—according to the Canon of Lek, an "oral code of custom," rooted in ancient notions of honor.[2]

Ahmed was sent away from the village for his formal education, initially to a nearby school that prepared students for government service and later to Turkey. There he adopted a more western-European style of clothing. At age sixteen Ahmed became chief of the Mati, following the death of his father, and his rise to power was swift. At age twenty-four he changed his name to Ahmed Zog and was appointed minister of the interior. In 1922, he became the first prime minister of Albania. Three years later, he became president of the Albanian Republic, and in 1928 he declared himself King Zog I. As king, Zog wore custom-made suits from England, silk shirts from Paris, and handmade shoes from Italy (fig. 6.2).[3]

Zog was especially interested in improving the lot of Albanian women. This focus on women can perhaps be explained by the fact that the king had six sisters. Brought up in the northern mountains of Albania, they had a rather rudimentary education, but their self-proclaimed royal brother transformed them into princesses. The Zog sisters "wore picturesque national costume at official functions" (fig. 6.3)[4] but at social events were seen dressed in the latest Paris fashions (fig. 6.4).

During his days as prime minister, Zog had asked C. Telford Erickson (1867–1966), an American missionary who had worked in Albania since 1908, to assist in the creation of a school for girls as well as one for boys. The American Board of Missions had decided in 1918 that Erickson had become too embroiled in the political turmoil of Albania and withdrew support for his activities. The missionary then "single-handedly set about the herculean task of organizing an American Committee in the United States to raise funds for the establishment of a far-reaching program of education—combining book knowledge and

practical experience—for Albanian youth with emphasis on agriculture for the boys and on household arts for the girls."[5] Erickson's efforts came to fruition in 1924 when the Albanian parliament set aside a thousand acres of land for the Albanian-American School of Agriculture.

On one of his fundraising visits to the United States Erickson met and recruited Emily Blackstone Camp (1900–1984), an idealistic young American woman (fig. 6.5), who had graduated from Massachusetts Agriculture College (now University of Massachusetts Amherst) with a major in animal husbandry. Emily—who according to Camp family lore initially thought she was being recruited to teach young girls in Albany, New York—[6] arrived in Albania on September 1, 1929, filled with excitement and looking forward to contributing to the formation of a new school. She confronted, however, poor living conditions, inadequate funding, few books, little food, not enough water, and almost no medicine, all of which made daily life difficult for her, the teachers, and the students. She described her ambivalent feelings in a letter:

> Here everyone moves slowly and everything is "*vesa*," the Albanian word for tomorrow.... Buying a spool of thread takes hours, and then you are apt to come away without it. Regardless of all of its drawbacks Albania is a place that "gets" you and certainly holds you by the throat.... There is a real love for this confounded country. I am eager to leave it and yet should hate like everything to get onto a ship and really know that I was leaving [it] forever. I would always want to come back.[7]

In another letter home dated October 21, 1929, Emily described a parade celebrating King Zog's birthday: "The whole of Albania came dressed in the national costume, some really lovely. The women were wearing the embroidered coats such as I am sending to you."[8] The following week she wrote: "The King is coming down to dedicate our school building. We are dressing all the children in Albanian costume [fig. 6.6] as we heard that Fox Movietone will be here for the big doings. So keep your eyes open for the news reels and you may see us all."[9] She followed up with a letter indicating everyone's disappointment because the king did not show up.[10]

Emily sent three Albanian coats to a friend in Santa Barbara, California with the explanation that

> the gold one without sleeves I bought for you thinking that you might find some use for it as a wall decoration—now I am not so sure. The others are my own unless you want them. The coats are over 100 years old as the sales slip shows—and are made with a thread covered with real gold— therefore they do not tarnish. It is not easy to find these now and they are going up in price all the time.[11] I would like to keep two of the robes I am sending because they give a very good idea of the different sections of Albania: the heavy gold coat is from Scutari in the north, and the long red one is from Korçë in southern Albania. You will notice that they both are very narrow in the shoulders due to the fact that the girls were only twelve to fourteen years old when married.[12]

The baggy trousers that women wore under their elaborately embroidered robes were made from enormous amounts of cloth (fig. 6.7). Cuffed holes were cut and sewn at the bottom corners of the bag-shaped garment causing the remaining fabric to gather and fall between the legs. An embroidered chemise was worn tucked into the trousers and

6.6 School girls dress in traditional Albanian costume in anticipation of a visit to their school by King Zog, circa 1928. They wear three-quarter length, elaborately embroidered sleeveless vests over full, baggy pants. EMILY BLACKSTONE CAMP ARCHIVE, FOWLER MUSEUM.

6.7 An Albanian woman and her daughter hold one pair of trousers made from ten yards of cloth. In time, the mother will re-tailor the cloth to make clothing for her younger children. NATIONAL GEOGRAPHIC (1931 [FEBRUARY] 59, NO. 2:155).

a sash was wound around the waist. The ensemble was completed with a specific headcover, which indicated whether or not the woman was married.[13]

Emily subsequently purchased additional gold-embroidered robes for herself and displayed them in her home (figs. 6.8–6.10). They were inherited by her cousin Nicolas Colasanti, who donated them to the Fowler Museum in 1984. These lavishly embroidered garments reflect Ottoman influence on Albanian textiles that lasted well into the twentieth century (see Jirousek, this volume). In the eighteenth and nineteenth centuries, such three-quarter length coats with full skirts and nonfunctional open sleeves were worn by both men and women. The finest examples were made of velvet elaborately decorated with silver or gold threads applied to the garments using several techniques: braiding, laid and couched work, or shaped rows of metallic thread, called *file*.[14]

Events leading up to World War II forced Emily to leave Albania. She moved to the San Francisco Bay area in 1938 and opened the Camp Poultry Ranch, a chicken farm in Mountain View, California. Although far away and creating a new life for herself, Emily kept track of events in Albania. Among her papers donated to the Fowler along with her gold-embroidered textiles is an article from the November 18, 1963, *San Francisco Chronicle*:

> The Albanians have big difficulties in making both ends meet. They are not in a position to dress up or go out for entertainment. A factory worker or a government official must spend two months' salary to buy a suit, and one month's pay to have a good pair of shoes. A working girl has to wait in a long queue when a new consignment of hosiery arrives from abroad. Then, to buy a pair of nylons, she must spend three day's pay.[15]

6.8A Woman's sleeveless coat
Albania, nineteenth century
Plain-weave black wool, metallic cord and ribbon; striped silk lining
111 X 174 cm
FOWLER MUSEUM X84.847; GIFT OF EMILY BLACKSTONE CAMP

This sleeveless coat is entirely covered with golden decoration.
The swirling motifs were created by couching masses of gold cord
and braid onto its surface, with patterned gold ribbons marking out
the structural lines. The lining is of red and white striped silk.

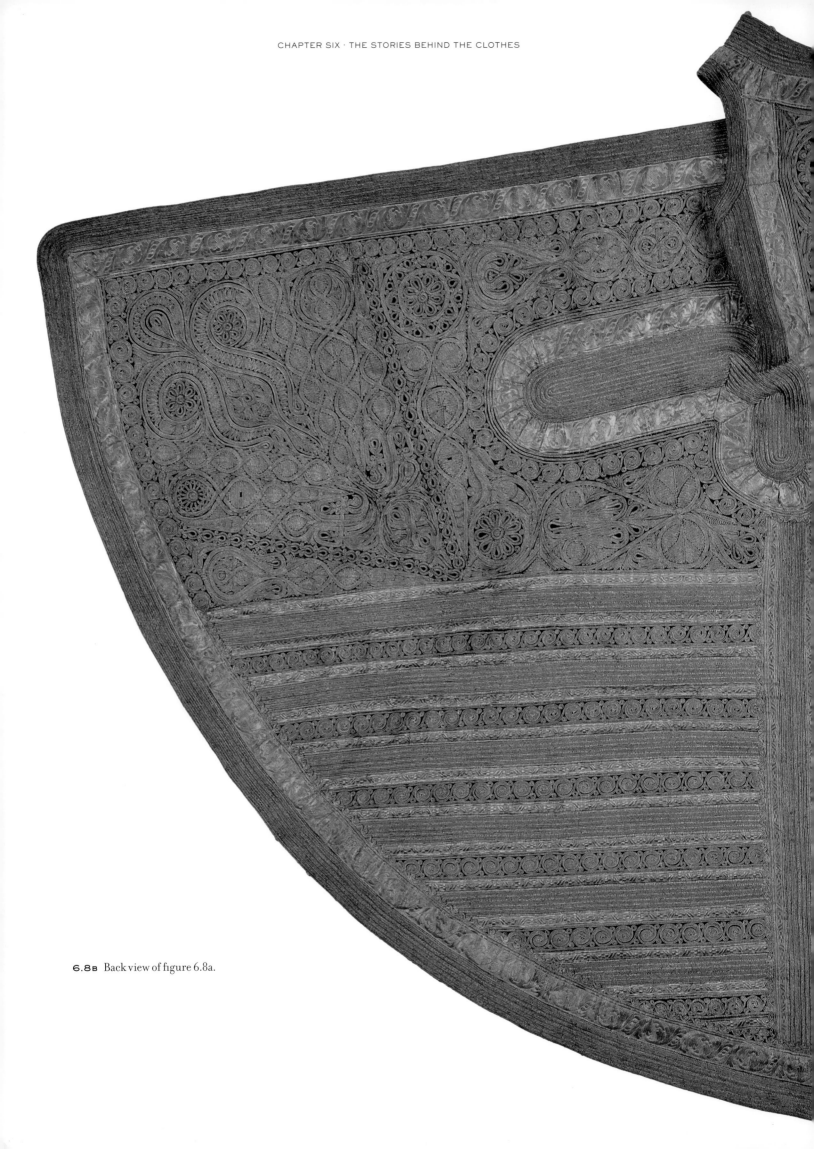

6.8B Back view of figure 6.8a.

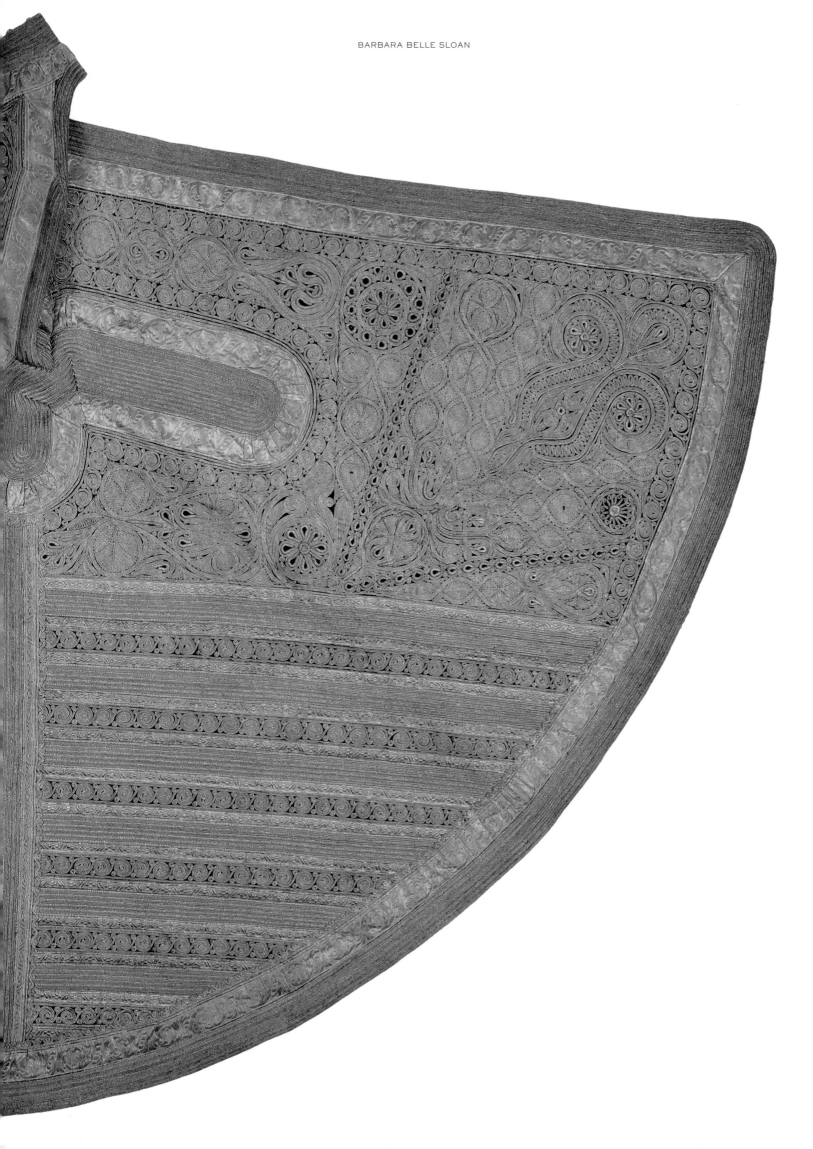

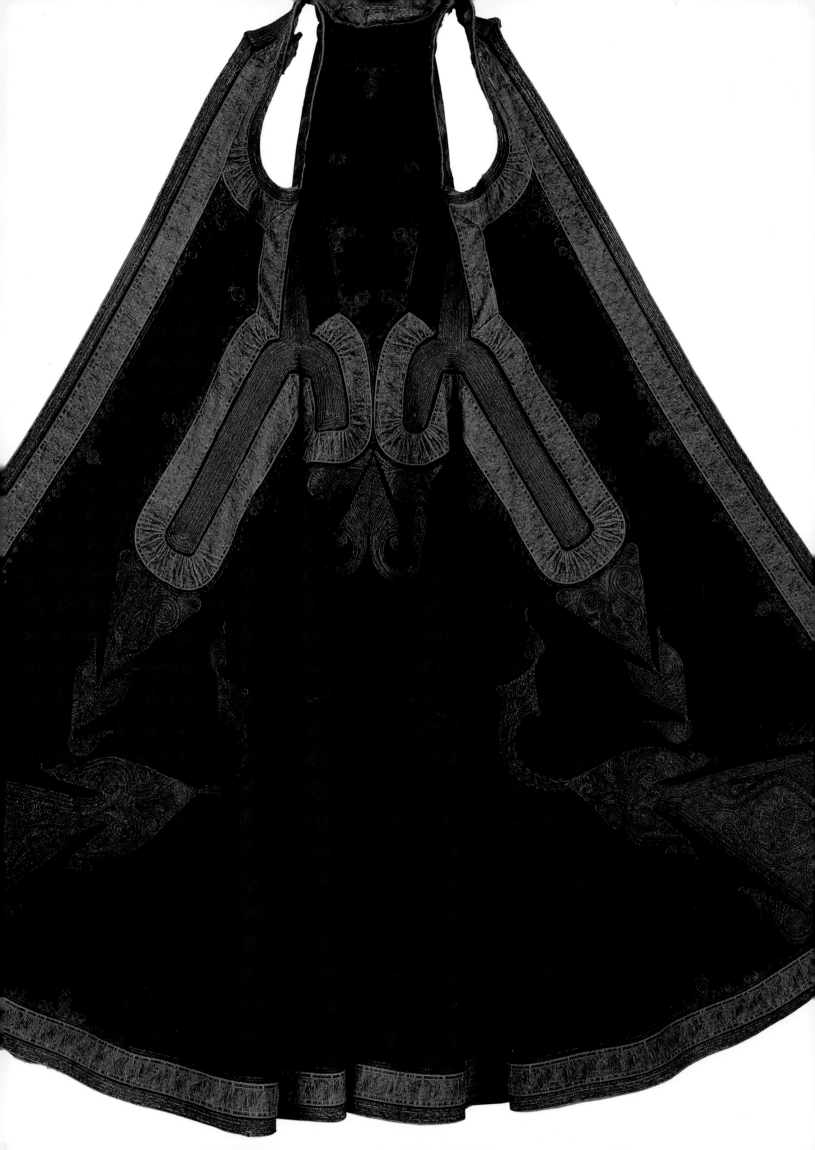

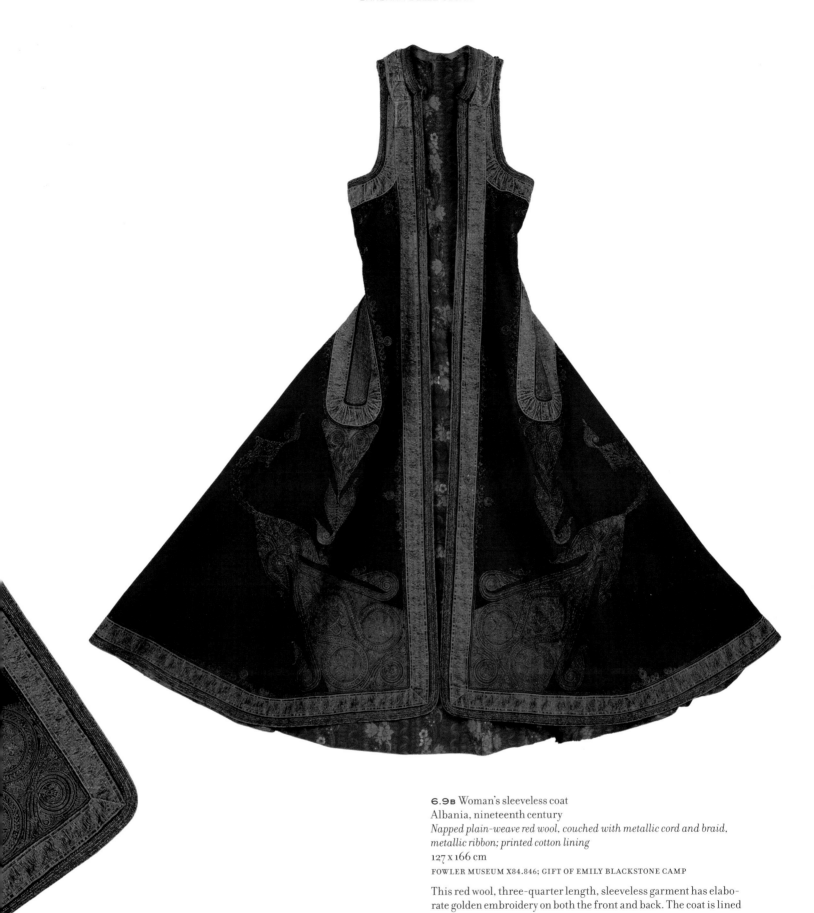

6.9B Woman's sleeveless coat
Albania, nineteenth century
Napped plain-weave red wool, couched with metallic cord and braid, metallic ribbon; printed cotton lining
127 x 166 cm
FOWLER MUSEUM X84.846; GIFT OF EMILY BLACKSTONE CAMP

This red wool, three-quarter length, sleeveless garment has elaborate golden embroidery on both the front and back. The coat is lined with a red floral cotton print cloth.

6.9A Back view of figure 6.9b.

6.10A Woman's coat with false sleeves
Albania, nineteenth century
*Black velvet, couched with metallic cord and braid, metallic ribbon;
satin weave silk lining (striped in body, plain golden yellow in false
sleeves): buttons braided with metallic thread, coral beads*
110 x 167 cm
FOWLER MUSEUM X84.848; GIFT OF EMILY BLACKSTONE CAMP

This magnificent coat has false sleeves of the flat type. They are
encrusted with elaborate designs in couched gold cord, lined with
golden silk, and have small buttons covered with gold braid. There
is a coral bead at the end of each button, believed to offer protection.
The body of the coat is lined with red, green, and gold silk.

6.10B Back view of figure 6.10a.

6.11 Niko Bachevich wears traditional dress and a celebratory sash bestowed upon him in Detroit, Michigan, in honor of his service to the community, circa 1916. DANILO BACH FAMILY PHOTOGRAPH.

6.12 This is the official wedding photograph of Milica Popovich and Niko Bachevich taken by the royal photographer of Montenegro in 1910. CHEYOVICH FAMILY PHOTOGRAPH.

NIKO J. BACHEVICH IN MONTENEGRO

Montenegrin traditional clothing reflected ethnic and religious affiliation, geography, economic circumstances, and specific historical events. While people in different regions of the country created their own unique patterns and ornamentation, generally speaking, two main styles of dress prevailed: one from the Dinaric, or mountain, areas and a second from the Adriatic Coast. Wool clothing was worn in the mountains by those who raised livestock, while cotton was the fabric of choice where livelihoods were linked to the sea.

The antecedents of a Montenegrin national festive costume can be discerned in the dress worn by privileged members of society for special occasions as early as the fourteenth and fifteenth centuries. At that time, non-Muslim Montenegrins were forbidden by the sumptuary laws of their Ottoman rulers to wear clothes of particular colors (red, blue, purple, green), especially red velvet, or to use gold embroidery on their clothing (see Jirousek, this volume).[16] With the passage of time, however, such laws disappeared, and more people had access to coveted velvet and gold thread.

Niko J. Bachevich was born the son of a mason in Ulcinj, Montenegro, near the Albanian border, in 1890 (fig. 6.11). In addition to his chores at home, he began to deliver messages for the postal service at an early age, and he was eventually taught how to telegraph. This led to his sending and receiving messages for Prince Nicholas of Montenegro, whose son was a childhood friend of Niko's father. In 1910 Prince Nicholas crowned himself King Nicholas I of Montenegro. The country was continuously fighting neighboring nations and struggling for autonomy, and at one juncture, Niko was called upon by the king to go to the neighboring Austrian-occupied Adriatic Coast to observe and to listen for word of any plots against his sovereign. When Austria overran Montenegro and Serbia in 1916, Niko followed the exiled king to Paris, leaving behind his wife and son. As an emissary of King Nicholas, Niko was sent to the United States to counter anti-Montenegrin propaganda and to help win the release of a group of Montenegrins in the Midwest who had been falsely accused of espionage against the United States, a mission in which he was successful.

6.13 Man's ensemble
Montenegro, twentieth century
FOWLER MUSEUM X2010.10.1,2,4,5,7; GIFT OF DANILO BACH IN MEMORY
OF NICHOLAS AND VASE N. BACHEVICH. X95.16.3 (HAT); GIFT OF PROFESSOR
ELSIE IVANCICH DUNIN. HENRY ART GALLERY, UNIVERSITY OF WASHINGTON,
SEATTLE, MARGARET J. HORD COLLETION, D262 (PANTS AND SHIRT)
(See Appendix for full details)

6.14 Metal plates called *toke* cover the front of this *jelek*. Rows and rows of rectangular and asymmetrical plates, called *kanate*, attached to each other with metal links, were sewn on to the upper part of the *jelek* with thread. The plates themselves were sometimes decorated with rosettes or crosses. REPRODUCED FROM MRVALJEVIĆ (1988, PL. 10). COURTESY OF HRVATSKI SABOR KULTURE/CROATIAN CULTURAL ASSOCIATION.

6.15 Man's vest (*dzamadan*)
Napped red wool twill, couched with metallic cord and braid; red silk braid, metallic-braided buttons, brass buttons
59 x 46 cm
FOWLER MUSEUM X2010.10.2; GIFT OF DANILO BACH IN MEMORY OF NICHOLAS AND VASE N. BACHEVICH

This is the gold-ornamented red wool vest that Niko Bachevich wore on his wedding day (see fig. 6.12). It is covered with intricate floral and leaf patterns couched in gold cord. This vest has also been incorporated in the ensemble illustrated in figure 6.13.

In 1918 the Treaty of Versailles established Yugoslavia, or the "Kingdom of Serbs, Croats and Slovenes," which resulted in the elimination of an independent Montenegro. King Nicholas I died in Paris in 1921, and the monarchy was never restored. Meanwhile, Niko, who had remained in the United States, had joined the U.S. Army in 1918 and become an American citizen. He brought his wife, Milica Popovich (fig. 6.12), and son to join him in the United States, where they had four more children. After Milica's death, Niko wrote to his best friend in Ulcinj, Jovan Djakonovich, asking him to recommend a new wife. His friend's sister, Vase Djakonovich, intercepted the letter and presented herself as a likely candidate. Together Nikolas and Vase had five children and raised the combined family in Detroit, Michigan, where Niko was a streetcar conductor for the Detroit Street Railways. He eventually shortened the family name to Bach and moved to Los Angeles in 1950, where he

held various jobs and died in 1985 at age ninety-five.[17] His son Danilo Bach brought the family's story—as well as part of his father's traditional Montenegrin costume (see fig. 6.11)—to the Fowler Museum in 2010. Danilo's half-sister Diane Cheyovich (by Niko's first wife) donated her mother's wedding costume to the Museum in 2011 (see fig. 6.12).

The Montenegrin man's national costume—primarily white, blue, and red—was especially luxurious and expensive (fig. 6.13). The shirt was made of white cotton, had long sleeves and frilled cuffs, and closed with simple white buttons. The trousers, which had a drawstring waist and side pockets embellished with braids in a floral motif, were of soft wool, known as baize, in blue. The full trouser legs reached below the knee (see fig. 6.11). The shirt and trousers were worn with a variety of outer garments (two types of vests and three styles of jackets) in different combinations, all with specific patterns and decorations (cf. figs. 6.11, 6.13).

6.16A,B Man's jacket (*dušanka*)
Montenegro, twentieth century
Napped plain-weave red wool, couched with black silk cord and braid,
braid-covered ball buttons; lined with felted plain-weave red wool, pink
cotton twill, tablet-woven polychrome silk band; metal buttons
44 x 159 cm
FOWLER MUSEUM X2010.10.1; GIFT OF DANILO BACH IN MEMORY
OF NICHOLAS AND VASE N. BACHEVICH

This jacket (*dušanka*) was worn by Niko Bachevich on his wedding
day (see fig. 6.12). The "false sleeves" of the jacket hang down in
back. Black silk cord has been used to decorate the back of the jacket
(see fig. 6.16b) with an intricate pattern. This jacket has also been
incorporated in the ensemble illustrated in figure 6.13.

The first style of vest, the *jelek*, was made of red baize
and was waist length and open in front. Small silver and
gilt plates (*toke*) sometimes covered the front (fig. 6.14).
Toke are reminiscent of medieval armor and were handed
down from father to son, whereas other parts of traditional
dress were sometimes buried with the deceased.[18] The back
of the *jelek* was elaborately decorated with golden embroidery.
The second type of vest, the *dzamadan*, was also made of red
baize, but the two front pieces of the garment overlapped,
forming a V-shaped neckline (fig. 6.15). The neckline was
ornamented with gold braid and embroidered with floral
motifs, circles, or stylized leaves. Another version of the
dzamadan was sometimes made with sleeves.

A vest was worn with one or two jackets. The *gunj*,
a long-sleeved jacket, usually made of fine, bright green
or white cloth, reached to the knees and was open in front
(see figs. 6.11, 6.12). It fit tightly around the upper body and
widened at the waist into a bell shape. The neckline and
open front edges were lightly ornamented with dark ribbon
and braid. Given its limited decoration, the *gunj* was usually
worn with an elaborately decorated vest or second jacket.

The *dušanka*, a waist-length, long-sleeved jacket, was
made of red baize, and like most Montenegrin men's jackets,
it hung open in the front rather than being buttoned. The
sleeves were also left open under the arm to allow for freedom
of movement. The round neck was embellished with golden
braid. The shoulders, wrists, and back of the *dušanka* were
decorated with golden leaves and flowers that form triangle-
shaped motifs in the center. Sometimes black thread and
braids, as opposed to gold, were used to decorate this jacket
type (figs. 6.16a,b).

The *dolama*, a long-sleeved jacket, reached below the
knees and was made of dark green baize. Like the *gunj*, it
was close fitting at the top and widened into a bell shape

6.17 The sleeves of the *dolama* were attached by a single button in the front so they could easily be allowed to hang freely behind the wearer. REPRODUCED FROM MRVALJEVIĆ (1988, TABLE VII.2). COURTESY OF HRVATSKI SABOR KULTURE/CROATIAN CULTURAL ASSOCIATION.

6.18 This Montenegrin man wears traditional dress. Note the sleeves of his jacket hang down behind him allowing his arms to move freely. His weapons are tucked into his leather belt (*silava*). Over this leather belt, the silk *trombolos*, a second belt, can be seen. REPRODUCED FROM MRVALJEVIĆ (1988, PL. 8). COURTESY OF HRVATSKI SABOR KULTURE/CROATIAN CULTURAL ASSOCIATION.

starting at the waist (figs. 6.17). The sleeves, however, were constructed in a different manner, being sewn to the back of the garment but attached in front by only a single button and loop. The sleeves could thus hang freely from the back of the jacket for a different, more dramatic look. Older men wore the *dolama* most frequently with the *jelek*, with or without *toke*, while younger men most often wore the V-necked *dzamadan* and short jacket (*dušanka*) with the sleeves falling freely (see fig. 6.13).

Generally, men wore two belts, the *trombolos* and the *silava* (fig. 6.18). The *trombolos*, made of three widths of silk (3–5 meters long), was purely decorative. Wrapping around the waist several times, it covered the *silava*, a wide leather belt with a buckle closure, which was used to hide money or hold a weapon. Montenegrin men considered a pistol or knife to be a symbol of freedom and dignity and an essential part of their national costume.[19] A celebratory sash, such as the one given to Niko Bach circa 1916 for service to his community, would also be proudly worn (fig. 6.19a,b). Today, such weapons and honorary garments are kept as prized trophies or souvenirs of the past.

Men also wore a variety of leg coverings: knee-length stockings, over-the-knee stockings, socks that covered the feet, as well as socks that covered just the toes. Stockings of white or black wool were knit with different stitches used for the sole, the heel and instep, the top of the foot, and the upper part of the sock. Leg coverings of white baize reached from ankle to knee and buckled at the back (see fig. 6.13). This type of covering was secured with garters (*podveze*), narrow strips of red baize decorated with golden thread. Men wore soft-soled shoes (*opanci*) with turned-up toes, which were made from ox hide or pigskin with lambskin straps; these were either made at home or by shoemakers. Men also wore knee-high leather boots.

The traditional men's woolen cap has always been a special symbol of Montenegro. In the first half of the nineteenth century the cap resembled the Turkish fez, but by the mid-nineteenth century the cap of choice—similar to hats found in other Balkan areas—was soft, round, and shallow, with a black edge and a red top that was embroidered with golden thread. Originally the golden embellishment on the flat top consisted of five nested arcs. Later the Cyrillic initials "HI" of the Montenegrin sovereign, King Nicholas were added in the center[20] (see fig. 6.13).

The traditional festive dress of Montenegrin women was also quite elegant (fig. 6.20a and see fig. 6.12). Its main elements consisted of a blouse, skirt, long-sleeved jacket (*jaketa*) or short-sleeved jacket (*dolaktica*), and long vest (*koret*). The sheer, long-sleeved blouse (*cenar*) was made of fine silk by the woman herself, whereas other garments were sewn by tailors. The blouse did not button but was slit in front and pulled over the head. Fine gold thread embroidery (*ošvice*) was stitched onto narrow pieces of cotton that were then attached to the neckline and center front of the blouse (fig. 6.20b). The *ošvice*, composed of small crossstitches, could be removed when the blouse was cleaned or, if necessary, could be transferred to a new blouse.

6.19A Celebratory sash
Detroit, Michigan, circa 1916
Satin, silk ribbon, metallic thread and braid, metallic spiral-wire tassels, sequins; satin-weave black cotton lining, with stenciled or printed silver cross
94 x 25 cm; fringe 4 cm
FOWLER MUSEUM X2010.10.5; GIFT OF DANILO BACH IN MEMORY OF NICHOLAS AND VASE N. BACHEVICH

The script on the sash is in Cyrillic and may be transliterated as "Presednik. S. R. P. Slobode. ODJ. Br. 270 S. S. S. Sloga. Detroit, Michigan, USA." This in turn may be translated as: "President, Serbian Volunteers of Freedom. Lodge #270. Only Unity Can Save Serbs. Detroit, Michigan, USA."

6.19B Detail of the lining of figure 6.19a. A silver cross was stenciled or printed on the reverse side of Niko Bachevich's celebratory sash. When worn, the cross covered the wearer's heart as a sign of protection.

6.20A Woman's ensemble
Montenegro, twentieth century
FOWLER MUSEUM X95.16.1A–F; GIFT OF PROFESSOR ELSIE IVANCICH
DUNIN. X2011.26.1 (JACKET); GIFT OF MICHELLE CHEYOVICH
(See Appendix for full details)

The traditional dress of a Montenegrin woman consisted of several
garments: a long vest (*koret*) and jacket over a skirt and blouse,
cinched by a belt and topped with a round hat.

OPPOSITE

6.20B Detail of the blouse in figure 6.20a. The transparency of the
woman's blouse necessitated a cotton undergarment. The fine gold
thread embroidery around the neckline and center is known as the
ošvice. It was stitched separately and then sewn to the blouse.

6.20c Detail of the skirt in figure 6.20a. Lace ruffles, called *karner*, ornament the center front of the skirt.

OPPOSITE
6.21 A photograph of Helenka Chlebeckova's kindergarten class. Helenka is seated in the center of the middle row; the girl seated second from the left is her cousin, Milena Chlebeckova; seated on her other side, cousin Irena Pilna. The black-embroidered collar worn in the photograph by cousin Irena was later given to Helenka. She in turn donated it to the Fowler Museum (see fig. 6.22a).

The ankle-length, bell-shaped skirt was also made of silk, sometimes in pastel colors but never black. It was decorated with handmade, crocheted lace ruffles (*karner*) sewn in parallel rows down the center front (fig. 6.20c).

A long-sleeved, waist-length jacket (*jaketa*), was worn over the blouse (see fig. 6.20a and fig. 6.12). It was made of dark red or purple velvet, open in front with rounded edges. The *jaketa* was elaborately decorated with golden braid and embroidery—floral motifs, leaves, and circles—around the neckline, front, shoulders and cuffs. A short-sleeved version of this long-sleeved jacket, the *dolaktica*, had the same type of golden decoration. The *jaketa* was usually worn by married women, the *dolaktica* by young girls.

The *koret*, a long, sleeveless vest made of bright green baize was worn over either style of jacket (see figs. 6.20a and 6.12). This garment was open at the front, fit snugly across the upper body, and widened from the waist to below the knees. The neck opening, armholes, and front were edged with red baize. Rows of golden thread and an abundance of golden, leaf-shaped embroidery covered the round neckline and bodice. The front bottom corners were sometimes embroidered with a floral motif. In addition to such floral motifs, the front bodice also carried small, round, gilt buttons each holding a tiny coral bead at its tip.

A two-inch wide belt, the *ćemer*, was constructed of several pieces of metal that were hinged together at the center front. The metal plate was decorated with floral or geometric motifs and often embellished with colorful stones. Silver chains were sometimes affixed to either side of the central plate. The *ćemer* might be used to hold small boxes for a mirror, needle, and thread.[21]

Like men, women wore white knitted stockings and shoes made of ox hide or leather. Decorative motifs in wool or cotton were sometimes added at the ankle and at the edges of their stockings. They also wore a smaller version of the men's headgear—a shallow cap with a red top and gold embroidery (see fig. 6.20a). At one time older women covered their heads with black scarves that hung down in back.[22]

After World War II, typical daily dress changed for men and women in both the mountain and coastal areas. Complete outfits of homemade traditional clothing were replaced for the most part by combinations of old-style items—caps and vests for the men, head scarves and aprons for the women—and store-bought or machine-made items purchased in local towns. Elaborate festive national costume, however, was still preserved for special occasions.

HELENKA CHLEBECKOVA FROST AND JOHN FROST IN THE CZECH REPUBLIC

In her mid-nineteenth-century novel *Granny*, Božena Němcová (1820–1862) presented a somewhat idealized view of her native Czechoslovakia. It nonetheless becomes clear that daily life was harsh, and major events in the life cycle— a new baby, marriage, death, harvests—offered reason to celebrate. These occasions required special costumes and accoutrements.

The costumes worn at celebrations, as well as traditions associated with them, were handed down from mother to daughter and father to son. Němcová describes a crowd attending a feast at harvest time as including festively dressed children, a youngster in an embroidered jacket, gentlemen wearing modern dress coats, a patriarch in a long coat, a neighbor in a coat fifty years old, ladies decked out in all their finery, townswomen in caps of lace or perhaps gold and silver thread, as well as country wives in starched caps and white headcloths. Dress revealed the wearer's station in life and often his or her occupation. It also identified those who adhered to custom and those who embraced change.[23]

Most households had a spinning wheel and a loom, and girls learned how to convert homegrown flax into thread and then to weave cloth. In Němcová's novel, Granny says to her granddaughter, "Come and sit down to the loom and learn, it'll stand you in good stead some day."[24] Some cloth was made into clothing, other stacks of linen accumulated year after year to save for children and grandchildren, or a trousseau: "linen and thread were the foundation of any household."[25] Sometimes, woven blankets were brought to town to sell.

John W. Frost was born in 1934 in Monterey, California. During his childhood, he experienced his family's struggles through the Great Depression and World War II. Since money was scarce his father took the family on camping trips, presented life as an adventure, read to them about the heroes of the past—especially sports figures like Babe Ruth—and told them about their own ancestors who had crossed the Great Plains in the nineteenth century.

John excelled at tennis and achieved success in the sport throughout his high school and college years. In 1959 he was asked by the U.S. State Department to participate in a goodwill tennis tour in Czechoslovakia, following that year's Wimbledon Championship in London.[26] Once in Prague John was assigned an interpreter who not only translated for him but followed his every move. On the second night of his stay, the interpreter invited John to join some of the Russian tennis players for dinner. The group enjoyed a good meal as

well as lively conversation made all the more so by the presence of yet another interpreter—this time to aid conversation with the Russians—a beautiful young Czech woman named Helenka Chlebeckova. She was fluent in Russian and Polish, but her English was limited. Helenka was from a small town of Brandýs nad Labem outside the city and was in Prague to interpret at the World Gymnastic Championships, which were taking place at the same time as the tennis tournament. Helenka welcomed the chance to practice her English when, at the end of the evening, John walked her to the streetcar station. As John tells the story:

> She ran for her tram and before she got on, she turned and looked at me and what I saw in her lovely brown eyes was: "You are the man on the white horse and I need you to rescue me." Of course, she may

have meant to convey something like "good night" or "thanks for dinner," but the message I got was precisely the one for which I had always waited.[27]

Returning to Prague a few weeks later, John saw Helenka again. Then he returned to California, continued to play tennis at home and abroad, and exchanged letters with Helenka. Her letters were long and written with great care. She usually enclosed a pressed flower. Helenka was an only child, and her father was a lawyer. Because of her "bourgeois" background, she had not initially been allowed to enter the university. Instead, for two years she worked as a locksmith in a factory in order to "prove herself" and finally received permission to sit for college entrance exams. She passed the required tests and attended Charles University in Prague where she studied languages.[28]

BARBARA BELLE SLOAN

OPPOSITE
6.22A Little girl's ensemble Czech Republic, twentieth century
FOWLER MUSEUM X2010.12.1.1–6; GIFT OF HELENKA AND JOHN FROST
(See Appendix for details)

This is the traditional costume made for Helenka Chlebeckova by her mother and seen in figure 6.21.

6.22B Back view of 6.22a.

John decided to telephone Helenka and ask her to marry him. His call came through at noon on Christmas Day 1963, but Helenka did not understand what he was asking. He sent his marriage proposal via telegram the next day and received an affirmative answer a couple of weeks later. Meanwhile, the future bride began the process of applying for permission from her government to marry an American and leave her country, and the waiting began. Finally, in 1964 John and Helenka received permission to marry. The wedding took place in Prague, and the couple moved to the United States in 1965. Helenka brought with her very few things from her life in Czechoslovakia. Among the items she carried was a picture of her kindergarten class (fig. 6.21) and the traditional costume that she wore on the day the picture was taken.

The children in the photograph are dressed in their finest clothes. Helenka, seated in the center of the middle row, wore traditional clothing that her mother made for her (figs. 6.22a,b), including a long-sleeved, white cotton, round-necked blouse that closed in the back with snaps. The wide cuffs were embroidered with black flowers, and the edges were trimmed with hand-crocheted lace. Her red cotton skirt was covered with a sprinkling of embroidered yellow and green flowers. The skirt had an ample hem so that it could be lengthened as Helenka grew, as well as pencil outlines for the placement of flowers that could be embroidered later. The short, red imitation silk, three-buttoned vest was decorated with red-and-green floral cotton appliqué outlined with golden rickrack in front and back. Three circles of golden rickrack were sewn onto the back of the vest, with a single silver bead attached to the

middle circle. Her apron was made of navy blue synthetic fabric, embroidered at the bottom with red, green, yellow, and white flowers, and trimmed with three inches of white cotton crocheted lace that incorporated red and green flowers in its pattern. The apron ties were made from inch-wide floral-patterned ribbon. A rectangular, white cotton collar decorated with black embroidery matched the handwork on the cuffs of the blouse. Finally, her hair decoration was made of wire, artificial flowers and ribbon. Helenka's cousins and other classmates in the photograph were also dressed in their "best" clothes.

It was not unusual for mothers and daughters to wear similar outfits (fig. 6.23). Interestingly, an adult version of this costume was donated to the Fowler Museum in 2006 (figs. 6.24.a–c). The woman's clothing differs only slightly from Helenka's. The form of the woman's blouse and collar is identical, but the black embroidery on the sleeves is more elaborate, and the lace trim at the cuff is done with black thread. The skirt is made of red cotton, embroidered with vertical stripes of golden flowers. The shape of the vest is the same as Helenka's but the appliqué is of much finer fabric and the golden rickrack thread is embellished with a row of sequins with the tiniest of glass beads at the center of each sequin. The white cotton petticoat is trimmed with openwork lace.

OPPOSITE
6.23 A mother and her daughter appear similarly attired.
PHOTOGRAPH BY HANS HILDENBRAND/NATIONAL GEOGRAPHIC STOCK, CZECHOSLOVAKIA, TWENTIETH CENTURY, NO. 1205889.

6.24A Detail of the embroidery of the apron hem on figure 6.24b.

6.24B Woman's ensemble
Kyjov, Moravia, Czech Republic, twentieth century
FOWLER MUSEUM X2006.11.2A–F,H,I; GIFT OF MARTHA ADAMS

This ensemble, which is from the village of Kyjov in Moravia, is the adult version of Helenka Chlebeckova's childhood dress (see figs. 6.22a,b).

6.24c Back view of figure 6.24b.

6.25 The Stojanović family poses for a portrait in Orasac. Front row, left to right, are Mileta Stojanović, grandson Milan, granddaughter Ruze, wife Radojka. In the back row are son Zarko and daughter-in-law Ljubica Stojanović. Note that the four adults wear traditional dress while the youngsters wear clothing typical of the 1950s. PHOTOGRAPH ©JOEL MARTIN HALPERN, 1953. JOEL M. HALPERN PAPERS. SPECIAL COLLECTIONS AND UNIVERSITY ARCHIVES, UNIVERSITY OF MASSACHUSETTS AMHERST LIBRARIES.

The adult size apron is truly exquisite—a magnificent garment with the date it was made, 1909, embroidered in a corner. In addition to elaborate bouquets and garlands of flowers composed of a variety of embroidery stitches, vertical stripes of small white blossom shapes have been created using the tie-dye process. The craftsmanship is superb, the work done by an experienced textile artist. The lace border contains vertical rows of red, green, and yellow flowers as well as tiny stitches of red and green meandering throughout the lace pattern. A floral-patterned hair ribbon and bow complement the woman's cap. Another highly decorated piece of the costume, the cap is made of white damask fabric with an embroidered floral pattern at the crown and a removable panel attached at the bottom that could be taken off and used on another cap at a later date. The highly embellished removable band of embroidery is covered with a bright array of flowers made of sparkling silver and blue beads and sequins surrounded by rows of silver and gold beads that are in turn surrounded by a silver crocheted border and trimmed with lace.

Mr. and Mrs. Frost donated Helenka's kindergarten photograph and childhood clothing to the Fowler Museum in 2010, pleased that this special attire reminiscent of earlier times and filled with family memories will be preserved in the Museum's collection.

DR. JOEL HALPERN IN SERBIA

American anthropologist Joel Halpern, now a professor emeritus at the University of Massachusetts, Amherst, spent more than fifty years studying life in the small Serbian village of Orasac. Dr. Halpern, his wife, and three daughters were initially welcomed into the home of the Stojanović family in 1953, and the Halperns have remained in touch with their Orasac "relatives" ever since (fig. 6.25). In exchange for a home base to use while working in the village, the Halperns helped their Serbian hosts with daily farming and household chores—feeding chickens, drawing water from the well, baking bread, spinning thread, and forking hay.

In their book *A Serbian Village in Historical Perspective* (1972), the Halperns cite nineteenth-century Serbian scholar Vuk Karadžić, who described life in his homeland in great detail. Karadžić noted that Serbian villages extended far up into mountain gorges and deep into forests, sometimes consisting of forty or fifty houses spread over a wide area and at considerable distance from one another. In each home lived a virtually self-sufficient, multigenerational family. Men built their own houses, made plows, wagons, yokes for their oxen, barrel hoops, and even shoes. Women spun wool, flax, and hemp; sewed, embroidered, knit stockings and gloves; dyed thread; and wove their homemade thread and yarn into cloth. They also worked in the fields with men threshing wheat, picking corn, raking hay, harvesting plums and grapes, and tending beehives

6.26A–C Front slats for beehives
Serbia, twentieth century
Wood, paint
Largest: 13 x 36 cm
FOWLER MUSEUM X67.2423 (A),
X67.2421 (B), X67.2419 (C); GIFT
OF MR. AND MRS. THEODORE
LOWENSTEIN

The front slats of wooden beehives were decorated with hand-painted scenes drawn from traditional tales, village life, and historical events.

6.27 Radojka Stojanović spins wool while tending her great-granddaughter in Orasac, 1966. PHOTOGRAPH ©JOEL MARTIN HALPERN. JOEL M. HALPERN PAPERS. SPECIAL COLLECTIONS AND UNIVERSITY ARCHIVES, UNIVERSITY OF MASSACHUSETTS AMHERST LIBRARIES.

(figs. 6.26a–c). In contrast, those who lived in towns were shopkeepers and craftsmen: furriers, tailors, bakers, gunsmiths, coppersmiths, blacksmiths, carpenters, rope makers and potters.[29]

In the 1950s radio and television had not yet reached Orasac. Women spun and wove (fig. 6.27), and at night men told stories and sang traditional songs. Evenings were still spent gathered around the living room fireplace. Families looked forward to the Saturday market in the nearby town of Arandjelovac, which gave villagers an opportunity to sell their livestock and produce and to purchase items from the town's vendors and artisans.

In their book, the Halperns describe the significant role that textiles played in the daily life of Orasac. A new-born boy or girl was tightly wrapped in cloth from "armpits to toes."[30] Small gowns with delicate ruffled, embroidered, and crocheted trim were worn for christenings (fig. 6.28). Babies who could crawl wore nondescript clothing indoors, but when they were taken outside the home, they were dressed as elaborately as possible. Children were status symbols, and the appearance of a child in a hand-knitted outfit and immaculate white stockings was a testimonial to the industry and pride of the family.[31] Textiles were also important at the end of life. In many instances the deceased was buried wearing traditional clothing that had been saved for this final celebration. Early nineteenth-century, hand-carved tombstones in village graveyards often depict the deceased as dressed in traditional clothing or supply a symbol of a trade or profession: "a soldier with his rifle, a hammer for an artisan, a book for a teacher, perhaps a distaff or sewing machine for women or girls"[32] (fig. 6.29). After a funeral service at the local church, the mourners proceeded to the graveyard where the bereaved family offered a celebratory feast to the attendees. These graveside celebrations were repeated on the anniversary of a family member's death.[33]

The people who lived in the mountainous regions of Serbia raised livestock, and the people of the lowlands were farmers. Generally, women used homegrown cotton and wool from their own sheep to weave household goods and clothing. Styles varied from village to village and town to town. The style and cut of garments may have been similar, but each community had its own distinctive type of decoration. In urban communities, clothes made of velvet with gold and silver embroidery were made by professional artisans and were greatly influenced by Ottoman styles of dress. Men's shirts (see fig. 1.7) were worn loose in summer and tucked in and worn with a vest or jacket in winter. Women wore a long vest called the *zubun* (fig. 6.30) over a chemise, front and back aprons, and a sash.

The *zubun* is one of the oldest and most distinctive Serbian garments.[34] Turkish in cut and decoration, it is sleeveless, traditionally made of wool, open in the front, and lacks fasteners. It was once worn all year round. The seams, armhole edges, and bottom of the front and back panels were decorated with embroidery and appliqué. Short versions of the *zubun* were sometimes made for men; both

6.28 Christening dress
Serbia, twentieth century
Commercial cotton and lace, embroidered and crocheted
95 × 53 cm
FOWLER MUSEUM X2011.4.42; GIFT OF DR. JOEL MARTIN HALPERN

6.29 A Serbian woman stands beside a gravestone carved with a spindle that attests to the proficiency of the deceased at spinning.
REPRODUCED FROM ALEKSIC (1966, 183).

6.30 Long vest (*zubun*)
Serbia, twentieth century
Felted wool, embroidery
93 x 59 cm
FOWLER MUSEUM X96.6.1; GIFT OF PROFESSOR ELSIE IVANCICH DUNIN

A black wool *zubun* is adorned with delicate strips of red, white, green, and yellow embroidery that outline the seams, armholes, and borders. Decorative embroidered circles ornament the sides and bottom.

styles were worn throughout Serbia up to the mid-twentieth century. The predominant color of the embroidery thread was red, but yellow, green, and blue—all created with vegetable dyes—were also used. Geometric shapes, hooks, lines, spirals, circles, wheels, feather shapes, and stylized floral motifs were embroidered at the seams and hem. Appliqué designs were created for the more elaborate *zubun* using sturdy black, gray, or red wool cloth, called *coha*, which was itself embellished and then sewn to the garment. Additional woolen cord trim and borders completed the design (see Corbett this volume).

The changing seasons and the associated farming activities regulated traditional village life. The feast day of the community's patron saint (*slava*) was celebrated with great fanfare as were weddings in the autumn after the crops were harvested. Until the beginning of World War I, young people would attend fairs and dances in nearby villages. Girls walked to the fair with their mothers, boys walked separately with their friends. The bachelors would leave home in their best clothes, while the girls traveled with their new dresses wrapped in kerchiefs carried by their mothers. When they neared the dance area, the girls

6.31A–C Bags
Serbia, twentieth century
FOWLER MUSEUM X2011.4.6 (A),
X2011.4.12 (B), X2011.4.10 (C); GIFT
OF DR. JOEL MARTIN HALPERN
(See Appendix for details)

6.32 Man's ensemble
Serbia, twentieth century
FOWLER MUSEUM X70.1231A–D;
MUSEUM PURCHASE
(See Appendix for details)

The sash shown in fig. 6.34
originally formed part of this
ensemble.

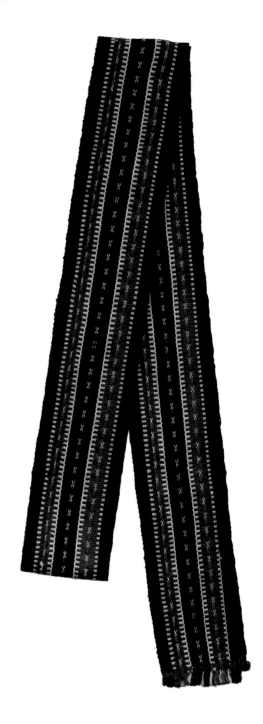

6.33 These men are dressed in traditional clothing and shoes and carry handwoven wool bags (see figs. 6.31a–c). They gather outside a church on Easter morning in Orasac in 1953. PHOTOGRAPH ©JOEL MARTIN HALPERN. JOEL M. HALPERN PAPERS. SPECIAL COLLECTIONS AND UNIVERSITY ARCHIVES, UNIVERSITY OF MASSACHUSETTS AMHERST LIBRARIES.

6.34 This long brown sash wound around the body several times. It would form part of the ensemble in fig. 6.32. (*See Appendix for details*)

would change into their fancy clothes, arrange their hair, and put on make-up. The old clothes were wrapped in the kerchiefs and left with a relative. Arriving at the fair all dressed up the girls were taken by the hand by the boys and invited to dance the *kolo*."³⁵ Such dances were still being held in the 1970s but with the young girls and boys attending separately, although the mothers still watched from the sidelines as before. The circle dances and music remained the same, but young men wore blue jeans, and the girls wore pantsuits and used lipstick rather than "dabbing their cheeks with bits of moistened red crepe paper."³⁶ Older village men however, still wore traditional clothing—brown homespun woolen trousers, a jacket, and an over-vest trimmed with black braid, or a suit of fine dark blue wool (figs. 6.32, 6.33). Both styles of dress were completed with a black sheared-lamb hat and pigskin sandals with turned up toes, often referred to as "noses." The trousers of the suit in

figure 6.32 have a drawstring waist and front flap that closes with an eye-hook at each side. The front closure creates attention-getting red-lined "false" pockets on both sides of the trousers. The center front, inseams, and cuffs are elaborately decorated with black wool thread. The matching long-sleeved jacket has an overlapping front closure, vents on both sides, and additional black decoration on the front and cuffs. The vest, however, is the most dramatic element of the suit. The front, back, and edges are filled with black couched-thread ornamentation, and the vest is worn over the jacket so that it can be admired. The full-cut, long-sleeved off-white cotton shirt has a small collar and a two-button opening with a small, pleated placket in front. The woven, multicolored (brown, green, white, yellow, blue) wool sash is long enough to wind around the man's waist more than once (fig. 6.34). Wool knit socks, cap, and leather shoes complete the man's traditional dress.

6.35 Women wear traditional dress on a Belgrade street in the early twentieth century.
PHOTOGRAPH BY LEWIS W. HINE/ NATIONAL GEOGRAPHIC STOCK, 603864.

OPPOSITE
6.36A Woman's ensemble
Serbia, twentieth century
FOWLER MUSEUM X93.23.20A,B,E–G;
GIFT OF PROFESSOR ELSIE IVANCICH
DUNIN. X70.1232A (CHEMISE);
MUSEUM PURCHASE
(See Appendix for details)

The women's costume consisted of several garments and was usually decorated with elaborate needlework (fig. 6.35). The collar, sleeves, and hem of the white cotton chemise in figures 6.36a,b are decorated with an embroidered floral and leaf motif. Serbs sometimes say that the red tones in the embroidered flowers symbolize the blood shed by Serbian soldiers in battle and that the dark colors represent the nation's sorrow at having lost its freedom.[37] The form-fitting, waist-length red velvet vest fastened in front with hooks. It is embellished on the front with swirls of golden braid and sequins and on the center back with an elaborate leaf pattern. Two aprons were worn: the black velvet front apron (prednja) is covered with three horizontal rows of multicolored flowers and trimmed with black lace. The multicolored striped, pleated back apron has a row of embroidered flowers along the bottom and is trimmed with blue crocheted lace. The black wool stockings also feature an elaborate display of flowers.

The history of the Stojanovič family survives in part through Dr. Halpern's written records as well as through the textiles he acquired from the family and from others in Serbia and donated to the Fowler Museum, which include many garments as well as a large number of woven bags (torpa). Each bag was made from a single piece of cloth that was folded in half with the sides sewn closed. Decorative woolen tassels were sometimes attached to the sides and top of the bag. Straps of wrapped or braided yarn of varying length were also added (figs. 6.31a–c). Dr. Halpern's donation also included stockings, slippers, and toe warmers of different sizes (figs. 6.37a–h), knit with a multitude of colored yarns in a variety of patterns. With increasing modernization and less available time, the complicated patterns of men's knit socks gave way to black socks with floral borders.

The hillside landscapes of long ago dotted with clusters of whitewashed houses with tile roofs have been replaced by modern homes in cities. Serbian men no longer hike to factory jobs in nearby towns and return home in the afternoon to work their land until sundown.[38] The daily bus service so welcomed in the 1970s to replace carts and bicycles has been supplanted by automobiles.[39] Economic development and industrialization have changed life in Serbia. After young people moved out of the countryside and into towns, the towns developed into cities. Village-wide celebrations, especially those involving processions through the town, disappeared. Likewise traditional costumes, once an important part of daily life, are now worn only occasionally by the elderly at family celebrations or to celebrate national holidays. In contemporary times, the traditional weaving, embroidery and knitting techniques once used for special family attire and household goods have been replaced by manufactured items.[40] ∞

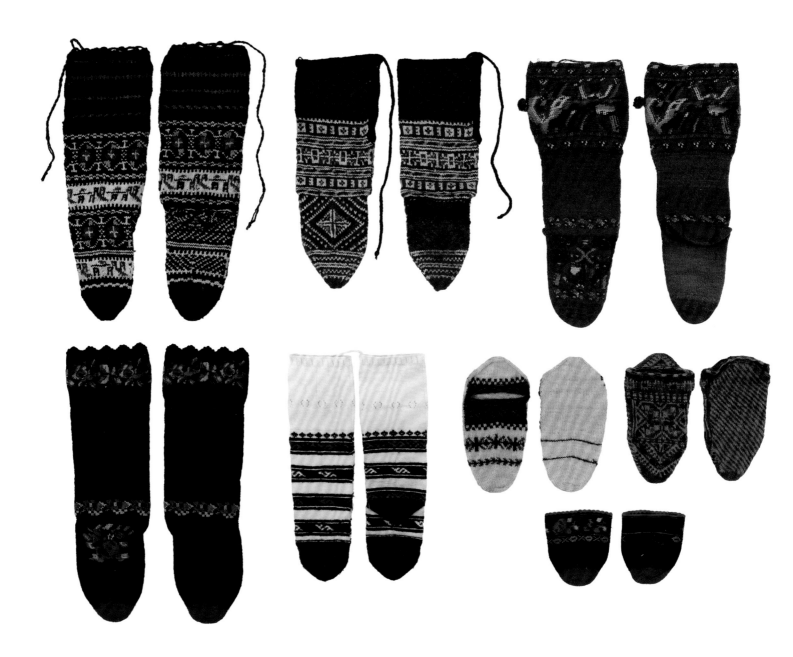

6.37A-H Socks, slippers, and toe warmers
Various, twentieth century
FOWLER MUSEUM: SOCKS—X2011.4.33A,B (A), X2011.4.21A,B (B),
X2011.4.20A,B (C), X2011.4.31A,B (D), X2011.4.24A,B (E); SLIPPERS—
X2011.4.25A,B (F), X2011.4.25A,B (G); TOE WARMERS—X2011.4.30A,B (H);
GIFT OF DR. JOEL MARTIN HALPERN
(See Appendix for details)

OPPOSITE
6.36B Front of figure 6.36a.

CHAPTER ONE

1.26 Woman's ensemble
Slatina, Sofia district, Bulgaria, twentieth century
FOWLER MUSEUM X99.50.1A,B; GIFT OF GAIL KLIGMAN

    a. Chemise
       Plain-weave cotton; cotton embroidery, cotton lace, plastic buttons
       122 x 91 cm

    b. Jumper/overdress
       Wool twill; couched cotton cord; wool braid
       104 x 91 cm

1.28 Woman's ensemble
Stara Zagora, southeastern Bulgaria (Thrace), twentieth century
FOWLER MUSEUM X93.14.4A–C; GIFT OF DOROTHY DAW

    a. Jumper/overdress
       Plain-weave wool; appliquéd stripes of velvet, plain-weave wool, twill
       cotton, felted woven wool; cotton, metallic, and silk rickrack; felt strips
       and cutouts; velvet ribbon; wool and cotton embroidery; sequins; plain-
       weave linen pocket
       101 x 110 cm

    b. Apron
       Wool twill (two panels sewn together vertically); looped wool embroidery;
       silk or synthetic lace
       70 x 70 cm

    c. Chemise
       Plain-weave linen, with thin beige and thick white linen weft stripes
       and altered tension for seersucker effects in sleeves; woolen and cotton
       embroidery in cross, straight, and buttonhole stitch; crocheted cotton
       lace; plastic button
       112 x 130 cm

1.30 Man's ensemble
Thrace, Bulgaria, twentieth century
FOWLER MUSEUM X93.23.15A–D; GIFT OF PROFESSOR ELSIE IVANCICH DUNIN

    a. Pants
       Wool woven in twill and heavily felted; couched silk braid; metal hooks
       and eyes
       100 x 113 cm

    b. Vest
       Heavily felted wool twill; couched wool braid, plain-weave linen; metal
       hooks and eyes
       47 x 41 cm

    c. Sash
       Bicolor wool twill; plied fringe
       432 x 37 cm

    d. Shirt
       Plain-weave cotton; chain-stitch embroidery
       74 x 150 cm

1.40 Man's jackets
Lazaropole, western Macedonia, twentieth century
FOWLER MUSEUM X99.34.21A,D; GIFT OF ROBERT LEIBMAN

    a. Long-sleeved jacket
       Fine worsted plain-weave wool, multicolored cotton machine-stitching;
       plastic buttons; plain-weave cotton lining
       61 x 155 cm

    d. Short-sleeved jacket
       Heavily felted wool twill
       55 x 96 cm

1.41 Woman's ensemble
Lazaropole, western Macedonia, twentieth century
FOWLER MUSEUM X99.34.15A–K; GIFT OF ROBERT LEIBMAN

    a. Jacket (mintan; hip length)
       Lightly felted plain-weave white wool, heavily felted maroon wool twill;
       couched with metal-over-fiber-core cord and braid, wool braid; metallic
       ribbon; filigree metal buttons, metal hooks and eyes
       152 x 64 cm

    b. Vest (waist length)
       Plain-weave, striped, and twill cotton; velvet, metallic braid, filigree
       metal buttons
       59 x 46 cm

    c. Coat with vestigial sleeves (klašenik; knee length)
       Heavily felted wool twill; velvet, couched with metal-over-fiber-core
       cord and braid; filigree metal buttons; couched wool cord and braid
       105 x 68 cm

    d. Chemise (košula; ankle length)
       Plain-weave linen body, with hemstitching, needle-netting; plain-
       weave silk stripes in linen sleeves
       119 x 128 cm

    e,f. Over-sleeves (rakavi)
       Plain-wave linen; embroidered with wool, silk, and metallic thread,
       tightly spun and plied wool fringe
       57 x 21 cm

    g. Apron (Stambulska futa)
       Plain-weave cotton with inlay-weave pattern; plain-weave printed cotton
       lining; striped interior cloth for strength; braided wool cord
       73 x 64 cm

    h. Apron (futa)
       Weft-faced woven wool, tightly spun and plied wool fringe
       61 x 46 cm

    i. Sash (pojas)
       Wool woven in rosepath; braided fringe
       363 x 14 cm

    j. Fringed sash (prepaška)
       Warp-faced woven wool; braided wool and cotton cord tassels; sequins,
       metallic thread
       347 x 10 cm

    k. Head cover (darpna)
       Plain-weave cotton, cotton embroidery, fringe
       142 x 94 cm

1.48 Woman's ensemble
Bitola, southwestern Macedonia, twentieth century
FOWLER MUSEUM X96.6.17A–I; GIFT OF PROFESSOR ELSIE IVANCICH DUNIN

    a. Chemise
       Plain-weave cotton, velvet ribbon, wool and perle cotton embroidery,
       silk lace
       112 x 109 cm

    b. Vest
       Heavily felted wool twill, embroidered and couched with silk cord and
       wool braid; silver coins
       71 x 52 cm

    c. Apron
       Two panels of weft-faced wool with tapestry lozenges, napped plain-
       weave wool, velvet ribbon, couched with wool and silk cord
       60 x 49 cm

    d. Head cover
       Plain-weave cotton, cotton embroidery and tassels, crocheted edging
       109 x 104 cm

    e. Dickie
       Plain-weave cotton, printed cotton, silk damask; plastic buttons,
       sequins, glass beads
       60 x 35 cm

    f,g. Sleeve(s)
       Plain-weave cotton, velvet, crochet; beads, sequins
       Each: 28 x 16 cm

    h,i. Stockings
       Knitted wool
       Each: 49 x 11 cm

1.61 Woman's ensemble
Mariovo, southwestern Macedonia, twentieth century
FOWLER MUSEUM X97.27.1A–E; BEQUEST OF MARSHA LIPMAN. X96.6.23E–H (SCARF,
DICKIE, STOCKINGS), X96.6.36A,B (SHOES); GIFT OF PROFESSOR ELSIE IVANCICH
DUNIN. PRIVATE COLLECTION (ubrus, COIN BELT, SILVER BUCKLE)

X97.27.1 (1930S–1970S)

    a. Chemise (košula)
       Heavy cotton twill, wool embroidery (mostly slant-stitch), printed cotton
       111 x 48 cm

    b. Apron (pregača, futa)
       Two vertical panels of weft-faced woven wool (with inlay designs) sewn
       together, wool and metallic fringe, metallic ribbon, lace, coins (1929–
       1940, Greek, Bulgarian, Turkish); braided wool cord
       68 x 58 cm

c. Vest (*saja*)
Plain-weave cotton, wool embroidery, metallic braid, wool fringe
93 x 43 cm

d,e. Over-sleeves
Plain-weave cotton, wool and metallic fringe, wool embroidery (mostly slant-stitch), plaited wool cord
Each: 35 x 21 cm

X96.6.23E–H

e. Head scarf
Plain-weave cotton, wool pompons, embroidery
124 x 122 cm

f. Dickie (*grlo*)
Plain-weave cotton, plastic buttons
61 x 40 cm

g,h. Stockings (*čorapi*)
Knitted wool, plaited wool cord
Each: 50 x 24 cm

X96.6.36A,B
Shoes (*opanci*)
Tanned leather, dyed leather
Each: 26 x 11 cm

PRIVATE COLLECTION (1970S; EARLY TWENTIETH CENTURY)
Head cover (*ubrus*)
Plain-weave cotton and linen, wool embroidery and fringe
276 (including fringe) x 31 cm

Belt (*pojas*)
Tablet-woven wool; coins (dating 1880s–1950s: Ottoman, Bulgarian, Serbian, Slovenian, Albanian, Italian, Yugoslav)
74 x 6 cm

Buckle
Metal
19 x 18 cm

1.62 Man's ensemble
Mariovo, southwestern Macedonia, early to mid-twentieth century
FOWLER MUSEUM X99.34.32A–D; GIFT OF ROBERT LEIBMAN

a. Pants
Plain-weave cotton, plastic buttons
98 x 90 cm

b. Shirt
Plain-weave cotton, cotton embroidery and braid
80 x 97 cm

c. Skirt (*fustan*)
Plain-weave cotton (gored and pleated), braided wool drawstring
55 x 93 cm

d. Vest
Heavily felted wool twill, silk braid, metal buttons; linen or hempen lining
41 x 44 cm

1.63 Man's ensemble
Skopje, northern Macedonia, twentieth century
FOWLER MUSEUM X99.34.27A–E; GIFT OF ROBERT LEIBMAN

a. Vest
Heavily felted wool twill
106 x 86 cm

b. Shirt
Plain-weave felted wool; knitted and embroidered wool cuffs, plain-weave cotton with wool embroidery, plastic buttons
57 x 143 cm

c. Pants
Heavily felted wool twill
70 x 110 cm

d,e. Leggings
Heavily felted wool twill, wool faggoting and braid, metal hooks
78 x 26 cm

1.64 Man's ensemble
Skopje, northern Macedonia, twentieth century
FOWLER MUSEUM X99.34.25A–D; GIFT OF ROBERT LEIBMAN

a. Pants
Plain-weave linen
89 x 106 cm

b. Shirt
Plain-weave linen, perle cotton embroidery, hemstitching, crocheted cotton lace, metal hooks and eyes
85 x 147 cm

c. Vest
Warp-faced striped wool, couched with silk cord and braid, metallic thread on cotton braid, cardboard backing
51 x 50 cm

d. Sash
Wool woven in zigzag twill, silk braid, damask silk ribbon, metallic thread and ribbon; beads, coins, plastic buttons
134 x 19 cm

1.65 Woman's ensemble
Debar, western Macedonia, twentieth century
FOWLER MUSEUM X99.34.6A–H; GIFT OF ROBERT LEIBMAN

a. Skirt (*suknja*)
Plain-weave cotton, eyelet lace, silk brocade ribbon
75 x 72 cm

b. Blouse (*mintan*)
Plain-weave cotton, napped plain-weave wool, velvet, silk trim; plastic buttons, metal snaps
59 x 142 cm

c. Coat (*klašenik*)
Heavily felted wool twill, plain-weave wool facing; velvet ribbon, silk tape, couched with silk cord and braid; filigree metal buttons
98 x 114 cm

d. Apron (*futa*)
Two tapestry-woven wool panels, faggoted together horizontally and embroidered with wool cord; silk ribbon, silk fringe, metallic rickrack with sequins; perle cotton fringe strung with glass beads and sequins
63 x 71 cm

e. Sash (*pojas*)
Wool twill, plaited warp-fringe
744 x 17 cm

f. Hat (*kapa*)
Velvet, couched with silk cord, braid; plain-weave cotton lining
Diam: 16.8 cm

g. Head cover (*darpna*)
Plain-weave cotton, perle cotton embroidery and tassels
109 x 99 cm

h. Scarf (*šamija*)
Damask-woven silk or synthetic, knotted and fringed
125 x 125 cm

1.66 Woman's ensemble
Skopje, northern Macedonia, twentieth century
FOWLER MUSEUM X96.6.41A,C,D; GIFT OF PROFESSOR ELSIE IVANCICH DUNIN. X69.108; MUSEUM PURCHASE

X96.6.41

a. Chemise
Plain-weave linen, wool embroidery
114 x 135 cm

c. Apron
Two panels of tapestry-woven wool (and metallic thread), lace, sequins; braided wool drawstring
68 x 262 cm

d. Head scarf
Plain-weave cotton, chain-stitch silk embroidery, woven and knotted silk fringe
140 x 137 cm

X69.108

Vest
Warp-faced striped wool, wool challis; couched with silk and metallic cord and braid, metallic thread on cotton braid; damask silk ribbon, lace, cotton and metallic rickrack, metallic ribbon; sequins
90 x 78 cm

1.67 Woman's ensemble
Debarski Drimkol, western Macedonia, twentieth century
FOWLER MUSEUM X99.34.1A–G, J; GIFT OF ROBERT LEIBMAN

a. Chemise
Plain-weave cotton; hemstitching, cotton rickrack, needle-netting, wool embroidery; plastic buttons
127 x 113 cm

b. Vest
Felted wool twill, napped plain-weave wool; wool braid, fringe, and cord
80 x 37 cm

c. Apron
Wool twill, napped plain-weave wool; metallic thread, cord, rickrack, braid, and ribbon; cotton cord; wool fringe
79 x 35 cm

d. Head cover
Plain-weave cotton, embroidered with wool; fringe of metallic thread and tightly plied wool
115 x 192 cm

e,f. Stockings
Knitted wool
Each: 50 x 18 cm

g. Belt
Warp-faced woven wool; belt hook made of 1925 Bulgarian coin
178 x 9 cm

j. Dickie
Plain-weave linen or cotton, wool embroidery
59 x 34 cm

1.68 Woman's ensemble
Bitola, southwestern Macedonia, twentieth century
FOWLER MUSEUM X99.34.19A–G; GIFT OF ROBERT LEIBMAN

a. Chemise
Plain-weave cotton, wool embroidery, silk rickrack, lace; glass beads, sequins, coins
114 x 93 cm

b. Vest
Heavily felted wool twill, pinked plain-weave wool, wool embroidery and couched braid, silk ribbon; sequins, beads, coins
82 x 62 cm

c. Apron
Two weft-faced wool panels (with tapestry and inlay designs) sewn together horizontally; lace, silk ribbon, commercial trim; beads, sequins, coins; plaited wool ties
68 x 59 cm

d. Dickie
Plain-weave linen, commercial silk and metallic braid, silk flowers, glass beads, coins, sequins; printed cotton ties
42 x 33 cm

e. Head cover
Plain-weave cotton, perle cotton embroidery, crochet, and tassels
106 x 103 cm

f,g. Stockings
Knitted wool
Each: 52 x 16 cm

1.69 Woman's ensemble
Ohrid, western Macedonia, twentieth century
FOWLER MUSEUM X2010.9.1A,B–5A,B; PURCHASED WITH FOWLER MUSEUM TEXTILE COUNCIL FUNDS FROM THE COLLECTION OF MARGARET HEMPSTEAD

1a. Chemise
Plain-weave linen or cotton, embroidery in wool and silk, commercial rickrack and lace; sequins, glass beads, coins, brass bells
130 x 58 cm

1b. Dickie
Plain-weave linen or cotton, commercial rickrack, glass beads, velvet tie, metal hook and eye
48 x 31 cm

2. Vest
Heavy felted wool twill, plain-weave wool, couched wool cord and braid
71 x 40 cm

3. Apron
Two horizontal panels of weft-faced wool (with inlay designs), commercial trim and lace, sequins
69 x 55 cm

4. Head cover
Plain-weave cotton, cotton embroidery and tassels
104 x 104 cm

5a,b. Stockings
Knitted wool (one row of silk)
Each: 46 x 13 cm

1.70 Woman's ensemble
Skopje, northern Macedonia, mid-twentieth century
FOWLER MUSEUM X96.6.19A–D,F,G; GIFT OF PROFESSOR ELSIE IVANCICH DUNIN

a. Chemise
Plain-weave cotton with textured warp-stripes, silk embroidery and faggoting, crocheted edging, hemstitching; sequins, glass beads
122 x 152 cm

b. Vest
Quilted striped plain-weave silk or rayon (batting unknown), cotton and metallic rickrack, metallic ribbon, metallic thread on cotton braid; plain-weave cotton lining, brass button
89 x 69 cm

c. Apron
Two panels of tapestry-woven wool sewn together horizontally; wool fringe, metallic braid and ribbon, beads; braided wool tie ending with printed cotton triangles with tatted and beaded edge, sequins
78 x 61 cm

d. Belt
Plain-weave cotton over cardboard, metallic ribbon, two-piece silver clasp
86 x 7 cm

f,g. Stockings
Knitted wool
Each: 32 x 13 cm

1.71 Woman's ensemble
Gostivar, northwestern Macedonia, twentieth century
FOWLER MUSEUM X99.34.5A–C,G–I; GIFT OF ROBERT LEIBMAN

a. Chemise
Plain-weave cotton or linen with tension-stripes
127 x 77 cm

b. Jacket
Velvet, couched metallic and silk cord, ball buttons covered with braided metallic thread; plain-weave cotton lining
56 x 136 cm

c. Apron
Two panels of weft-faced wool (with patterns in wool tapestry and cotton overshot) sewn together horizontally; crocheted cotton lace, braided wool tie
57 x 109 cm

g. Sash
Plaid wool twill, warp fringe
300 x 27 cm

h,i. Stockings
Knitted wool and cotton, with knitted and slant-stitched patterns
Each: 44 x 17 cm

1.74 Woman's ensemble
Trebovec village, Posavina, Croatia, circa 1900–1920
FOWLER MUSEUM X83.273A–C; GIFT OF PROFESSOR ELSIE IVANCICH DUNIN

a. Skirt
Plain-weave linen with supplementary cotton weft patterns, pleating
91 x 98 cm

b. Apron
Plain-weave linen with supplementary cotton warp and weft pattern, cotton lace
94 x 290 cm

c. Blouse/jacket
Plain-weave linen with supplementary cotton weft pattern, pleated, hemstitched; brocade silk ribbon, braided cotton ties
44 x 169 cm

1.75 Woman's ensemble
Croatia, twentieth century
FOWLER MUSEUM X70.1592A–D; GIFT OF MIA SLAVENSKA

a. Skirt
Plain-weave linen, plain-weave cotton, wool embroidery
92 x 177 cm

b. Apron
Plain-weave linen, wool and silk embroidery
87 x 170 cm

c. Blouse
Plain-weave linen, smocking; plain-weave cotton; wool embroidery
47 x 133 cm

d. Head cover/shawl
Plain-weave linen, wool embroidery, mending
99 x 93 cm

1.76 Woman's ensemble
Posavina, Croatia, twentieth century
FOWLER MUSEUM X99.39.1A–C; GIFT OF HELEN, JAMES, JERRY, AND NICHOLAS MAROTT

a. Blouse
Plain-weave linen, patterned vertical tucks, plain-weave white silk cutwork, silk embroidery, shell buttons
55 x 144 cm

b. Apron
Plain-weave linen, pleating; satin-stitch silk embroidery, silk embroidery on netting; twill cotton ties
97 x 95 cm

c. Skirt
Plain-weave linen, pleating, drawnwork hemstitching, silk-embroidered netting
104 x 76 cm

1.77 Woman's ensemble
Bonavina, Posavina, Croatia, twentieth century
FOWLER MUSEUM X99.39.2A–C; GIFT OF HELEN, JAMES, JERRY, AND NICHOLAS MAROTT

a. Blouse
Plain-weave linen, smocked and pleated; silk satin-stitch embroidery, drawnwork, hemstitching; plastic buttons
56 x 155 cm

b. Apron
Plain-weave linen, smocked and pleated; silk satin-stitch embroidery, cutout and embroidered lace
96 x 102 cm

c. Skirt
Plain-weave linen, smocked and pleated; silk satin-stitch embroidery, drawnwork, hemstitching
98 x 78 cm

1.78 Woman's ensemble
Posavina, Croatia twentieth century
FOWLER MUSEUM X99.34.10A,B; GIFT OF ROBERT LEIBMAN. X93.14.5 (APRON); GIFT OF DOROTHY DAW

X99.34.10

a. Blouse
Plain-weave linen, tucks; cotton and silk satin-stitch embroidery, silk-thread cutwork; appliquéd silk cutwork on white damask silk; metal snaps
51 x 136 cm

b. Skirt
Plain-weave linen, pleated; cotton and silk satin-stitch embroidery, silk-thread cutwork, braided cotton ties
98 x 76 cm

X93.14.5

Apron
Plain-weave linen, cotton embroidery, cotton lace
96 x 197 cm

1.79 Woman's ensemble
Posavina, Croatia, twentieth century
FOWLER MUSEUM X2008.4.1 (BLOUSE), X2008.4.2 (APRON), X2008.3.2 (SKIRT); GIFT OF JEAN AND GARY CONCOFF

a. Blouse
Plain-weave linen with tucks and pleats; silk ribbon, silk satin-stitched embroidery, cotton lace, drawnwork hemstitching; metal snaps
62 x 155 cm

b. Apron
Plain-weave linen, pleating; satin-stitched silk and cotton embroidery, perle cotton and silk bobbin lace
94 x 75 cm

c. Skirt
Plain-weave linen, pleating; synthetic lace, cotton twill ties
106 x 111 cm

1.80 Woman's ensemble
Donja Bebrina area, Baranja, Croatia, twentieth century
FOWLER MUSEUM X69.29 (DRESS), X69.30 (APRON), X69.986 (CAP); GIFT OF ANTHONY SHAY

a. Dress
Woven strips of warp-float-patterned cotton, plain-weave cotton; silk and satin ribbon, several types of lace, silk embroidery; metallic thread, trim, and fringe; sequins, glass beads
149 x 129 cm

b. Apron
Brocade silk, satin-stitch silk embroidery, ribbon, metallic lace; pleating
71 x 33 cm

c. Cap
Plain-weave black linen, white damask cotton; looped wool embroidery, silk embroidery, ribbon, metal-wrapped thread; plastic stars, rhinestones, sequins, glass beads
33 x 43 cm

1.81 Woman's ensemble
Baranja, Croatia, twentieth century
FOWLER MUSEUM X72.186A–E; GIFT OF VILMA MACHETTE

a. Skirt
Plain-weave cotton or linen, pleating; looped cotton embroidery, drawnwork, crocheted lace
113 x 127 cm

b. Blouse
Plain-weave cotton, pleating; cotton embroidery, couching, and faggoting; crocheted cotton edging
54 x 143 cm

c. Pantaloons
Plain-weave cotton, crocheted cotton edging
94 x 83 cm

d. Apron
Wool woven in slit tapestry, wool fringe
82 x 65 cm

e. Head cover
Plain-weave cotton, cutwork, crocheted lace
102.2 x 95 cm

1.82 Women's ensemble
Baranja, Croatia, probably ethnic Hungarian; early twentieth century
FOWLER MUSEUM X97.27.6A–F; GIFT OF MARSHA LIPMAN

a. Blouse
Plain-weave linen, strips of silk embroidery, silk-embroidered netting, metallic lace and rickrack trim, sequins
67 x 55 cm

b. Skirt
Black velvet, black cotton sateen, silk embroidery, metallic trim, sequins; braided wool cord
83 x 61 cm

c. Apron
Bicolor silk brocade (red and white), silk embroidery, metallic lace and trim, cotton lace
77 x 43 cm

d. Belt
Woven cotton, couched metallic thread and braid, embroidery with metal strips and cotton thread

e. Underskirt
Plain-weave cotton, hand-crocheted cotton lace
21 x 25 cm

f. Cap
Black velvet, silk embroidery, metallic trim
21 x 25 cm

1.83 Man's ensemble
Lika area, Dalmatia, southern Croatia, twentieth century
FOWLER MUSEUM X72.187A–F,I,J; GIFT OF VILMA MACHETTE

a. Pants
Plain-weave cotton or linen, fringe, hemstitching, braided cotton drawstring
97 x 85 cm

b. Shirt
Plain-weave cotton or linen, tucks, plastic buttons
85 x 161 cm

c. Vest
Plain-weave wool, commercial cotton lining in striped plain-weave, machine-stitched decoration, plastic buttons
85 x 64 cm

d. Hat
Felted wool
Diam: 19 cm

e,f. Shoes (opanci)
Rawhide bottoms, twined rawhide thongs, tanned leather strap, iron buckles
Each: 28 x 11 cm

i.j. Stockings
Knitted wool
Each: 55 x 11 cm

1.84 Woman's ensemble
Posavina, Croatia, twentieth century
FOWLER MUSEUM X95.50.2A,D,F,G,K,L; GIFT OF PROFESSOR ELSIE IVANCICH DUNIN

a. Vest
Sheepskin with fleece inside; appliquéd leather patches and strips, woven leather strips, leather "buttons"; mixed cotton and wool braid, pompoms, toggles, and buttons
39 x 47 cm

d. Apron
Plain-weave linen with cotton overshot patterns, cross-stitch cotton embroidery (on waistband), twill cotton ties
62 x 122 cm

f,g. Ribbon (on blouse)
Polychrome brocade silk ribbon
106 x 9 cm

k. Blouse
Plain-weave cotton, cotton and wool overshot designs, smocking, grosgrain ribbon
53 x 121 cm

l. Dress
Plain-weave linen with cotton and wool overshot designs; smocking
99 x 127 cm

1.85 Man's ensemble
Posavina, Croatia, twentieth century

a. Hat
Fiber felt; silk embroidery, plain-weave felted wool appliqués; satin lining
Diam: 18 cm

b. Vest
Plain-weave wool, couched silk braid, silk embroidery; metal studs, brass buttons with enamel; plain-weave linen lining, basket-weave wool tape; braided cotton cords wrapped with metallic thread; metallic and silk cords plaited, knotted, and tasseled
51 x 47 cm

c. Shirt
Plain-weave linen or cotton; yoke of cotton with overshot designs; lapels embroidered in cross-stitch
95 x 119 cm

d. Pants
Plain-weave linen, hemstitched and fringed; plain-weave cotton; cotton shoestring as drawstring
112 x 72 cm

1.89 Man's ensemble
Mezőkövesd, northern Hungary, twentieth century

218. Shirt
Plain-weave cotton; perle-cotton embroidery
85 x 189 cm

219. Pants
Plain-weave cotton, fringed; twill cotton drawstring
90 x 374 cm

220. Vest
Plain-weave wool, couched silk braid, silk ribbon; plastic buttons
157 x 42 cm

221. Apron
Black cotton sateen, printed wool challis, silk embroidery, brocade silk ribbon, knotted silk fringes
157 x 63 cm

222. Hat
Felt, ribbon, rickrack, artificial flowers
13 x 46 cm

1.90 Woman's ensemble
Kalocsa, Hungary, twentieth century

X69.979

a. Skirt
Plain-weave cotton or rayon, pleated; silk-embroidered plain-weave (synthetic?) "lace," silk embroidery; plain-weave cotton and printed cotton facing of waistband
81 x 122 cm

b. Blouse
Plain-weave cotton, eyelet cutwork, perle-cotton embroidery; metal snaps
54 x 87 cm

e. Vest
Plain-weave cotton, perle-cotton embroidery, metal snaps
31 x 44 cm

f. Apron
Plain-weave cotton, eyelet cutwork, perle-cotton embroidery
74 x 80 cm

g. Woman's cap
Plain-weave cotton, perle-cotton embroidery
23 x 42 cm

X68.248

Girl's headdress
Polychrome brocade ribbons, paper flowers, florist's wire
27 x 6 cm

1.91 Man's ensemble
Northern Croatia, twentieth century

a. Pants
Plain-weave cotton, drawnwork, eyelet cutwork, metallic thread embroidery and rickrack; sequins, beads; commercial elastic and grosgrain suspenders
107 x 105 cm

d. Shirt
Plain-weave cotton, pleating; drawnwork, eyelet, cutwork, plastic buttons
84 x 182 cm

e. Belt
Cotton, metallic thread, braid, fringe, pompoms
213 x 5 cm

f. Vest
Cotton, silk, wool, metallic thread, appliqué
47 x 45 cm

1.92 Woman's ensemble
Slavonia, Croatia, twentieth century

a. Blouse
Plain-weave cotton, vertical tucks, cutwork, faggoting; metallic wire embroidery on plain-weave synthetic(?) as appliqué, sequins; button
50 x 155 cm

b. Apron
Black damask silk, black cotton bobbin-lace, metallic wire embroidery on plain-weave synthetic(?) as appliqué, sequins
Woven, crocheted,
79 x 109 cm

c. Skirt
Plain-weave cotton, eyelet and other cutwork, faggoting; metallic wire embroidery on plain-weave synthetic(?) as appliqué, sequins
103 x 131 cm

d. Shawl
Plain-weave silk, machine lace, metallic wire embroidery
76 x 208 cm

e. Head cover
Velvet, metallic wire and thread; sequins, glass beads
48 x 105 cm

1.93 Woman's ensemble
Slavonia, Croatia, twentieth century

1. Dress
Plain-weave cotton, cotton lace; plain-weave cotton embroidered with metal wire, sequins, glass beads, metallic rickrack; metallic ribbon, drawnwork, hemstitching, cotton bobbin-lace
129 x 173 cm

2. Apron
Satin, appliquéd sections of metallic thread embroidery, further embroidered with metal wire, sequins, glass beads; black eyelet cutwork "lace"
82 x 127 cm

3. Head cover
Velvet, appliquéd sections of metallic thread embroidery with sequins, glass beads; black net backing
46 x 112 cm

4. Shawl
Velvet, appliquéd sections of metallic thread embroidery, metal fringe, sequins, glass beads
46 x 144 cm

CHAPTER TWO

2.5 Man's ensemble
Sarajevo, Bosnia-Herzegovina, mid-twentieth century

b. Fez
Fiber-felted wool, spool-knitted wool cord, silk tassel
Diam: 20 cm

c. Shirt
Striped satin of rayon or silk, plastic buttons
66 x 136 cm

d. Vest
Black wool twill front, heavily felted red wool back, plain-weave wool facing; couched with silk cord and braid; plain-weave linen lining and inner pocket
54 x 49 cm

f. Jacket
Fine felted plain-weave wool, couched with silk cord; red felted plain-weave wool lining, black cotton sateen lining of upper sleeves
49 x 165 cm

g. Pants
Black plain-weave wool, red felted plain-weave wool facing, white plain-weave cotton lining, black twill cotton waistband; couched silk cord, metal hooks and eyes
58 x 176 cm

h. Sash
Synthetic (?) warp-faced cloth and tassels
108 x 76 cm

2.18 Man's ensemble
Bosnia-Herzegovina, twentieth century
FOWLER MUSEUM X66.1061A–K; MUSEUM PURCHASE

a. Pants
Plain-weave wool, fringed; braided wool cord (drawstring)
50 x 143 cm

b. Shirt
Heavy cotton seersucker, crocheted lace
91 x 119 cm

c. Vest
Heavily felted wool twill, couched silk braids, wool embroidery
45 x 42 cm

d. Sash
Striped warp-faced wool, rolled hem, fringe
298 x 12 cm

e,f. Leggings
Heavily felted wool twill, couched wool braids, wool embroidery; metal hook and eye
Each: 35 x 17 cm

g,h. Socks
Knitted wool, embroidered wool designs on cuffs
Each: 31 x 15.5 cm

i,j. Shoes
Tanned leather, dyed leather appliqués and braiding; metal studs (under heels)
Each: 28 x 10.5 cm

k. Hat
Black wool fleece outside, white wool fleece inside
25 x 28 cm

2.19 Woman's ensemble
Kosovo, late nineteenth century
FOWLER MUSEUM X83.259A–F, H–J, L–Q; MUSEUM PURCHASE

a. Headband
Wool needlepoint on synthetic mesh; elastic
7 x 51 cm

b. Hairpiece
Black twill cotton (unknown stiffening inside), brown hair
73 x 11 cm

c. Scarf
Warp-striped plain-weave cotton, wool and metallic embroidery, crochet, fringing
204 x 45 cm

d. Blouse
Plain-weave cotton with texture and tension stripes in warp; glass beads, sequins
71 x 137 cm

e. Under-sleeves
Plain-weave cotton, embroidered in wool, metallic thread, and silk; cotton lace; sequins, glass beads; plastic buttons
41 x 17 cm

f. Vest
Machine-quilted plain-weave silk; commercial rickrack, silk braid frogs, plastic and metal buttons, metal eyes; plain-weave cotton lining (batting unknown)
34 x 44 cm

h. Skirt
Plain-weave cotton with texture and tension (seersucker) stripes in warp
69 x 104 cm

i. Hip harness
Printed plain-weave cotton, sheet plastic, burlap; over wooden frame padded with foam rubber and knitted cotton
11 x 55 cm

j. Sash
Wool twill
166 x 20 cm

l. Back apron
Weft-faced silk, with silk and metallic overshot weft patterns, silk and metallic trim, silk fringed trim, woven silk cord, plastic button
70 x 140 cm

m. Front apron
Tapestry-woven wool and metallic thread; glass beads, shell buttons
75 x 57 cm

n. Pantaloons
Upper part: plain-weave cotton with texture and tension (seersucker) stripes in warp. Lower parts: plain-weave red cotton with in-woven weft stripes (black and white silk thread twisted as woven in)
95 x w 69 cm

o. Socks
Knitted wool, wool and metallic thread chain-stitch embroidery, crocheted edge
Each: 24 x 15 cm

p. Slippers
Knitted wool; cotton and metallic thread chain-stitch embroidery
Each: 29 x 16 cm

q. Shoes
Rawhide bottoms, cotton woven, crocheted, and plaited uppers with chain-stitched metallic and wool thread; cotton fringe
Each: 30 x 8 cm

2.20 Woman's ensemble
Bosnia-Herzegovina, twentieth century
FOWLER MUSEUM X93.23.16A–G, X69.103 (METAL BELT); GIFTS OF PROFESSOR ELSIE IVANCICH DUNIN

X93.23.16

a. Pants
Plain-weave cotton or linen legs with plaid texture-striping; checkered plain-weave and basket-weave cotton top half; twill cotton and plied cord drawstrings
131 x 50 cm

b. Head scarf
Plain-weave and damask cotton; satin-stitch embroidery; cotton lace
107 x 104 cm

c. Chemise
Plain-weave white linen with designs inlaid with yellow and white supplementary weft; embroidery; bobbin lace edging
110 x 99 cm

d. Vest
Velvet, couched with metallic cord; striped plain-weave cotton lining
37 x 48 cm

e. Sash
Tablet-woven warp-faced wool and cotton, warp fringe
1,272 x 12 cm

f,g. Stockings
Knitted cotton
Each: 44 x 10 cm

X69.103

Belt
Metal, wire
186 x 6 cm

2.21 Woman's ensemble
Travnik, Sarajevo area, Bosnia-Herzegovina, twentieth century
FOWLER MUSEUM X66.1062A–G; MUSEUM PURCHASE. X93.23.17C, E, F (HEAD COVER, APRON, SASH); GIFTS OF PROFESSOR ELSIE IVANCICH DUNIN

X66.1062

    a. Chemise
       Plain-weave and seersucker cotton; pleats; green silk trim, crocheted
       lace (on sleeve ends), cutwork eyelet lace (at hem)
       123 x 114 cm

    b. Short vest
       Green velvet; couched silk cord and braid; sequins; gray sateen silk
       or synthetic lining
       35 x 48 cm

    c. Vest
       Heavily felted black woven wool; black silk cord and braid, appliquéd
       red felt, chain-stitched embroidery
       56 x 50 cm

    d,e. Socks
       Knitted wool; ankle bands embroidered in slant- and chain-stitch
       Each: 27 x 14 cm

    f,g. Shoes
       Leather; buckle at ankle, upper decorated with red, white, blue,
       and black strips woven geometric designs
       Each: 27 x 11 cm

X93.23.17

    c. Head cover
       Handspun, handwoven cotton with multicolor supplementary weft
       designs (overshot and brocaded); embroidery (unfinished!); warp fringe
       90 x 86 cm

    e. Apron
       Horizontally striped plain-weave wool apron; knitted or plaited border
       extended as ties
       55 x 60 cm

    f. Sash
       Warp-faced wool, probably card woven, fringed ends
       111 x 9 cm

CHAPTER THREE

3.3 Woman's ensemble
    Čičmany, Zilina, Slovakia, circa 1918
    FOWLER MUSEUM X66.1863–65; MUSEUM PURCHASE

    X66.1863
       Skirt
       Plain-weave cotton, densely smocked and pleated
       71 x 174 cm

    X66.1864
       Apron
       Plain-weave linen; embroidery, drawnwork, bobbin lace
       54 x 130 cm

    X66.1865
       Blouse
       Plain-weave cotton, pleated; embroidery, cutwork, faggoting, bobbin lace
       36 x 146 cm

3.6 Woman's partial ensemble
    Piešťany, Slovakia, twentieth century
    FOWLER MUSEUM X70.1225A,B; GIFT OF ERIC BARKER

    a. Blouse
       Plain-weave linen, smocking, eyelet cutwork, crochet, brocade ribbon,
       bobbin lace, metallic trim; elastic
       36 x 146 cm.

    b. Cap
       Plain-weave linen, eyelet cutwork
       30 x 50 cm

3.8 Woman's ensemble
    Hel'pa, Gemer County, Slovakia, twentieth century
    FOWLER MUSEUM X2006.11.3A–D; GIFT OF MS. MARTHA ADAMS

    a. Blouse
       Plain-weave linen, couching, embroidery, lace (embroidered netting),
       plain-weave synthetic (ruff)
       55 x 183 cm

    b. Vest
       Wool challis, satin ribbon, synthetic(?) plain-weave ribbon,
       commercial trim, sequins; plain-weave linen lining
       28 x 40 cm

    c. Skirt
       Printed plain-weave cotton, pleated; machine embroidery, ribbon,
       bobbin lace
       66 x 78 cm

    d. Apron
       Plain-weave linen, plain-weave cotton appliqué, hand and machine
       embroidery, woven cotton ribbon; embroidered and cutout lace;
       cotton twill tape ties
       61 x 41 cm

CHAPTER FOUR

4.5 Woman's ensemble
    Čilipi, Konavle, twentieth century
    FOWLER MUSEUM X2010.26.2.1–4,6,7,11,13A,B; GIFT OF PROFESSOR ELSIE IVANCICH DUNIN

    1. Chemise
       Plain-weave cotton, smocked; appliquéd *ošvice* (at lapels and cuffs)
       embroidered in silk on fine plain-weave linen; silk braid and tassels,
       satin ribbon, gold-plated metal buttons
       137 x 77 cm

    2. Vest
       Wool twill, couched with silk braid and cord; black cotton sateen lining
       131 x 39 cm

    3. Apron
       Twill cotton, with inwoven wool weft-stripes; wool braid edging;
       twill cotton ties
       183 x 59 cm

    4. Skirt
       Plain-weave cotton
       187 x 89 cm

    6. Belt
       Twill cotton, with inwoven stripes; synthetic ribbon bindings
       170 x 10 cm

    7. Sash
       Warp-faced striped cotton, warp fringe
       104 x 3 cm

    11. Purse
       Plain-weave linen; silk embroidery, silk tassels; plaited wool loops,
       cotton cord
       12 x 11 cm

    13a,b. Stockings
       Knitted synthetic
       Each: 150 x 9 cm

CHAPTER FIVE

5.1 Woman's ensemble
    Skopje, Macedonia, 1960s
    FOWLER MUSEUM X69.100A,B–103; GIFT OF PROFESSOR ELSIE IVANCICH DUNIN

    X69.100A
       Pants (*čintiani*)
       Floral-print plain-weave nylon or polyester
       115 x 302 cm

    X69.100B
       Jacket (*mintan*)
       Floral-print plain-weave nylon or polyester; pleating, shirring;
       plain-weave cotton lining
       26 x 150 cm

    X69.101
       Blouse
       Modified cellulose imitating silk, in texture-striped plain-weave;
       tatted edgings
       162 x 139 cm

    X69.102
       Scarf (*šamija*)
       Plain-weave polyester, tatted edging
       181 x 81 cm

    X69.103
       Belt
       Filigree metal, partly gilded; colored glass
       186 x 6 cm

5.2 Woman's ensemble
    Skopje, Macedonia, 2011
    FOWLER MUSEUM X2011.33.1–9; GIFT OF PATRICIA ANAWALT

    X2011.33.1
    a. Jacket (*mintan*)
       Blue synthetic netting; sequins; plain-weave polyester lining
       90 x 36 cm

    b. Pants (*kuli*)
       Blue synthetic netting; sequins
       112 x 70 cm

c. Handkerchief
Blue synthetic netting, sequins, metallic rickrack loop
26 x 29 cm

X2011.33.2

a,b. Pair of hand covers
Red synthetic netting, embroidery, ribbon, sequins
23 x 23 cm

c. Shawl
Red synthetic netting, embroidery, ribbon, sequins
97 x 97 cm

X2011.33.3

Belt
Cast metal links, elastic band
175 x 4.5 cm

X2011.33.4

Handkerchief
Red plain-weave silk, knotted silk cord, sequins
28 x 30 cm

X2011.33.5

Puff
Looped and knotted white plastic thread, sequins
36 x 36 cm

X2011.33.6

Handkerchief
Silver plastic/metallic thread, sequins
24 x 24 cm

X2011.33.7

Flour Sifter
Plastic and wire-mesh flour sifter, covered with red satin, artificial flowers (silk, plastic), commercial trim, sequins
Diam: 29 cm

X2011.33.8

Camisole
Polyester/cotton knit, machine lace; rhinestones
59 x 36.5 cm

X2011.33.9

Hair combs
Plastic, rhinestones
8 x 24 cm

CHAPTER SIX

6.16 Man's ensemble
Montenegro, twentieth century
FOWLER MUSEUM X2010.10.1,2,4,5,7; GIFT OF DANILO BACH IN MEMORY OF NICHOLAS AND VASE N. BACHEVICH. X95.16.3 (HAT); GIFT OF PROFESSOR ELSIE IVANCICH DUNIN. HENRY ART GALLERY, UNIVERSITY OF WASHINGTON, SEATTLE, MARGARET J. HORD COLLECTION, D262 (PANTS AND SHIRT)

HENRY GALLERY

Shirt
Plain-weave cotton, plastic buttons
79 x 182 cm

HENRY GALLERY

Pants
Felted plain-weave blue wool, silk and metallic cord and braid; plain-weave red synthetic fiber
84 x 46 cm

X2010.10.1

Jacket (dušanka)
Napped plain-weave red wool, couched with black silk cord and braid, braid-covered ball buttons with red glass bead; lined with felted plain-weave red wool, pink cotton twill, tablet-woven polychrome silk band; metal buttons
44 x 159 cm

X2010.10.2

Vest (dzamadan)
Napped red wool twill, couched with metallic cord and braid; red silk braid and frogs, metallic-braided buttons, brass buttons
59 x 46 cm

X2010.10.4

Sash (trombolos)
Plain-weave silk with stripes in both warp and weft; lightly braided and knotted warp-fringe
296 x 93 cm

X2010.10.5

Celebratory sash
Satin, silk ribbon, metallic thread and braid, metallic spiral-wire tassels, sequins; satin-weave black cotton lining, with stenciled silver cross
94 x 25 cm; fringe: 4 cm

X2010.10.7.1A,B

Leggings
Heavily felted white wool twill; red wool twill, brown wool braid, metal hooks and eyes
35 x 38 cm

X2010.10.7.2A,B

Garters (podveze)
Woven red wool couched with gold cord; red silk braid edging; warp-faced striped cotton band as backing; metal hooks and eyes
38 x 3 cm

X95.16.3

Hat
Felted plain-weave red wool top, black satin sides, red satin lining; couched with gold cord and braid
Diam: 18 cm

6.20 Woman's ensemble
Montenegro, twentieth century
FOWLER MUSEUM X95.16.1A–C,E,F; GIFT OF PROFESSOR ELSIE IVANCICH DUNIN; X2011.26.1; GIFT OF MICHELLE CHEYOVICH

X95.16.1

a. Blouse
Texture-striped plain-weave modified cellulose (imitating silk); gold-wrapped thread and colored silk embroidery on applied synthetic plain-weave strips (ošvice)
63 x 50 cm

b. Skirt
White satin, machine-lace, elastic waistband
107 x 81 cm

c. Hat
Felted plain-weave red wool top, black satin sides, red satin lining; couched with gold cord
Diam: 19 cm

e. Vest (koret)
Napped plain-weave white and red wool, couched with metallic cord; buttons braided with metallic wire, coral beads; plain-weave cotton lining in lapels
114 x 106 cm

f. Belt (ćemer)
Warp-faced cotton band; filigree metal belt-ornament; metal hooks and eyes
84 x 9 cm

X2011.26.1

Jacket (jaketa)
Red velvet, couched with metallic cord and braid; plain-weave cotton lining
39 x 138 cm

6.22 Little girl's ensemble
Czech Republic, twentieth century
FOWLER MUSEUM X2010.12.1.1–6; GIFT OF HELENKA AND JOHN FROST

X2010.12.1.1

Blouse
Plain-weave cotton, cutwork, cotton embroidery, cotton lace, metal snaps
41 x 46 cm

X2010.12.1.2

Skirt
Plain-weave rayon(?) skirt, plain-weave cotton waistband; perle cotton embroidery (note patterns for further embroidery marked near hemline)
41 x 28 cm

X2010.12.1.3

Vest
Printed wool challis, weft-faced silk and/or synthetic ribbon, metallic trim, buttonhole stitching in perle cotton, plastic buttons; plain-weave linen or hempen lining
29 x 33 cm

X2010.12.1.4

Apron
Plain-weave blue synthetic; perle cotton embroidery; pillow lace; brocade ribbon
32 x 51 cm

X2010.12.1.5

Collar
Plain-weave cotton, cutwork, cotton embroidery, cotton lace
23 x 57 cm

X2010.12.1.6

Headdress
Silk flowers, paper-covered wire, silk brocade ribbon
76 x 17 cm

6.24 Woman's ensemble
Kyjov, Moravia, Czech Republic, twentieth century
FOWLER MUSEUM X2006.11.2A–F,I; GIFT OF MARTHA ADAMS

a. Vest
Green and white bichrome brocade, watered-silk ribbon, metallic-
thread rickrack with sequins, silk embroidery, plastic buttons
25 x 46 cm

b. Blouse
Fine plain-weave cotton, silk embroidery and lace, cotton needle-lace,
cross-stitched cotton ribbon, elastic, shell button
56 x 116 cm

c. Collar
Plain-weave cotton, hemstitched cutwork, silk embroidery and lace
65 x 42

d. Skirt
Cotton brocade, linen net lining (backing), silk-embroidered linen
waistband with hempen (?) lining, cotton twill ties; sequins, metal
hooks and eyes
65 x 209 cm

e. Apron
Tie-dyed (with indigo) polished cotton, pillow lace, perle cotton
embroidery and smocking, cotton twill ties
69 x 121 cm

f. Cap
Damask silk, silk ribbon, cotton lace, metallic rickrack, glass beads,
pearls, sequins; plain-weave cotton lining, cotton twill ties
33 x 44 cm

i. Hair bow and ribbon
Polychrome brocade silk ribbon
45 x 30 cm

6.31 Bags
Serbia, twentieth century
FOWLER MUSEUM X2011.4.6 (A), X2011.4.12 (B), X2011.4.10 (C);
GIFT OF DR. JOEL MARTIN HALPERN

X2011.4.6

Woven wool
32 x 28 cm

X2011.4.12

Woven wool
43 x 44 cm (folded in photograph)

X2011.4.10

Woven wool
36 x 28 cm

6.32 Man's ensemble
Serbia, twentieth century
FOWLER MUSEUM X70.1231A–D, F (FIG. 6.34); MUSEUM PURCHASE

a. Pants
Plain-weave felted wool, couched wool braid, synthetic braided cord,
twill cotton facing, printed plain-weave cotton waistband
99 x 54 cm

b. Shirt
Plain-weave linen with texture-stripes in warp, vertical tucks on front,
shell buttons
98 x 169 cm

c. Vest
Felted and napped wool twill, couched with silk cord and braid,
plain-weave napped wool lining and inner pockets, plaited cotton tape
54 x 44 cm

d. Jacket
Felted and napped plain-weave wool, couched with silk cord and braid,
gauze-weave cotton lining, twill wool lining (in sleeve ends and
under collar)
66 x 164 cm

f. Sash (fig. 6.34 in essay)
Warp-faced tablet-woven wool with polychrome pattern stripes
293 x 11 cm

6.36 Woman's ensemble
Serbia, twentieth century
FOWLER MUSEUM X93.23.20A,B,E–G; GIFT OF PROFESSOR ELSIE IVANCICH DUNIN.
X70.1232A (CHEMISE); MUSEUM PURCHASE

X70.1232A

Chemise
Plain-weave linen or cotton, perle-cotton embroidery, crocheted cotton
lace, plastic button
146 x 121 cm

X93.23.20

a. Vest
Velvet, couched with metallic thread, cord, and braid; sequins;
silk or synthetic plain-weave lining, metal hooks and eyes
37 x 49 cm

b. Apron
Velvet, wool (slant-stitch) embroidery, lace; plain-weave cotton lining,
braided cotton cord
70 x 55 cm

e,f. Stockings
Knitted wool, cross-stitched wool embroidery
Each: 49 x 15 cm

g. Back-apron
Weft-faced and weft-striped wool, wool embroidery, crocheted wool
edging; braided wool cord
82 x 123 cm

6.37 Stockings, slippers, and toe warmers
Various, twentieth century
FOWLER MUSEUM: *STOCKINGS*—X2011.4.33A,B (A), X2011.4.21A,B (B), X2011.4.24A,B (C),
X2011.4.31A,B (D), X2011.4.20A,B (E); *SLIPPERS*— X2011.4.26A,B (F), X2011.4.25A,B (G);
TOE WARMERS—X2011.4.30A,B (H); GIFT OF DR. JOEL MARTIN HALPERN

X2011.4.33

a,b. Stockings
Macedonia, twentieth century
Knitted wool and cotton; crochet; double-plied wool cord
Each: 51 x 17 cm

X2011.4.21

a,b. Stockings
Macedonia, twentieth century
Knitted wool; plaited wool cord
Each: 42 x 16 cm

X2011.4.24

a,b. Stockings
Šumadija, Serbia, twentieth century
Knitted wool (tops carded, legs and feet combed); woolen embroidery
and crochet
Each: 51 x 16 cm

X2011.4.31

a,b. Stockings
Knitted wool, metallic thread, plaited wool cord, tassels; metal beads
49 x 18 cm

X2011.4.20

a,b. Stockings
Probably Albanian from Kosovo, twentieth century
Knitted synthetic yarn
41 x 13 cm

X2011.4.26

a,b. Slippers
Macedonia, twentieth century
Knitted wool
Each: 25 x 13 cm

X2011.4.25

a,b. Slippers
Macedonia, twentieth century
Knitted wool
Each: 25 x 13 cm

X2011.4.30

a,b. Toe warmers
Šumadija, Serbia, twentieth century
Knitted wool, woolen embroidery and crochet
Each: 14 x 12 cm

CHAPTER ONE · BARBER

1. For the social and economic "prehistory" of cloth and clothing in Europe and the Near East, see Barber (1994). For the technical history and its copious data, see Barber (1991). For further analysis of the string skirt (and *panyova*), see Barber (1999b).
2. Barber (1991, 79–83); Barber (1994, 78–83).
3. Barber (1991, 20–30).
4. For example, Prošić-Dvornić(1989).
5. Barber (1991, 235–39).
6. In some areas, e.g., parts of Macedonia, the red fringes were seen chiefly as protecting the woman's fertility from the evil eye (Mladenović 1999). I have found no way to confirm how old that exact aspect of the belief is; but in many parts of western Eurasia, throughout the Upper Paleolithic and the Neolithic, people often went to great lengths to place red pigment—usually red ochre—in graves. So we do know that red has been deeply significant in this area for many tens of millennia.
7. For Albanian women's costumes with "manes" of fringes on the shoulders, see, e.g., Gjergji (1988, figs. 117, 153, 167, 180, 186, 197, and front cover).
8. Zelenin (1927, 207–8). Farther west, South Slavic women in some areas also donned a special back apron at puberty. In Serbian Šumadija it was permanently pleated with hot water and stones (fig. 1.24); in Croatian Baranja it was called a *ponjavka*; in the mountains just east of Slovenia women even wove their heavily fringed red aprons on a special traditional loom not used for their other cloth (a vertical two-beam loom). See Prošić-Dvornić (1989, 64, 86); Šistan (1986, 29); Muraj (1988, 42).
9. Bogatyrev (1971, 49).
10. Barber (1999a, 37–39).
11. Kličkova and Petruševa (1963, pls. XVII–XXIV, and 13–20).
12. Knauer (1978) presents a splendidly data-rich analysis of the history of sleeved and vestigial-sleeved coats.
13. Denisov (1969); see especially color photograph 14.
14. Kličkova and Petruševa (1963, 33). The local names for the Mariovo costume pieces have been culled from this same book.
15. For a fuller description and photographs of numerous Croatian costumes—some of which already were and more of which now are in the Fowler collection—see Dunin (1984).
16. Information from paper given by John Irwin, September 8, 1983; see also Irwin and Brett (1970, 19, 29 [for crewel], 30 [for prohibition dates]).
17. Bogatyrev (1971, 89).
18. Bogatyrev (1971, 83).

CHAPTER TWO · JIROUSEK

1. Fine (1994, 25).
2. Fine (1994, 29–43).
3. Fine (1994, 43–44, 66–69).
4. Fine (1994, 208–11).
5. Fine (1994, 211, 225, 226).
6. This vintage photograph and others illustrating this chapter were taken from *Yilinda Turkiye'de Halk Giysileri: Elbese-I Osmaniyye* (*Dress of the Ottomans*) by Osman Hamdi Bey and Marie de Launay (1873). This book was created at the order of the sultan to accompany an Ottoman exhibition designed for an International Fair held in Vienna. Hamdi Bey was commissioned to collect costumes representative of all the peoples of the Ottoman Empire. Although they were photographed on models in Constantinople, the costumes are authentic. This volume represents the earliest systematic photographic record of the dress of the Ottoman Empire.
7. Inalcik (2000, 915).
8. For further details about the structure and governance of Ottoman sumptuary law, see Quataert (2000, 174–78).
9. Quataert (1997, 403–25).
10. Göçek (1996, 156).
11. Göçek (1996, 39).
12. Finkel (2005, 436).
13. Baker (1986, 72–85).
14. Barber (1999b).

CHAPTER THREE · CORBETT

I would like to offer special thanks to Dr. Inez Giles for technical information on embroidery and to Helene Baine Cincebeaux, Carol Bowdoin Gil, Stefano Ionescu, Jan Letowski, and Edward Maeder, all of whom assisted me in various ways in the preparation of this essay.

CHAPTER FOUR · DUNIN

1. At the time, the Fowler Museum was known as the Museum of Cultural History.
2. The walled city of Dubrovnik is a UNESCO World Heritage Site, and the region of Konavle was under Dubrovnik's domain since the early fifteenth century.
3. The county (*općina*) of Konavle in the 2011 census had a population of 8,571, and Čilipi had 934.
4. My own association with the area of Konavle began with what has become a three-generational dance study of a South Slavic diaspora. Emigrants from the coastal area of today's Croatia began to arrive in California shortly after the mid-nineteenth century discovery of gold. At the time, the Croatian coastal area was under Austrian administration, and large numbers of local men left for California to seek their fortunes with the intention to return eventually to their ancestral homes. By the early 1900s, however, most every village in Konavle and along the southern Adriatic coastal strip of Croatia had family members who had stayed on in California. The emigrant population from Konavle centered primarily in Watsonville, California. These emigrants maintained contacts with their families in Croatia and assisted them economically into the mid-twentieth century. For studies about the Croatian emigrants in California's Watsonville area, see Mekis and Miller (2009), for Croatians in California see Adam Eterovich (2000) and recent, but as yet unpublished, sources by Tom Ninkovich.
5. Dunin (1984, 33).
6. "Yugoslavia ranks among the Bank's five largest borrowers.... The World Bank helped Yugoslavia to meet the challenge of post-war [World War II] development both through its lending program and its encouragement of structural reforms to assist development" (Cullen 1979, iii).
7. Kobašić (2001) provides an overview of the building construction, such as the hotels (pages 142–43), and public works in Dubrovnik and surrounding area after World War II.
8. Ceribašić (2003) lists Čilipi among numerous village groups in festival programs sponsored by the Peasant Unity organization in 1938, 1946, 1947, and 1951.
9. Jadran Film (1948) with Potkolo performed by the Čilipi villagers. See on YouTube <http://www.youtube.com/watch?v=Jhne3kPre3E>.
10. The International Folk Music Council (the name was changed in 1981 to International Council for Traditional Music [ICTM]) organized a major meeting in the northern Adriatic coastal town of Opatija in 1951. Representative dance and music groups from throughout former Yugoslavia, based on the groups of the 1930s and 1940s that had participated in regional festivals, were selected to perform their repertoire for this international body of dance and music scholars. The Čilipi and Popovići villages were part of this program, dancing Potkolo accompanied by bagpipe (Žganec 1951, 77). The four professional folk dance and music ensembles of Yugoslavia, established in 1948 and 1949, had not yet influenced village groups with theatricalized performances of rural dances.
11. Stijepo Vezelić Mijovov (1907–2000) directed the group from 1967 until the late 1980s. Personal communication with Dunin in 1976, 1983, and 1993.
12. The KUD Čilipi was originally formed as KPD, an acronym for Kulturno Prosvjetno Društvo (Cultural and Educational Society), Vladimir Nazor in 1954. The name was changed to KUD Čilipi in 1967 when the group began its touristic program.
13. Ivančan (1966, 399).
14. Perić (1957, 20).
15. Described in the Dubrovnik newspaper *Crvena Hrvatska* of March 24, 1900, cited in Hajdić (2010, 33).
16. A catalog of an exhibition featuring Jelka Miš and held in Dubrovnik, shows a photograph of the Dalmatian pavilion in the Viennese exposition 1907 (Hajdić 2010, 22).
17. Hajdić (2010, 20).
18. Katica Benc-Bošković states that this fabric, known as Czech *rumburg*, was highly esteemed (1983, 61).
19. Benc-Bošković (1982, 158).
20. This cistern was not in use and dry, but in most homes the water supply is collected from rain water draining off the roofs and filtered into their own cisterns.
21. Born in Konavle of an old family, Marina Desin completed her undergraduate studies in ethnology and Italian language in Zagreb. She then worked as a conservator with the Institute for the Protection of Historical Monuments in Dubrovnik before being hired to manage the Čilipi regional museum in 1984. As the museum's curator she carries out research and presents local ethnoculture through tourism. She continues in this role in 2012.
22. The "breakup" of the "former" Yugoslavia began with a declaration of independance by Croatia (and Slovenia) in June 1991. Federal power in Serbia opposed the breakup and sent the Yugoslav People's Army (JNA), combined with Montenegrin reserve forces, to seize the Croatian coast. The invasion of Konavle from Montenegro's border began September 29, 1991, and the attack on Čilipi occurred October 1–2 (Brautović 2009).
23. See Čale (1993) for personal accounts and letters of displaced persons collected by researchers at the Institute of Ethnology and Folklore Research in Zagreb during the 1991–1992 period.
24. The three who continued as performers from 1967 to 2011 were Luko Novak, Katica Stankovič, and Marko Matić.

25. In the former Yugoslavia, the dates for the performances were set on Sundays between May 1 and October 31. The current schedule beginning in 1993 is based on the religious calendar and runs from Palm Sunday to All Saints Day.

26. Luko Novak assumed the leadership of the dance group in the late 1980s. Born 1947, he began to dance with KPD Vladimir Nazor (see note 12, above) at age nine. He was a young man of twenty in 1967 when the same group (now named KUD Čilipi) began to perform their weekly Sunday programs. Leaving his displaced family in a Cavtat hotel room, he returned to his damaged home in November 1992 to begin reorganizing the KUD Čilipi (interview by Dunin in Čilipi, 2008.07.08).

27. Marina Desin oversaw the reconstruction and inventory of the museum. In addition she has spoken at international conferences and has written about the plight and needs of the destroyed regional museum (see Desin 1993, 1994, 1998). She also managed to organize and mount the exhibitions in the rebuilt museum in time for its reopening in 2007.

28. The annual festival in Zagreb was continued throughout 1991–1995 despite the threats posed by the war, in particular the shelling of the city itself and nearby areas.

CHAPTER FIVE · DUNIN

I would like to acknowledge the assistance and support of: Daniel Petrovski and his bride, Sabina (2006); Simon Petrovski and his bride, Mersina (2011); Šakija and Ramče Ismailov (1967) in Topaana, and their extended family (2011) in Šuto Orizari; Romano Ilo for arranging the exhibition of Saint George's Day/Erdelezi photographs and sponsoring its catalog/monograph in 1998; and Patricia Anawalt for sponsoring the acquisition of the 2011 Romani outfit for the Fowler Museum that is shown in the exhibition accompanying this book.

1. Following Victor Friedman's linguistic definitions (1998, 2001), the appropriate terms for *Gypsy* in English are *Rom* (singular), *Roms* (plural, instead of *Roma*), and *Romani* (adjective). The term *Roma* was indiscriminately introduced into written English during the 1970s.

2. Roms are reported in northern Greece in the late thirteenth century, and in Prizren and Dubrovnik (in today's Kosovo and Croatia, respectively) in the early fourteenth century (Kenrick 2007). Large numbers of Roms also accompanied and served the victorious Ottomans in their military campaigns. Early Roms of Skopje in the Ottoman period are identified as living in a neighborhood known as the place of the cannons, Topaana.

3. Earlier statistics did not include a separate Romani listing in Serbia. Greece also does not have clear statistics. Bulgaria's 2011 census, however, identifies Roms as third in number, while Macedonia's census statistics show Roms as fourth in number since 1971.

4. The subgroups are differentiated based on language, religion, and occupation.

5. The earthquake registered 6.9 on the Richter scale and destroyed 80 percent of the city with over a thousand fatalities and three thousand injured.

6. The *kale* was the site of fortresses used by those occupying the region. The Ottoman Turks were among the longest to hold the site, controlling the city for half a millenium, from 1392 until 1912.

7. Census statistics in Macedonia and even more so in other European countries are not wholly reliable. Roms are often reluctant to state their ethnic identities because of discriminatory attitudes and their experiences during the Holocaust in World War II.

8. My observations and participation in the dance events of the Gypsies in Skopje took place in 1967 with the support of a United States Office of Education Small Contract Grant. Subsequent visits continued over forty-five years—during the summer months of 1969–1973, and in May of 1977, 1987, 1997, 2007, 2012 to observe the Saint George's Day/Erdelezi holiday, and in July 2011 to observe weddings.

9. In 1967 women and men identified themselves as Turski Cigani. The term Romi or Roma (Slavic plural for Rom) was initiated by Romani activists at the time of the organizing of the First World Romani Congress held in London 1971, and the 1971 census in Macedonia included a category of "Roma." Outcomes of this Congress included the acceptance of a Romani flag and a sung anthem, *Gjelem Gjelem*.

10. Another term for the jacket is *elek*.

11. Many Muslim Turkish and Albanian women continue to differentiate themselves in public by covering their clothing with long coats and head coverings. Romani women, however, dress the same as other non-Muslim urban women on a daily basis.

12. During the 1970s, when passports became available to Yugoslav citizens, many took advantage of the guest worker programs (*Gastarbeiter* in German) offered in these countries, which had temporary worker agreements with Turkey, Greece, and Yugoslavia. Many temporary workers settled permanently prior to Macedonia's secession in 1991. Romani families live in Romani enclaves in industrial cities such as Düsseldorf and use their summer vacations to join families in Skopje, especially for weddings.

13. The Slavic term *svadba* means literally "wedding," but here it has come closer to meaning a family celebration, which is further defined as a *sunet* (circumcision) or as a *nevesta* (bride) celebration.

14. This *amam* (one of several) was located near the large open market, about a ten-minute walk from Topaana. Although damaged in the 1963 earthquake, it was still serviceable in 1967. Every Romani bride was brought here as part of the wedding cyle to have the henna washed from her hair, hands, and feet. By 1977 this *amam* was no longer functioning as a bathing site.

15. *Apušme* from 1967 are included in the Fowler collection.

16. A photographic exhibition of the Saint George's Day/Erdelezi event spanning thirty years (1967, 1977, 1987, 1997) was organized in Skopje on the occasion of an international symposium "Spiritual and Material Culture among the Roma." The May 1998 exhibition was mounted in central Skopje and then moved to the Šuto Orizari suburb so that the local Romani community could more easily see the exhibited pictures. Upon viewing the photographs of the 1967 and 1977 celebrations, the Romani teens of the 1990s expressed surprise at seeing that what they identified as Romani "wedding" outfits were worn by their elders during community holidays in prior decades.

CHAPTER SIX · SLOAN

1. Tomes (2003, 7–8).
2. Tomes (2003, 10–11).
3. Tomes (2003, 2); Powell (1951, 20).
4. Powell (1951, 20); Tomes (2003, 135).
5. Orr (n.d., 5).
6. Personal communication from Nicolas Colasanti, Emily Blackstone Camp's cousin, 2010.
7. Emily Blackstone Camp, correspondence, undated. Emily Blackstone Camp Archive, Fowler Museum.
8. Emily Blackstone Camp, correspondence, October 21, 1929. Emily Blackstone Camp Archive, Fowler Museum.
9. Emily Blackstone Camp, correspondence, undated. Emily Blackstone Camp Archive, Fowler Museum.
10. Emily Blackstone Camp, correspondence, undated. Emily Blackstone Camp Archive, Fowler Museum.
11. Emily Blackstone Camp, correspondence, October 21, 1929. Emily Blackstone Camp Archive, Fowler Museum.
12. Emily Blackstone Camp, correspondence, October 21, 1929. Emily Blackstone Camp Archive, Fowler Museum.
13. *National Geographic* (1932, 59, no. 2:155).
14. Gervers (1982, 86).
15. *San Francisco Chronicle* (1963, 58).
16. Mrvaljević (1988, 46).
17. Danilo Bach, personal communication, 2010.
18. Mrvaljević (1988, 23, 48).
19. Žunić-Baš (1966, 65); Mrvaljević (1988, 49).
20. Mrvaljević (1988, 46, 49); Deliso (2009, 97–98).
21. Mrvaljević (1988, 47).
22. Mrvaljević (1988, 47). In the past, it was said that the black color of the cap and scarf symbolized sorrow in the countries occupied by Turkey.
23. Němcová (1962, 147).
24. Němcová (1962, 49).
25. Němcová (1962, 181).
26. This was possibly the first time during the Cold War that American tennis players were invited to Prague. (John Frost, personal communication, 2010.)
27. John Frost, personal communication, 2010.
28. Helenka had used her wages from the factory to pay for private English lessons in the event that the opportunity for advanced education might present itself (Helenka Frost, personal communication, 2010).
29. Halpern and Halpern (1972, 11, 12).
30. Halpern and Halpern (1972, 87).
31. Halpern and Halpern (1972, 88).
32. Žunić-Baš (1966, 118).
33. Halpern and Halpern (1972, 108).
34. Menković (2009, 85).
35. Halpern and Halpern (1972, 95).
36. Halpern and Halpern (1972, 95).
37. Žunić-Baš (1966, 114).
38. Halpern (1972, 40).
39. Halpern (1972, 41).
40. Halpern (1958, 126–27).

Aleksić, Božo
1966   *Yugoslavia*. Zagreb: Graficki Zavoid Hrvatske.

Baker, Patricia
1986   "The Fez in Turkey: A Symbol of Modernization?" *Costume* (20): 72–85.

Banatceanu, Tancred
1977   "Romania." *The Thesaurus of the Traditional Popular Costume*. Bucharest: Editura Sport-Turism.

Barber, Elizabeth J. W.
1991   *Prehistoric Textiles*. Princeton: Princeton University Press.
1994   *Women's Work: The First 20,000 Years*. New York: W.W. Norton.
1999a   *The Mummies of Ürümchi*. New York: W.W. Norton.
1999b   "On the Antiquity of East European Bridal Clothing." *Folk Dress in Europe and Anatolia*, edited by Linda Welters: 13–31. Oxford: Berg.
2013   *The Dancing Goddess*. New York: W.W. Norton.

Becatti, Giovanni
1957   *Colonna di Marco Aurelio*. Milan: Domus.

Benc-Bošković, Katica
1982   "Konavoski vez u prošlosti i danas" [Konavle embroidery in the past and present]. *Konavoski zbornik*: 155–66. Dubrovnik: Konavle. (Summary in English.)
1983   *Konavle: tekstilno rukotvorstvo i narodna nošnja* [Konavle: textile handicrafts and folk costumes]. Zagreb: Etnografski Muzej. (Summary in English.)
1986   *Narodna nošnja Konavla Čilipi: priručnik za rekonstrukciju nošnje*. Zagreb: Kulturno-Prosvjetni Sabor Hrvatske. (Text in Croatian, English, French, German.)

Bey, Osman Hamdi; de Launay, Marie
1873   *Yilinda Turkiye'de Halk Giysileri: Elbese-I Osmaniyye* [Dress of the Ottomans]. N.p.

Bjeladinovic, Jasna
2011   *Serbian Ethnic Dress in the Nineteenth and Twentieth Centuries*. Belgrade: Ethnographic Museum.

Bogatyrev, Petr.
1971   *The Functions of Folk Costume in Moravian Slovakia*. The Hague: Mouton.

Brautović, Julijana Antić; Brautović, Mato
2009   *Napad na Konavle/Attack on Konavle* (booklet for exhibition of photographs and documental materials). Močići: Brautović with Municipality of Konavle. (Exhibition held 8 August–4 September in KUD Čilipi Gallery.)

Čale Feldman, Lada, editor
1993   *Fear, Death and Resistance: An Ethnography of War: Croatia 1991-1992*. Zagreb: Institute of Ethnology and Folklore Research.

Ceribašić, Naila
2003   *Hrvatsko, seljačko, starinsko i domaće: povijest i etnografija javne prakse narodne glazbe u hrvatskoj* [Croatian, rustic, antique, and home: the history and ethnography of the public practice of folk music in Croatia]. Zagreb: Institut za etnologiju i folkloristiku. (Summary in English.)

Cullen, Tim
1979   *Yugoslavia and the World Bank*. Washington, D.C.: World Bank, Information and Public Affairs Department.

Deliso, Christopher
2009   *Culture and Customs of Serbia and Montenegro*. Westport, Connecticut: Greenwood Press.

Denisov, P. V.
1969   *Etnokul'turnye paraleli dunajskikh bolgar i chuvashej*. Cheboksary: Chvashskoe knizhnoe izdatel'stvo.

Desin, Marina
1993   "Muzej u Čilipima: stradanje i obnova" [Museum in Čilipi: distress and revival]. *Informatica museologica 23(1–4) 1992*: 72–75. Zagreb: Muzejski Dokumentacijski Centar. (Summary in English.)
1994   "Museum in Čilipi—Distress and Revival." (Paper presented to the second global conference, International Institute for Peace through Tourism, held in Montreal, Canada.)

1998   "Čilipi—Presentation of Culture Historical Heritage through Tourism: War, Destruction, and Revitalization." (Paper for International Council of Museums, held in Dubrovnik, Interuniversity Centre). Online: <http://www.maltwood.uvic.ca/tmr/desin.html> (accessed 15 September 2011).

Dunin, Elsie Ivancich
1984   *Dance Occasions and Festive Dress in Yugoslavia*. Los Angeles: University of California.
1998   *St. George's Day—Coming of Summer 1967-1997*. Skopje, Republic of Macedonia: Association of Admirers of Rom Folklore Art "Romano Ilo" [Gypsy Heart]—Skopje.

Eterovich, Adam S.
2000   *Croatians in California, 1849-1999*. San Carlos, California: Ragusan Press.

Fine, John V. A., Jr.
1994   *The Late Medieval Balkans: A Critical Survey from the Late Twelfth Century to the Ottoman Conquest*. Volume 1. Ann Arbor: University of Michigan Press.

Finkel, Caroline
2005   *Osman's Dream: The Story of the Ottoman Empire 1300-1923*. London: John Murray.

Friedman, Victor
1998   "The Romani Language in the Republic of Macedonia: Status, Usage, and Sociolinguistic Perspectives." *Acta Linguistica Hungarica*. Budapest: Akadémiai Kiadó.
2001   "Foreword." *Identity Formation among Minorities in the Balkans: The Cases of Roms, Egyptians, and Ashkali in Kosovo*. Sofia: Minority Studies *Studii Romani*.

Gervers, Veronika
1982   *The Influence of Ottoman Turkish Textile and Costume in Eastern Europe*. Historic, Technology and Art Monograph 4. Toronto: Royal Ontario Museum.

Gimbutas, Marija
1982   *Goddesses and Gods of Old Europe*. Berkeley: University of California Press.

Gjergji, Andromaqi
1988   *Veshjet Shqiptare ne Shekuj*. Tiranë: Akademia e Shkencave e RPS të Shqipërisë, Instituti i Kulturës Popullore.

Göçek, Fatma Müge
1996   *Rise of the Bourgeoisie, Demise of Empire: Ottoman Westernization and Social Change*. New York: Oxford University Press.

Hajdić, Branka
2010   *Jelka Miš: Life Dedicated to Heritage*. Dubrovnik: Etnografski Muzej. (Text in Croatian and English.)

Halpern, Joel Martin
1958   *A Serbian Village*. New York: Columbia University Press.

Halpern, Joel M.; Halpern, Barbara Kerewsky
1972   *A Serbian Village in Historical Perspective*. New York: Holt, Rinehart and Winston.

Hoernes, M.
1898   *Urgeschichte der bildenden Kunst in Europa*. Vienna: Holzhausen.

Inalcik, Halil
2000   *The Ottoman Empire: The Classical Age 1300-1600*. London: Phoenix.

Irwin, John; Brett, Katherine
1970   *Origins of Chintz*. London: Her Majesty's Stationery Office.

Ivančan, Ivan
1966   «Konavoski narodni plesovi» [Folk dances from Konavle]. *Anali 10–11*: 363–416. Dubrovnik: Historijskog Instituta Jugoslavenske Akademije Znanosti i Umjetnosti. (Summary in German.)

Jadran Film
1948   *Podkolo by Čilipi Dance Group*. Zagreb: Jadran Film. Online: YouTube: <http://www.youtube.com/watch?v=Jhne3kPre3E> (accessed September 26, 2011.)

Kenrick, Donald
2007 *Historical Dictionary of the Gypsies*. Second edition. Historical Dictonaries of Peoples and Cultures 7. Lanham, Maryland: Scarecrow Press.

Kirin, Vladimir
n.d. *Narodne Nošnje Jugoslavije*. Zagreb: RVI.

Kličkova, Vera; Petruševa, Anica
1963 *Makedonski Narodni Nosii*. Skopje: Ethnological Museum.

Knauer, Elfriede
1978 "Toward a History of the Sleeved Coat." *Expedition* 21 (1): 18-36.

Kobašić, Antun
2001 "Što i kako se gradilo u Dubroviku poslije II. svjetskog rata" [What and how Dubrovnik was built after World War II]. *Dubrovački horizonti 41/32*: 136-162. Zagreb: Društvo Dubrovčana i Prijatelja Dubrovačke Starine u Zagrebu.

Magyar Nemzeti Múzeum
2001 *A szépség dicsérete: 16-17. századi magyar főúri öltözködés és kultúra* [The praise of beauty: costumes and habits of Hungarian aristocracy in the 16th-17th centuries]. Budapest: Magyar Nemzeti Múzeum.

Marinatos, Spyridon; Hirmer. Max
1960 *Crete and Mycenae*. New York: Abrams.

Mekis, Donna F.; Mekis Miller, Kathryn
2009 *Blossoms into Gold: The Croatians in the Pajaro Valley*. Capitola, California: Capitola Book Company.

Menković, Mirjana
2009 *Zubun Chemise: Belgrade's Ethnographic Museum's Nineteenth to Mid-Twentieth Century Collection*. Belgrade: Ethnographic Museum in Belgrade.

Mladenović, Vesna
1999 "Threads of Life: Red Fringes in Macedonian Dress." In *Folk Dress in Europe and Anatolia*, edited by Linda Welters, 97-110. Oxford: Berg.

Moser, Henri
1885 *À travers l'Asie centrale*. Paris: Plon, Nourrit et Cie.

Mrvaljević, Zorica
1988 *Narodna Nošnja Crne Gore*. Zagreb : Kulturno-Prosvjetni Sabor Hrvatske.

Müller-Karpe, Hermann
1980 *Handbuch der Vorgeschichte. IV: Bronzezeit*. Munich: C. H. Beck.

Munksgaard, Elisabeth
1974 *Oldtidsdragter*. Copenhagen: Nationalmuseet.

Muraj Aleksandra
1988 *Narodna Nošnja Žumberka: Stojdraga*. Zagreb: Kulturno- Prosvjetni Sabor Hrvatske

Myers, J. L.
1902-1903 "Excavations at Palaikastro II." *Bulletin of the British School at Athens* 9: 356-87. pl. VII-XIII.

Němcová, Božena
1962 *Granny: Scenes from Country Life*. Translated by Edith Pargeter. Prague: Artia.

Nielsen, Erica
2011 *Folk Dancing*. Santa Barbara, California: Greenwood.

Orr, William
n.d. Albanian American School of Agriculture Newsletter. New York.

Parrot, André
1961 *Sumer*. New York: Golden.

Perić, Ivo
1957 *Sto godina narodne škole u Čilipima (1857-1957)* [One hundred years of school education in Čilipi (1857-1957)]. Čilipi: N.p.

Powell, E. Alexander
1951 "The Girl Who Is Almost a Queen." *Liberty*. 14 November: 16-21.

Prošić-Dvornić, Mirjana
1989 *Narodna Nošnja Šumadije*. Zagreb: Kulturno-Prosvjetni Sabor Hrvatske.

Quataert, Donald
1997 "Clothing Laws, State and Society in the Ottoman Empire, 1720-1829." *International Journal of Middle Eastern Studies* 29: 403-25.

2000 *The Ottoman Empire, 1700-1922, New Approaches to European History*. Cambridge: Cambridge University Press.

Ramanjuk, Mikhas
2003 *Belaruskija narodnyja stroi*. Minsk: Dzianys Ramanjuk.

Renfrew, Colin; Gimbutas, Marija; Elster, Ernestine S.
1986 *Excavations at Sitagroi*. Volume 1. Los Angeles: Institute of Archaeology, UCLA.

Robinson, Naeda; Canavarro, Maria
2009 *Macedonian Village Dress, Going Going Gone*. Bitola: International Music and Arts Foundation, Vaduz.

Šistan, Ivica
1986 *Narodna NošnjaBaranje: Topolje*. Zagreb: N.p.

Snowden, James
1979 *The Folk Dress of Europe*. New York: Mayflower.

Tarasov, L.
1965 "Paleoliticheskaja stojanka Gagarino." *Materialy i issledovanija po arkheologii SSSR* (131): 111-40.

Tomes, Jason
2003 *King Zog: Self-Made Monarch of Albania*. Gloucestershire: Sutton.

Vinogradova, N.
1969 *Russkij narodnyj kostjum*. Moscow: Izobrazitel'noe iskkusstvo.

Welters, Linda, editor
1999 *Folk Dress in Europe and Anatolia*. Oxford: Berg.

Williams, Patricia
1999 "Protection from Harm: The Shawl and Cap in Czech and Slovak Wedding, Birthing, and Funerary Rites." In *Folk Dress in Europe and Anatolia*, edited by Linda Welters, 135-54. Oxford: Berg.

Zelenin, D.
1927 *Russische (Ostslavische) Volkskunde*. Berlin: Walter de Gruyter.

Žganec, Vinko
1951 "Narodne pjesme, plesovi i običaji Narodne republike Hrvatske" [Folk songs, dances and customs in the People's Republic of Croatia]. Petar Bingulac; Nikola Hercigonja; Slobodan Zečević (editors), *Pjesme, plesovi i običaji Jugoslavenskih naroda, na festival 9-13.IX.1951. u Opatiji*. Zagreb: Hrvatska Seljačka Tiskara. (Program for the International Folk Music Council meeting in Yugoslavia.)

Žunić-Baš, Leposava
1966 *Folk Traditions in Yugoslavia: Ten Tours*. Translated by Karin Radovanović. Belgrade: N.p.

CONTRIBUTORS

ELIZABETH WAYLAND BARBER is professor emerita of Archaeology and Linguistics at Occidental College, Los Angeles, and a research associate at the Cotsen Institute of Archaelogy at UCLA. She received her bachelor's degree from Bryn Mawr in archaeology and Greek and her doctorate from Yale in linguistics. Dr. Barber has published numerous essays in the fields of archaeology, linguistics, and Classics, as well as several very highly regarded books: *Archaeological Decipherment* (1974), *Prehistoric Textiles* (1991), *Women's Work—The First 20,000 Years* (1994), *The Mummies of Ürümchi* (1999), *When They Severed Earth from Sky: How the Human Mind Shapes Myth* (2005, with her husband Paul), and *The Dancing Goddesses: Folklore, Archaeology, and the Origins of European Dance* (2013). Her research interests include the origin and development of textiles and costume in western Eurasia, the interfaces between archaeology and linguistics, and cognitive archaeology (archaeology of brain and language; evolution of myth, ritual, dance, writing, clothing, and other modes of transmitting information).

JOYCE CORBETT received her MFA in art history from the University of Washington and has been a Fulbright Research Scholar in Slovakia and Hungary and an IREX Scholar (International Research and Exchanges Board) in Romania and Hungary. She works as an independent scholar and curatorial consultant specializing in central and eastern European art with a focus on traditional dress and textile history, having curated exhibitions on Hungarian, Slovak, and Romanian dress and textiles, as well as twentieth-century Hungarian artists Eva Zeisel and Joseph Domjan. Her exhibition-related publications include: *Romanian Folk Textiles* (1978); *Dowry: Eastern European Painted Furniture, Textiles, and Related Folk Art* (1998); and *Between East and West: Folk Art Treasures of Romania* (2010).

ELSIE IVANCICH DUNIN is professor emerita in the Department of World Arts and Cultures/Dance (formerly the Department of Dance) at UCLA and invited dance research associate at the Institute of Ethnology and Folklore Research in Zagreb, Croatia. Dunin's research interests and numerous publications focus upon continuities and changes in dance events of coastal Croatians in diaspora (California, Chile, Peru, Australia), as well as in dance events of Slavic Macedonian and Romani (Gypsy) populations in the Republic of Macedonia. In the year of the 1984 Olympics in Los Angeles and Sarajevo, Yugoslavia, Professor Dunin curated a multimedia exhibition with costumes, slides, and video showings, held at the UCLA Museum of Cultural History (now the Fowler Museum at UCLA) and authored the accompanying monograph *Dance Occasions and Festive Dress in Yugoslavia*. Two of the articles in the volume of 1984 form the basis for Dunin's essays in the present volume.

CHARLOTTE JIROUSEK received her doctorate at the University of Minnesota and is presently an associate professor at Cornell University where she teaches historical and cultural aspects of textiles and dress, as well as design foundations and theory. She is also curator of the Cornell Costume and Textile Collection. Her research explores the relationship of world dress to the history of western dress with special attention to Ottoman and Islamic influences. She has also been documenting traditional textile technologies throughout Turkey in the context of historical world textile trade and production networks. Jirousek contributed substantially to *The Fabric of Life: Cultural Transformations in Turkish Society* (2005). She was also a contributor to *The Berg Encyclopedia of World Dress and Fashion* (2010); *Encyclopedia of Clothing and Fashion* (2005); and *Consumption Studies and the History of the Ottoman Empire, 1550-1922* (2000).

BARBARA SLOAN is associate director at the Center for the Study of Regional Dress, Fowler Museum at UCLA. She received her bachelor's degree in art education from the University of Wisconsin, Madison, and her master's degree in Costume History from UCLA. She has served as president of Region V of the Costume Society of America and a member of the board of the Textile Society of America. Sloan has also developed and supervised the teaching of the textile classes offered to UCLA undergraduate students through the Center for the Study of Regional Dress and coordinated the activities of the Fowler Textile Council. She worked with Dr. Patricia Anawalt on the development of *The Worldwide History of Dress* (2008).

Resplendent Dress from Southeastern Europe

A HISTORY IN LAYERS

FOWLER MUSEUM AT UCLA

Marla C. Berns, *Shirley & Ralph Shapiro Director*
David Blair, *Deputy Director*

Stacey Ravel Abarbanel, *Director of External Affairs*
David Acevedo, *Financial Services Coordinator*
Patricia Rieff Anawalt, *Director, Center for the Study of Regional Dress*
Gassia Armenian, *Curatorial and Research Associate*
Manuel Baltodano, *Operations Supervisor/Technical Coordinator*
Sam Bartels, *Technical Support Consultant*
Danny Brauer, *Director of Publications*
Sebastian M. Clough, *Director of Exhibitions*
Don Cole, Museum Photographer
Christian de Brer, *Head of Conservation*
Pablo Dominguez, *Financial Services Coordinator (through July, 2012)*
Bridget DuLong, *Project Manager, Exhibitions*
Luis Figueroa, *Weekend Operations Supervisor*
Susan Gordon, *Director of Development*
Roy W. Hamilton, *Senior Curator/Curator of Asian and Pacific Collections*
Isabella Kelly-Ramirez, *Collections Manager*

Lynne Kostman, *Managing Editor*
Stella Krieger, *Store Manager*
Lori LaVelle, *Membership Coordinator*
Sophia Livsey, *Executive Assistant*
Charles 'Joey' Mann, IV, *Graphics Assistant*
Patrick A. Polk, *Curator of Latin American and Caribbean Popular Arts*
Greg Sandoval, *Curator of Public Programs*
Betsy D. Quick, *Director of Education and Curatorial Affairs*
Rachel Raynor, *Director of Registration and Collections Management*
Gemma Rodrigues, *Curator of African Arts*
Linda Rondinelli, *Associate Director of Development*
Roberto Salazar, *Human Resources Coordinator*
Justin Scoltock, *Exhibitions Production Supervisor*
Corrie Siegel, *Education Manager*
Barbara Belle Sloan, *Associate Director, Center for the Study of Regional Dress*
Agnes Stauber, *Head of Digital Media*
Wendy Teeter, *Curator of Archaeology*
Emry Thomas, *Facilities Supervisor*

Library of Congress Cataloging-in-Publication Data

Barber, E. J. W., 1940-
  Resplendent dress from southeastern Europe : a history in layers / Elizabeth
Barber and Barbara Sloan ; with essays by Elizabeth Wayland Barber, Joyce Corbett,
Elsie Dunin, Charlotte Jirousek, Barbara Belle Sloan, Fowler Museum at UCLA.
      pages cm — (Fowler museum textile series ; No. 11)
  Includes bibliographical references and index.
    ISBN 978-0-9847550-3-5 (soft cover) — ISBN 978-0-9847550-4-2 (hard cover)
1. Clothing and dress—Balkan Peninsula—History. 2. Clothing and dress—
Social aspects—Balkan Peninsula. 3. Balkan Peninsula—Social life and customs.
I. Fowler Museum at UCLA. II. Title.
    GT1280.B37 2013
    391.009496--dc23
                                                            2012047633